D1585483

Cloud Computing
FOR
DUMMIES®

Cloud Computing FOR DUMMIES®

by Judith Hurwitz, Robin Bloor,
Marcia Kaufman, and Dr. Fern Halper

John Wiley & Sons, Inc.

Cloud Computing For Dummies®

Published by
John Wiley & Sons, Inc.
111 River Street
Hoboken, NJ 07030-5774

www.wiley.com

Copyright © 2010 by John Wiley & Sons, Inc., Hoboken, New Jersey

Published by John Wiley & Sons, Inc., Hoboken, New Jersey

Published simultaneously in Canada

No part of this publication may be reproduced, stored in a retrieval system or transmitted in any form or by any means, electronic, mechanical, photocopying, recording, scanning or otherwise, except as permitted under Sections 107 or 108 of the 1976 United States Copyright Act, without either the prior written permission of the Publisher, or authorization through payment of the appropriate per-copy fee to the Copyright Clearance Center, 222 Rosewood Drive, Danvers, MA 01923, (978) 750-8400, fax (978) 646-8600. Requests to the Publisher for permission should be addressed to the Permissions Department, John Wiley & Sons, Inc., 111 River Street, Hoboken, NJ 07030, (201) 748-6011, fax (201) 748-6008, or online at http://www.wiley.com/go/permissions.

Trademarks: Wiley, the Wiley logo, For Dummies, the Dummies Man logo, A Reference for the Rest of Us!, The Dummies Way, Dummies Daily, The Fun and Easy Way, Dummies.com, Making Everything Easier, and related trade dress are trademarks or registered trademarks of John Wiley & Sons, Inc. and/or its affiliates in the United States and other countries, and may not be used without written permission. All other trademarks are the property of their respective owners. John Wiley & Sons, Inc. is not associated with any product or vendor mentioned in this book.

LIMIT OF LIABILITY/DISCLAIMER OF WARRANTY: THE PUBLISHER AND THE AUTHOR MAKE NO REPRESENTATIONS OR WARRANTIES WITH RESPECT TO THE ACCURACY OR COMPLETENESS OF THE CONTENTS OF THIS WORK AND SPECIFICALLY DISCLAIM ALL WARRANTIES, INCLUDING WITHOUT LIMITATION WARRANTIES OF FITNESS FOR A PARTICULAR PURPOSE. NO WARRANTY MAY BE CREATED OR EXTENDED BY SALES OR PROMOTIONAL MATERIALS. THE ADVICE AND STRATEGIES CONTAINED HEREIN MAY NOT BE SUITABLE FOR EVERY SITUATION. THIS WORK IS SOLD WITH THE UNDERSTANDING THAT THE PUBLISHER IS NOT ENGAGED IN RENDERING LEGAL, ACCOUNTING, OR OTHER PROFESSIONAL SERVICES. IF PROFESSIONAL ASSISTANCE IS REQUIRED, THE SERVICES OF A COMPETENT PROFESSIONAL PERSON SHOULD BE SOUGHT. NEITHER THE PUBLISHER NOR THE AUTHOR SHALL BE LIABLE FOR DAMAGES ARISING HEREFROM. THE FACT THAT AN ORGANIZATION OR WEBSITE IS REFERRED TO IN THIS WORK AS A CITATION AND/OR A POTENTIAL SOURCE OF FURTHER INFORMATION DOES NOT MEAN THAT THE AUTHOR OR THE PUBLISHER ENDORSES THE INFORMATION THE ORGANIZATION OR WEBSITE MAY PROVIDE OR RECOMMENDATIONS IT MAY MAKE. FURTHER, READERS SHOULD BE AWARE THAT INTERNET WEBSITES LISTED IN THIS WORK MAY HAVE CHANGED OR DISAPPEARED BETWEEN WHEN THIS WORK WAS WRITTEN AND WHEN IT IS READ.

For general information on our other products and services, please contact our Customer Care Department within the U.S. at 877-762-2974, outside the U.S. at 317-572-3993, or fax 317-572-4002.

For technical support, please visit www.wiley.com/techsupport.

Wiley publishes in a variety of print and electronic formats and by print-on-demand. Some material included with standard print versions of this book may not be included in e-books or in print-on-demand. If this book refers to media such as a CD or DVD that is not included in the version you purchased, you may download this material at http://booksupport.wiley.com. For more information about Wiley products, visit www.wiley.com.

Library of Congress Control Number: 2009938254

ISBN 978-0-470-48470-8 (pbk); ISBN 978-0-470-59740-8 (ebk); ISBN 978-0-470-59741-5 (ebk); ISBN 978-0-470-59742-2 (ebk)

10 9 8 7 6 5 4

WILEY

About the Authors

Judith Hurwitz is a technology strategist and thought leader. She is the president of Hurwitz & Associates, a business technology strategy firm that helps companies gain business benefit from their technology investments. Her area of focus is on cloud computing and all the related distributed computing technologies that enable the cloud. In 1992, she founded the Hurwitz Group, a technology research group. She has worked in various corporations, such as John Hancock, Apollo Computer, and Patricia Seybold's Group. She publishes a regular blog. Judith holds a BS and an MS degree from Boston University. She is a coauthor of *Service Oriented Architecture For Dummies,* Second Edition (Wiley), *Information on Demand For Dummies* (2009), *Service Management For Dummies* (2009), and *Collaboration For Dummies* (2009).

Marcia Kaufman, a founding partner of Hurwitz & Associates, has 20 years of experience in business strategy, industry research, and analytics. She has written many industry white papers and publishes a regular technology blog. Marcia has worked extensively on financial services industry modeling and forecasting in various research environments, including Data Resources, Inc. (DRI). Marcia holds an AB from Connecticut College in mathematics and economics and an MBA from Boston University. Marcia is coauthor of *Service Oriented Architecture For Dummies,* Second Edition (Wiley), *Information on Demand For Dummies*(2009), *Service Management For Dummies* (2009), and *Collaboration For Dummies* (2009).

Dr. Fern Halper, a partner with Hurwitz & Associates, has over 20 years of experience in data analysis, business analysis, and strategy development. Fern has published numerous articles on data and content management. She has done extensive research, writing, and speaking on the topic of text analytics. She publishes a regular technology blog. She has held key positions at AT&T Bell Laboratories and Lucent Technologies and directed strategy and product line planning for Lucent's Internet Software Unit. Fern received her BA from Colgate University and her Ph.D. from Texas A&M University. Fern is coauthor of *Service Oriented Architecture For Dummies,* Second Edition (Wiley), *Information on Demand For Dummies* (2009), and *Service Management For Dummies* (2009).

Robin Bloor, President of Bloor Group, an IT analyst company and an affiliate of Hurwitz & Associates, has been an IT consultant and technology analyst for almost 20 years. He lived and worked in the U.K. until 2002, founding the IT analysis company Bloor Research, which published comparative technology reports that covered everything from computer hardware architecture to e-commerce. Robin is the author of the U.K. business bestseller, *The Electronic B@zaar: From the Silk Road to the E-Road* (Nicholas Brealey Publishing), which analyzed and explained the field of e-commerce. He is a coauthor of *Service Oriented Architecture For Dummies,* Second Edition (Wiley) and *Service Management For Dummies* (2009).

Dedications

Judith dedicates her part of the book to her family — her husband, Warren; her children, Sara and David; and her mother, Elaine. She also dedicates this book in memory of her father, David.

Robin dedicates his part of the book to Judy, for her encouragement, support, and advice.

Marcia dedicates her part of the book to her husband, Matthew; her daughters, Sara and Emily; and her parents, Larry and Gloria.

Fern dedicates her part of the book to her husband, Clay, and her daughters, Katie and Lindsay. She also dedicates this book in memory of her parents, Stanley and Phyllis.

Authors' Acknowledgments

Amazon's Jeff Barr; Bell Aliant's Tony Lodge; CA's Brian Bonazzoli, Nicole Buffalino, Debra Cattani, Stephen Elliott, Jay Fry, Ajei Gopal, Joanne Moretti, Roger Pilc, and John Swainson; Cisco's William Scott; Citrix's Ian Platt; Cloud Camp's David Nielson; Computer Sciences Corporation's (CSC) Brian Boruff; Desktone's Jeff Fisher and Harry Ruda; Distributed Management Task Force's (DMTF) Winston Bumpus; EMC's Chuck Hollis and Irene Mirageas; Good Data's Roman Stanek; GSK Pharmaceuticals' Ivan Hislaire; HP's Magdy Assem, Russ Daniels, Cheryl Rose Hayden, Tom Hogan, Rebecca Lawson, Scott McClellan, Joanne McMenoman, and Scott Pace; IBM's Lee Ackerman, Ruthie Amaru, Erich Clementi, Latha Colby, Teresa Cook, Jim Corgel, Dave Dworkin, Leon Katznelson, Martha Leversuch, Dave Lindquist, Amy Loomis, Steve Maher, Mike McCarthy, David Mitchell, Harold Moss, David Parker, Hamid Pirahesh, Sean Poulley, John Simonds, Toby Sirota, Zarina Lam Stanford, Lauren States, Tim Vincent, Marie Weeks, and David Yockelson; Intuit's Anna Lane, Bill Lucchini, and Angus Thomson; JBoss's Aaron Darcy; MDot's Mike Kavis; Metro Health's Bill Lewkowski; Microsoft's Prashaut Ketkar, Niraj Nagrani, Steve Sloan, and Mike Werner; National Institute of Standards and Technology; Pervasive's John Bernard, Kimberli Daugherty, David Inbar, Jim Falgout, and Hollis Tibbetts; Platform Computing's Randy Clark; RightScale's Michael Crandell; Salesforce's Marc Benioff, Alex Chris, Ariel Kelman, and Bill Lukini; Savvis's Bryan Doerr; ServiceNow's Rhett Glauser; Sisters of Mercy Health System's Jeff Bell and John Treadway; State Street Corporation's David Saul; THINKStrategies's Jeff Kaplan; Virtual Bridges's Jim Curtin and Dan Perlman; VMware's Dawn Giusti, Neena Joshi, Wendy Perilli, and Jiam Zhen; Verizon's Joe Crawford and Tim Gillen; Wavemaker's Chris Keene; WorkXpress's Treff LaPlante; and 3tera's Paul Brennan.

Publisher's Acknowledgments

We're proud of this book; please send us your comments at http://dummies.custhelp.com. For other comments, please contact our Customer Care Department within the U.S. at 877-762-2974, outside the U.S. at 317-572-3993, or fax 317-572-4002.

Some of the people who helped bring this book to market include the following:

Acquisitions and Editorial

Project Editor: Tonya Maddox Cupp

Development Editor: Linda Morris, Tonya Maddox Cupp

Senior Acquisitions Editor: Katie Feltman

Technical Editor: Brenda Michelson

Editorial Manager: Jodi Jensen

Editorial Assistant: Amanda Graham

Sr. Editorial Assistant: Cherie Case

Cartoons: Rich Tennant
(www.the5thwave.com)

Composition Services

Project Coordinator: Patrick Redmond

Layout and Graphics: Ashley Chamberlain, Joyce Haughey, Christine Williams

Proofreaders: John Greenough, Bonnie Mikkelson

Indexer: Sharon Shock

Publishing and Editorial for Technology Dummies

Richard Swadley, Vice President and Executive Group Publisher

Andy Cummings, Vice President and Publisher

Mary Bednarek, Executive Acquisitions Director

Mary C. Corder, Editorial Director

Publishing for Consumer Dummies

Kathleen Nebenhaus, Vice President and Executive Publisher

Composition Services

Debbie Stailey, Director of Composition Services

Contents at a Glance

Introduction *1*

Part 1: Introducing Cloud Computing *5*

Chapter 1: Grasping the Fundamentals 7
Chapter 2: Discovering the Value of the Cloud for Business 17
Chapter 3: Getting Inside the Cloud 27
Chapter 4: Developing Your Cloud Strategy.. 39

Part 11: Understanding the Nature of the Cloud *47*

Chapter 5: Seeing the Advantages of the Highly Scaled Data Center 49
Chapter 6: Exploring the Technical Foundation for Scaling
        Computer Systems.. 59
Chapter 7: Checking the Cloud's Workload Strategy 67
Chapter 8: Managing Data 75
Chapter 9: Discovering Private and Hybrid Clouds... 87

Part 111: Examining the Cloud Elements *105*

Chapter 10: Seeing Infrastructure as a Service... 107
Chapter 11: Exploring Platform as a Service.. 119
Chapter 12: Using Software as a Service.. 137
Chapter 13: Understanding Massively Scaled Applications
        and Business Processes 153
Chapter 14: Setting Some Standards 161

Part 1V: Managing the Cloud *171*

Chapter 15: Managing and Securing Cloud Services 173
Chapter 16: Governing the Cloud 187
Chapter 17: Virtualization and the Cloud.. 197
Chapter 18: Managing Desktops and Devices in the Cloud 209
Chapter 19: Service Oriented Architecture and the Cloud.............................. 221
Chapter 20: Managing the Cloud Environment 231

Part V: Planning for the Cloud 243

Chapter 21: Banking on Cloud Economics 245

Chapter 22: Starting Your Journey to the Cloud 255

Part VI: The Part of Tens 265

Chapter 23: Ten (Plus One) Swell Cloud Computing Resources 267

Chapter 24: Ten Cloud Dos and Don'ts 271

Glossary 275

Index 291

Table of Contents

Introduction *1*

About This Book...2
Foolish Assumptions...2
How This Book Is Organized 2
    Part I: Introducing Cloud Computing 3
    Part II: Understanding the Nature
      of the Cloud..3
    Part III: Examining the Cloud Elements..............................3
    Part IV: Managing the Cloud..3
    Part V: Planning for the Cloud..3
    Part VI: The Part of Tens..3
Icons Used in This Book 4
Where to Go from Here...4

Part 1: Introducing Cloud Computing *5*

Chapter 1: Grasping the Fundamentals 7

Considering Perspectives...8
Computing on the Cloud..8
Defining the Cloud 9
    Elasticity and scalability 10
    Self-service provisioning...10
    Application programming interfaces (APIs)......................11
    Billing and metering of services...11
    Performance monitoring and measuring...........................12
    Security 12
Comparing Cloud Providers with Traditional IT Service Providers 12
Addressing Problems...13
Discovering the Business Drivers for Consuming Cloud Services..........14
    Supporting business agility 15
    Reducing capital expenditures...15

Chapter 2: Discovering the Value of the Cloud for Business 17

Modeling Services..17
Understanding Infrastructure as a Service................................18
Exploring Platform as a Service...20
Seeing Software as a Service 21
    Software as a Service modes 22
    Massively scaled Software as a Service 23
    Economies of scale 23
Management and Administration 24

Chapter 3: Getting Inside the Cloud 27

    Feeling Sensational about Organization 27
        Deciding on a strategy. 28
        Coping with governance issues 28
        Monitoring business processes 29
        Managing IT costs 30
    Administering Cloud Services. 30
        Service level agreements and monitoring 31
        Support. 32
        Billing and accounting. 32
    Looking at the Technical Interface. 32
        APIs and data transformations. 33
        Data and application architecture. 33
        Security in the cloud 34
    Managing Cloud Resources. 34
        IT security. 35
        Performance management. 35
        Provisioning. 36
        Service management 37
    Untangling Software Dependencies. 37

Chapter 4: Developing Your Cloud Strategy .39

    Seeing the Many Aspects of Your Cloud Strategy 40
    Questioning Your Company's Strategy. 41
    Assessing Where You Are Today 42
        How tangled is my computing environment?. 42
        What's my data center environment? 42
        What data supports my strategy? 43
    Assessing Your Expense Structure 44
    Checking Up on Rules and Governances. 44
    Developing a Road Map 45

Part II: Understanding the Nature of the Cloud **47**

Chapter 5: Seeing the Advantages of the Highly
Scaled Data Center 49

    Comparing Financial Damage: Traditional versus Cloud 50
        Traditional data center 50
        Cloud data center 51
    Scaling the Cloud. 52
    Comparing Traditional and Cloud Data Center Costs 55
        Examining labor costs and productivity. 56
        Wondering where you are 56

Chapter 6: Exploring the Technical Foundation for Scaling Computer Systems 59

Server-ing Up Some Hardware 60
   Tradition! versus clouds 60
   Considering cloud hardware 61
   Open-source dynamic 63
Economies of Scale 63
   Benefitting enormously 64
   Optimizing otherwise 64
Keeping the Bottom Line in Mind 65

Chapter 7: Checking the Cloud's Workload Strategy 67

Managing Workloads in the Cloud 67
   Thinking of workloads as well-planned services 68
   Creating interfaces between containers 70
   Discovering how XML fits in 70
   Using container workloads: Case study 71
Balancing Risk and Practical Models 71
Testing Workloads in the Real World 73

Chapter 8: Managing Data 75

Declaring Data Types 75
Securing Data in the Cloud 76
   Data location in the cloud 77
   Data control in the cloud 78
   Securing data for transport in the cloud .79
Looking at Data, Scalability, and Cloud Services 81
   Large-scale data processing 81
   Databases and data stores in the cloud 82
   Data archiving 84
Sorting Out Metadata Matters 84
Talking to Your Cloud Vendor about Data 84

Chapter 9: Discovering Private and Hybrid Clouds 87

Pining for Privacy 88
   Defining a private cloud 88
   Comparing public, private, and hybrid 89
Examining the Economics of the Private Cloud 92
   Assessing capital expenditures 92
   Vendor private cloud offerings 93
Offering Up Key Vendors 94
   Services-led technology companies 95
   Systems integrators companies 98
   Technology enabler companies 99

Part III: Examining the Cloud Elements 105

Chapter 10: Seeing Infrastructure as a Service 107
Tracing IaaS to ISP 107
    Renting (but not to own) 108
    Following the ISP pattern 109
Exploring Amazon EC2: Case Study 109
    EC2 Compute Units 110
    Platforms and storage 110
    EC2 pricing... 112
    EC2 customers... 112
Checking Out Other IaaS Companies 113
    Rackspace 113
    GoGrid 114
    Others.. 114
Examining IaaS-Enabling Technology 114
    AppLogic 115
    Eucalyptus 115
Trusting the Cloud.. 116
What Infrastructure as a Service Means to You 117

Chapter 11: Exploring Platform as a Service 119
Putting Platform as a Service on a Pedestal... 120
    Integrated lifecycle platforms 121
    Anchored lifecycle platforms 122
    Enabling technologies as a platform 122
Getting Inside the Integrated Lifecycle Platform................................... 122
    Google App Engine.. 123
    Microsoft Azure... 125
Getting Inside Anchored Lifecycle Platform as a Service...................... 127
    Salesforce.com's Force.com platform 127
    Intuit 130
    LongJump 132
Enabling Technologies as a Platform.. 133
    Testing in the cloud 134
    Service management for the cloud.. 134
    Integration and configuration platforms...................................... 134
    Social network, framework, and portal platforms....................... 135

Chapter 12: Using Software as a Service 137
SalesForce.com's Approach to Evolving Software as a Service 138
    Salesforce.com software environment 138
    SalesForce.com ecosystem 140
Characterizing Software as a Service... 140
Understanding the Economics and the Ecosystem................................. 142
    Pretending you're a customer... 142
    The value of the ecosystem... 144

Examining Types of SaaS Platforms 145
    Packaged Software as a Service 147
    Collaboration as a Service 148
    Enabling and management tools 149

Chapter 13: Understanding Massively Scaled Applications and Business Processes 153

Naming Names: Companies with Massively Scaled Applications 154
    Listing the companies 154
    Looking at Web-based business services 156
Delivering Business Processes from the Cloud 157
    Business process examples...................................... 157
    Business processes destined for the cloud................ 158
    Hidden in the cloud 158
    Business processes already flying high 158
    Predicting the future 159

Chapter 14: Setting Some Standards 161

Understanding Best Practices and Standards 161
    Best practicing makes perfect.................................. 162
    Setting your sites on standards 162
Clouding the Standards and Best Practices Issue 163
    Interoperability 164
    Portability 164
    Integration 164
    Security 164
Standards Organizations and Groups................................. 166
    Cloud Security Alliance 166
    Distributed Management Task Force (DMTF)............... 167
    National Institute of Standards and Technology (NIST)............. 167
    Open Cloud Consortium (OCC)................................. 168
    Open Grid Forum (OGF).. 168
    The Object Management Group (OMG) 169
    Storage Networking Industry Association (SNIA)......... 169
    Cloud Computing Interoperability Forum (CCIF) 169
    Vertical groups.. 170

Part IV: Managing the Cloud 171

Chapter 15: Managing and Securing Cloud Services 173

Putting Security on the Spot with Questions 174
Understanding Security Risks... 175
Reducing Cloud Security Breaches 177
Implementing Identity Management 179
    Benefits of identity management 179
    Aspects of identity management 180

Playing Detective: Detection and Forensics 182
Activity logs 182
HIPS and NIPS 182
Data audit 184
Encrypting Data 184
Creating a Cloud Security Strategy 185

Chapter 16: Governing the Cloud 187
Looking at IT Governance 188
Deciding on a Governor 189
Imagining a scenario 190
Imagining another scenario 190
Knowing the Risks of Running in the Cloud 190
Understanding risk 191
Measuring and monitoring performance 193
Measurement methods 193
Making Governance Work 194
Establishing your governance body 194
Monitoring and measuring IT service performance 195
Cataloging control and compliance data 195

Chapter 17: Virtualization and the Cloud 197
Visualizing Virtualization 197
Characteristics 198
Using a hypervisor in virtualization 199
Abstracting hardware assets 201
Managing Virtualization 202
Foundational issues 202
Abstraction layer 203
Provisioning software 204
Virtualizing storage 205
Hardware provisioning 205
Security issues 206
Taking Virtualization into the Cloud 208

Chapter 18: Managing Desktops and Devices in the Cloud 209
Virtualizing the Desktop 209
Across industries 210
The client desktop 210
Putting Desktops in the Cloud 212
Further pros 213
Desktop as a Service (DaaS) 213
Managing Desktops in the Cloud 215
Watching four areas 215
Managing assets 216

Monitoring services 217
Change management 218
Security 218
Getting a Reality Check.. 219

Chapter 19: Service Oriented Architecture and the Cloud 221

Defining Service Oriented Architecture................................... 221
Combining the cloud and SOA 222
Characterizing SOA.. 222
Loosening Up on Coupling 223
Making SOA Happen... 224
Catching the Enterprise Service Bus.............................. 225
Telling your registry from your repository 225
Cataloging services.. 227
Understanding Services in the Cloud...................................... 228
Serving the Business with SOA and Cloud Computing 230

Chapter 20: Managing the Cloud Environment 231

Managing the Cloud.. 232
The service provider 232
Customers.. 234
Hybrid environments 236
Building Up Support Desks... 237
Service desk goals.. 237
Varying support levels 238
Examining support services 238
Gaining Visibility... 240
Ensuring adequate performance levels 241
Monitoring service availability 241
Tracking Service Level Agreements.. 241

Part V: Planning for the Cloud..................................... 243

Chapter 21: Banking on Cloud Economics 245

$eeing the Cloud's Allure.. 245
Filling the need for capacity.. 246
Getting the work done without capital investment...... 246
Selecting a SaaS for common applications 247
Selecting the massively scaled application 247
When it's not black and white.. 247
Creating an Economic Model of the Data Center 248
Listing application costs.. 248
Recovering costs... 250

Adjusting the Economic Model even Further 251
    Private cloud and allocation costs 251
    Service levels and compliance costs...252
    Strategic considerations and costs 253
Summarizing an Economic Cost Model 253

Chapter 22: Starting Your Journey to the Cloud 255

Putting the Kibosh on Cloud Cultural Issues 255
    Anticipating (but not with relish)...256
    Smoothing the transition 257
Measuring Twice: Assessing Risks 258
    Playing risk with categories..258
    Top company concerns 259
Picking the Right Targets for Success..260
    Picking the low-hanging fruit..261
    Approaching other areas 261
Planning for Leveraging the Cloud 262
    Example 1...262
    Example 2...263

Part VI: The Part of Tens............................. 265

Chapter 23: Ten (Plus One) Swell Cloud Computing Resources 267

Hurwitz & Associates 267
National Institute of Standards and Technology 268
CloudCamp..268
SaaS Showplace..268
TechTarget...268
The Cloud Standards Wiki..269
Finding OASIS 269
The Eclipse Foundation 269
The Cloud Security Alliance 269
Open Cloud Manifesto 270
Vendor Sites 270

Chapter 24: Ten Cloud Dos and Don'ts 271

Don't Be Reactive 271
Do Consider the Cloud a Financial Issue 271
Don't Go It Alone..272
Do Think about Your Architecture...272
Don't Neglect Governance..272

Don't Forget about Business Process 272
Do Make Security the Centerpiece of Your Strategy 273
Don't Apply the Cloud to Everything 273
Don't Forget about Service Management 273
Do Start with a Pilot Project 273

Glossary **275**

Index *291*

Introduction

Welcome to *Cloud Computing For Dummies*. You can't read a technology journal or blog — or even your local newspaper — without coming upon a reference to cloud computing. While there's been a lot of debate about what cloud computing is and where it's headed, no one has doubts that it is real.

In fact, we think that cloud computing, in all of its forms, is transforming the computing landscape. It will change the way we deploy technology and how we think about the economics of computing. We hope this book provides a perspective on cloud computing and starts your journey of exploration.

Cloud computing is more than a service sitting in some remote data center. It's a set of approaches that can help organizations quickly, effectively add and subtract resources in almost real time. Unlike other approaches, the cloud is as much about the business model as it is about technology. Companies clearly understand that technology is at the heart of how they operate their businesses. Business executives have long been frustrated with the complexities of getting their computing needs met quickly and cost effectively. In a sense, cloud computing has started to become mainstream because these business executives have forced the issue into the forefront.

Cloud computing isn't a quick fix. It requires a lot of thought: Which approach is most appropriate for your company? For example, companies have to decide if they want to use *public* (external) cloud services or if they want to have private clouds behind their firewalls. How should you architect your internal environment to support the cloud?

The cloud environment itself requires a strong foundation of best practices in software development, software architecture, and service management foundations. This strong foundation is especially important because most organizations combine public and private cloud services. You want to be informed before you start your search. We think this book will give you the context to make informed decisions.

About This Book

Cloud computing is a big new area and requires that a lot of people get familiar with it in a fairly short period of time. That's why we wrote this book. Some people may want to get deeper into the technological details, while others may care only about the business implications.

We recommend that you read the first five chapters, regardless of how deeply you want to wander into the cloud. These chapters give you context about the cloud and what's behind the concept. If you want to begin understanding the economics and the available approaches to the cloud, you should read the later chapters.

You can read from cover to cover, but if you're not that kind of person, but we've tried to adhere to the *For Dummies* style of keeping chapters self-contained so you can go straight to the topics that interest you most. Wherever you start, we wish you well.

Foolish Assumptions

Try as we might to be all things to all people, when it came to writing this book, we had to pick who we thought would be most interested in *Cloud Computing For Dummies*. Here's who we think you are:

- **You're smart.** You're no dummy, yet the topic of service oriented architecture gives you an uneasy feeling; you can't quite get your head around it, and if you're pressed for a definition, you might try to change the subject.

- **You're a businessperson who wants little or nothing to do with technology,** but you live in the 21st century and find that you can't escape it. Everybody's saying, "It's all about moving to the cloud," so you think that you better find out what they're talking about.

- **You're an IT person who knows a heck of a lot about technology,** but who is new to this cloud stuff. Everybody says it's something different. Once and for all, you want the whole picture.

Whoever you are, welcome. We're here to help.

How This Book Is Organized

We divide our book into six parts for easy consumption. Feel free to skip about.

Part I: Introducing Cloud Computing

In this part, we explain the fundamentals of cloud computing from a business and technology perspective. We also introduce you to the major concepts and components so you can hold your own in any meaningful cloud conversation.

Part II: Understanding the Nature of the Cloud

Part II is for more technically oriented people. In this section, we dive deeper into the actual foundational elements of the cloud.

Part III: Examining the Cloud Elements

What types of clouds are there and how do they work? This part delves into areas critical to your cloud plans.

Part IV: Managing the Cloud

The rubber meets the road right here. A cloud computing environment can't work if it isn't well managed. This section gives you plenty to think about in this critical area.

Part V: Planning for the Cloud

When you understand what the cloud is all about, you can start planning. You need to think about the financial implications of clouds as well as the steps that get you going.

Part VI: The Part of Tens

If you're new to the *For Dummies* treasure trove, you're no doubt unfamiliar with "The Part of Tens." In "The Part of Tens," Wiley editors torture *For Dummies* authors into creating useful bits of information easily accessible in lists containing ten (or more) elucidating elements. We started these chapters kicking and screaming but are ultimately very glad they're here. We think you'll be glad, too.

Icons Used in This Book

Pay attention. The bother you save may be your own.

You may be sorry if this little tidbit slips your mind.

We think this a particularly useful point to pay attention to.

Tidbits for the more technically inclined.

Where to Go from Here

We've created an overview of cloud computing and introduce you to all of its significant components. Many of these chapters could be expanded into full-length books of their own. Cloud computing and the entire distributed technology landscape is a big focus for us at Hurwitz & Associates, and we invite you to visit our site and read our blogs and insights at www.hurwitz.com.

Part I
Introducing Cloud Computing

The 5th Wave — By Rich Tennant

"Oh, I'll get us in — I used to run tech support at an internet access company."

In this part . . .

*T*he phrase *cloud computing* implies something, but exactly what is it? In this part, we introduce the concept and provide a simple graphic that describes the layers of cloud computing. We also examine the value that the cloud can bring to your organization and look at some of the associated business issues.

Chapter 1

Grasping the Fundamentals

In This Chapter

▶ Doing your computing on the cloud

▶ Seeing what the cloud's made of

▶ Comparing the cloud to tradition

▶ Driving your business

*I*n a dynamic economic environment, your company's survival may depend on your ability to focus on core business and adapt quickly. Yesterday's profitable business model can't be counted on to translate into future growth and profits. As your business adapts to changing government and industry regulations, evaluates new business partnerships, and anticipates competitive threats, IT needs to help the business find new ways to respond.

At the same time, plans for change must often be made in the context of limited resources for finances, people, technology, and power. In this chapter, we introduce you to cloud computing — what it is and how it helps companies rethink how they deploy technology.

While there are a lot of technical considerations, keep in mind the fundamental truth: Cloud computing is a business and economic model. Is cloud computing a replacement for the traditional data center? The answer is complicated. In some cases, yes; in some cases, no.

Are we suggesting that the traditional data center goes away to be replaced with a cloud? Not necessarily. Sometimes the traditional data center is the best fit. However, for business agility and economic reasons, the cloud is becoming an increasingly important option for companies. We see cloud computing as the foundation for the industrialization of computing. Yes, it is that important.

Considering Perspectives

In this book, we look at cloud computing from three perspectives: the strategy from both the customer and the provider's point of view, business and economic considerations, and the technical underpinnings. We also examine how companies are using the cloud to control IT expenditures as they prepare to move to a service-centric world.

Many players make up the world of cloud computing:

- ✔ The **vendors** providing applications and enabling technology, infrastructure, hardware, and integration
- ✔ The **partners** of these vendors that are creating cloud services offerings and providing support services to customers
- ✔ The **business leaders** themselves who are either using or evaluating various types of cloud computing offerings

This book addresses each of these audiences because they're all a fundamental part of this fabric of the future of computing.

Computing on the Cloud

What is cloud computing? Cloud computing is the next stage in evolution of the Internet. The *cloud* in cloud computing provides the means through which everything — from computing power to computing infrastructure, applications, business processes to personal collaboration — can be delivered to you as a service wherever and whenever you need.

Cloud computing is offered in different forms:

- ✔ Public clouds
- ✔ Private clouds
- ✔ Hybrid clouds, which combine both public and private

In general the cloud — similar to its namesake of the cumulus type — is fluid and can easily expand and contract. This *elasticity* means that users can request additional resources on demand and just as easily *deprovision* (or release) those resources when they're no longer needed. This elasticity is one of the main reasons individual, business, and IT users are moving to the cloud.

In the traditional data center it has always been possible to add and release resources. However, this process couldn't be done in an automated or self-service manner.

This evolution to cloud computing — already underway — can completely change the way companies use technology to service customers, partners, and suppliers. Some businesses already have IT resources almost entirely in the cloud. They feel that the cloud model provides a more efficient, cost-effective IT service delivery.

This doesn't mean that all applications, services, and processes will necessarily be moved to the cloud. Many businesses are much more cautious and are taking a hard look at their most strategic business processes and intellectual property to determine which computing assets need to remain under internal company control and which computing assets could be moved to the cloud.

Defining the Cloud

The *cloud* itself is a set of hardware, networks, storage, services, and interfaces that enable the delivery of computing as a service. *Cloud services* include the delivery of software, infrastructure, and storage over the Internet (either as separate components or a complete platform) based on user demand.

The world of the cloud has lots of participants:

- ✔ The **end user** doesn't really have to know anything about the underlying technology. In small businesses, for example, the cloud provider becomes the de facto data center. In larger organizations, the IT organization oversees the inner workings of both internal resources and external cloud resources.

- ✔ **Business management** needs to take responsibility for overall governance of data or services living in a cloud. Cloud service providers must provide a predictable and guaranteed service level and security to all their constituents.

- ✔ The **cloud service provider** is responsible for IT assets and maintenance.

Therefore, we have written this book to include the concerns of all the players in the evolving cloud ecosystem.

Cloud services must enable *multi-tenancy* — different companies sharing the same underlying resources. This topic is discussed further in Chapter 12.

Companies are finding some important new value in cloud services. The cloud can eliminate many of the complex constraints from the traditional computing environment, including space, time, power, and cost.

Cloud services like social networks (such as Facebook or LinkedIn) and collaboration tools (like video conferencing, document management, and webinars) are changing the way people in businesses access, deliver, and understand information. Cloud computing infrastructures make it easier for companies to treat their computing systems as a pool of resources rather than a set of independent environments that each has to be managed.

Overall, the cloud embodies the following four basic characteristics:

- ✔ Elasticity and the ability to scale up and down
- ✔ Self-service provisioning and automatic deprovisioning
- ✔ Application programming interfaces (APIs)
- ✔ Billing and metering of service usage in a pay-as-you-go model

Each of these characteristics is described in more detail in the following sections.

Elasticity and scalability

The service provider can't anticipate how customers will use the service. One customer might use the service three times a year during peak selling seasons, whereas another might use it as a primary development platform for all of its applications.

Therefore, the service needs to be available all the time (7 days a week, 24 hours a day) and it has to be designed to scale upward for high periods of demand and downward for lighter ones. *Scalability* also means that an application can scale when additional users are added and when the application requirements change.

This ability to scale is achieved by providing *elasticity*. Think about the rubber band and its properties. If you're holding together a dozen pens with a rubber band, you probably have to fold it in half. However, if you're trying to keep 100 pens together, you will have to stretch that rubber band. Why can a single rubber band accomplish both tasks? Simply, it is elastic and so is the cloud.

In Chapter 2, we give you some concrete examples of how providers are using this characteristic.

Self-service provisioning

Customers can easily get cloud services without going through a lengthy process. The customer simply requests an amount of computing, storage, software, process, or other resources from the service provider. Chapter 7 explains this process in detail.

Contrast this on-demand response with the process at a typical data center. When a department is about to implement a new application, it has to submit a request to the data center for additional computing hardware, software, services, or process resources. The data center gets similar requests from departments across the company and must sort through all requests and evaluate the availability of existing resources versus the need to purchase new hardware. After new hardware is purchased, the data center staff has to configure the data center for the new application. These internal procurement processes can take a long time, depending on company policies.

Of course, nothing is as simple as it might appear. While the on-demand provisioning capabilities of cloud services eliminates many time delays, an organization still needs to do its homework. These services aren't free; needs and requirements must be determined before capability is automatically provisioned.

Application programming interfaces (APIs)

Cloud services need to have standardized APIs. These interfaces provide the instructions on how two application or data sources can communicate with each other.

A standardized interface lets the customer more easily link a cloud service, such as a customer relationship management system with a financial accounts management system, without having to resort to custom programming. For more information on standards see Chapter 14.

Billing and metering of services

Yes, there is no free lunch. A cloud environment needs a built-in service that bills customers. And, of course, to calculate that bill, usage has to be *metered* (tracked). Even free cloud services (such as Google's Gmail or Zoho's Internet-based office applications) are metered.

In addition to these characteristics, cloud computing must have two overarching requirements to be effective:

  ✔ A comprehensive approach to service management

  ✔ A well-defined process for security management

Performance monitoring and measuring

A cloud service provider must include a service management environment. A *service management environment* is an integrated approach for managing your physical environments and IT systems. This environment must be able to maintain the required service level for that organization.

In other words, service management has to monitor and optimize the service or sets of services. Service management has to consider key issues, such as performance of the overall system, including security and performance. For example, an organization using an internal or external email cloud service would require 99.999 percent uptime with maximum security. The organization would expect the cloud provider to prove that it has met its obligations.

Many cloud service providers give customers a dashboard — a visualization of key service metrics — so they can monitor the level of service they're getting from their provider. Also, many customers use their own monitoring tools to determine whether their service level requirements are being met.

Security

Many customers must take a leap of faith to trust that the cloud service is safe. Turning over critical data or application infrastructure to a cloud-based service provider requires making sure that the information can't be accidentally accessed by another company (or maliciously accessed by a hacker).

Many companies have compliance requirements for securing both internal and external information. Without the right level of security, you might not be able to use a provider's offerings. For more details on security, see Chapter 15.

Comparing Cloud Providers with Traditional IT Service Providers

Traditional IT service providers operate the hardware, software, networks, and storage for its clients. While the customer pays the licensing fees for the software, the IT service provider manages the overall environment. The service provider operates the infrastructure in its own facilities. With the traditional IT service provider, the customer signs a long-term contract that specifies mutually agreed-upon service levels. These IT providers typically customize an environment to meet the needs of one customer.

In the cloud model, the service provider might still operate the infrastructure in its own facilities (except in the case of a private cloud, which we discuss in Chapter 9). However, the infrastructure might be *virtualized* across the globe, meaning that you may not know where your computing resources, applications, or even data actually reside. (We talk more about virtualization in Chapter 17.) Additionally, these service providers are designing their infrastructure for scale, meaning that there isn't necessarily a lot of customization going on. (We talk more about the scale issue in Chapter 13.)

Addressing Problems

There is an inherent conflict between what the business requires and what data center management can reasonably provide. Business management wants optimal performance, flawless implementation, and 100 percent uptime. The business leadership wants new capability to be available immediately, frequent changes to applications, and more accessibility to quality data in real time — but their organizations have limited budgets.

Getting on board with cloud computing

Although opinions differ about how quickly technology will migrate to the cloud, without doubt the interest level is high. Lots of business folks are asking questions about the cloud approach when they hear about the data center efficiencies achieved by companies like Amazon (www.amazon.com) and Google (www.google.com).

For example, a smart CEO was under a lot of pressure to improve profitability by cutting capital expenditures. One day he read an article about the economic advantages of cloud computing in a business journal and began to wonder, "Hey, if Amazon can offer computing on demand, why can't our own IT department act like that?" The CEO paid a visit to the CIO and asked that very question. The CIO wasn't quite sure how to answer his boss. His only reply was that things are more complicated than that. The CIO pointed out issues related to data security and privacy. In addition, there are applications running in the data center that are one-of-a-kind and not easily handled. At the same time, he recognized that the department needed to provide better service to internal customers. The CIO did agree that there were other areas of IT that might be appropriate for the cloud model. For example, areas such as testing, software development, storage, and email were good candidates for cloud computing.

Over time, it became easier for IT to add hardware to the data center rather than to focus on making the data center itself more effective. And this plan worked. By pouring more resources into the data center, IT ensured that critical applications wouldn't run out of resources. At the same time, these companies built or bought software to meet business needs. The applications that were built internally were often large and complex. They had been modified repeatedly to satisfy changes without regard to their underlying architecture.

Between managing a vast array of expanding hardware resources combined with managing huge and unwieldy business software, IT management found itself under extraordinary pressure to become much more effective and efficient.

This tug of war between the needs of the business and the data center constraints has caused friction over the past few decades. Clearly, need and money must be balanced. To meet these challenges, there have been significant technology advancements including virtualization (see Chapter 17), service-oriented architecture (see Chapter 19), and service management (see Chapter 20). Each of these areas is intended to provide more modularity, flexibility, and better performance for IT.

While these technology enablers have helped companies to become more efficient and cost effective, it isn't enough. Companies are still plagued with massive inefficiencies. The promise of the cloud is to enable companies to improve their ability to leverage what they've bought and make use of external resources designed to be used on demand.

We don't want to give you the idea that everything will be perfect when you get yourself a cloud. The world, unfortunately, is more complicated than that. For example, complex, brittle applications won't all be successful if they are just thrown up on the cloud. Virtualization adds performance implications. And many of these applications lack an architecture to achieve scale. A database-bound application will remain database bound, regardless of the additional compute resources beneath it.

Discovering the Business Drivers for Consuming Cloud Services

In the beginning of this chapter, we name reasons companies are thinking about cloud services and some of the pressures coming from management. Clearly, business management is under a lot of pressure to reduce costs while providing a sophisticated level of service to internal and external customers. In this section, we talk about the benefits of cloud services.

Supporting business agility

One of the most immediate benefits of cloud-based infrastructure services is the ability to add new infrastructure capacity quickly and at lower costs. Therefore, cloud services allow the business to gain IT resources in a self-service manager, thus saving time and money. By being able to move more quickly, the business can adapt to changes in the market without complex procurement processes.

A typical cloud service provider has *economies of scale* (cost advantages resulting in the ability to spread fixed costs over more customers) that the typical corporation lacks. As mentioned earlier, the cloud's self-service capability means it's easier for IT to add more *compute cycles* (more CPU resources added on an incremental basis) or storage to meet an immediate or intermittent needs.

With the advent of the cloud, an organization can try out a new application or develop a new application without first investing in hardware, software, and networking.

Reducing capital expenditures

You might want to add a new business application, but lack the money. You might need to increase the amount of storage for various departments. Cloud service providers offer this type of capability at a prorated basis. A cloud service vendor might rent storage on a per-gigabyte basis.

Companies are often challenged to increase the functionality of IT while minimizing capital expenditures. By purchasing just the right amount of IT resources on demand the organization can avoid purchasing unnecessary equipment. There are always trade-offs in any business situation.

A company may significantly reduce expenses by moving to the cloud and then may find that its operating expenses increase more than predicted. In other situations, the company may already have purchased significant IT resources and it may be more economically efficient to use them to create a private cloud. Some companies actually view IT as their primary business and therefore will view IT as a revenue source. These companies will want to invest in their own resources to protect their business value.

Chapter 2

Discovering the Value of the Cloud for Business

In This Chapter

▶ Introducing a model of the cloud

▶ Getting familiar with *as a service*

▶ Measuring the cloud value to your business

A s soon as you start reading about cloud computing, you run into the words *as a service* an awful lot. Examples include *Infrastructure as a Service, hardware as a Service, social networks as a service, applications as a service, desktops as a service,* and so on.

The term *service* is a task that has been packaged so it can be automated and delivered to customers in a consistent and repeatable manner. These services may be delivered by a cloud service vendor or through your own internal data center.

Modeling Services

We include the various types of cloud services into three distinct models, illustrated as different layers in Figure 2-1. The reality is that there is a blending between the types of service delivery models that are available from cloud vendors. For example, a Software as a Service vendor might decide to offer separate infrastructure services to customers. The purpose of grouping these services into three models is to aid in understanding what lies beneath a cloud service. All these service delivery models require management and administration (including security), as depicted by the outer ring in Figure 2-1.

The three cloud service delivery models are Infrastructure as a Service, Platform as a Service, and Software as a Service, and the purpose of each model is as follows:

✔ The Infrastructure as a Service layer offers storage and compute resources that developers and IT organizations use to deliver custom business solutions.

✔ The Platform as a Service layer offers development environments that IT organizations can use to create cloud-ready business applications.

✔ The Software as a Service layer offers purpose-built business applications.

In this chapter we provide an introduction to each model. In addition, because an understanding of each model is critical to developing an understanding of cloud computing, each model is covered in separate chapters in Part II.

The customer accesses those services with defined interfaces. These interfaces are, in fact, all that the user ever comes in contact with. The customer never sees the infrastructure that provides a movie on demand, for example — they only see the screen that enables the user to select and purchase the movie. Likewise, in cloud computing the underlying infrastructure that provides the service may be very sophisticated indeed. However, the user doesn't necessarily need to understand this infrastructure to use it.

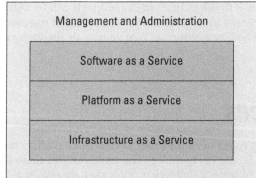

Figure 2-1:
Cloud service delivery models.

Understanding Infrastructure as a Service

Infrastructure as a Service (IaaS) is the delivery of computer hardware (servers, networking technology, storage, and data center space) as a service. It may also include the delivery of operating systems and virtualization technology to manage the resources.

The IaaS customer rents computing resources instead of buying and install-ing them in their own data center. The service is typically paid for on a usage basis. The service may include *dynamic scaling* so that if the customer winds up needing more resources than expected, he can get them immediately (probably up to a given limit).

Dynamic scaling as applied to infrastructure means that the infrastructure can be automatically scaled up or down, based on the requirements of the application.

Additionally, the arrangement involves an agreed-upon *service level.* The ser-vice level states what the provider has agreed to deliver in terms of availabil-ity and response to demand. It might, for example, specify that the resources will be available 99.999 percent of the time and that more resources will be provided dynamically if greater than 80 percent of any given resource is being used.

Currently, the most high-profile IaaS operation is Amazon's Elastic Compute Cloud (Amazon EC2). It provides a Web interface that allows customers to access virtual machines. EC2 offers scalability under the user's control with the user paying for resources by the hour. The use of the term *elastic* in the naming of Amazon's EC2 is significant. The elasticity refers to the ability that EC2 users have to easily increase or decrease the infrastructure resources assigned to meet their needs. The user needs to initiate a request, so this ser-vice provided isn't dynamically scalable. Users of EC2 can request the use of any operating system as long as the developer does all the work. Amazon itself supports a more limited number of operating systems (Linux, Solaris, and Windows). For an up-to-the-minute description of this service, go to `http://aws.amazon.com/ec2`.

Service delivery models defined

You have probably noticed a multitude of com-panies providing all kinds of cloud services, using their own resources. Services you pur-chase from these cloud service providers are offered to you the same way your TV cable provider offers services. Your cable contract provides you with access to watch a specific set of television channels. In addition to receiv-ing your standard channels, you may have a self-service option where you can purchase a movie to watch on demand.

Companies with research-intensive projects are a natural fit for IaaS. Cloud-based computing services allow scientific and medical researchers to perform testing and analysis at levels that aren't possible without additional access to computing infrastructure.

Other organizations with similar needs for additional computing resources may boost their own data centers by renting the computer hardware — appropriate allocations of servers, networking technology, storage, and data center space — as a service. Instead of laying out the capital expenditure for the maximum amount of resources to cover their highest level of demand, they purchase computing power when they need it.

Exploring Platform as a Service

With *Platform as a Service (PaaS),* the provider delivers more than infrastructure. It delivers what you might call a *solution stack* — an integrated set of software that provides everything a developer needs to build an application — for both software development and runtime.

PaaS can be viewed as an evolution of Web hosting. In recent years, Web-hosting companies have provided fairly complete software stacks for developing Web sites. PaaS takes this idea a step farther by providing *lifecycle management* — capabilities to manage all software development stages from planning and design, to building and deployment, to testing and maintenance. The primary benefit of PaaS is having software development and deployment capability based entirely in the cloud — hence, no management or maintenance efforts are required for the infrastructure. Every aspect of software development, from the design stage onward (including source-code management, testing, and deployment) lives in the cloud.

PaaS is inherently multi-tenant and naturally supports the whole set of Web services standards and is usually delivered with dynamic scaling. In reference to Platform as a Service, *dynamic scaling* means that the software can be automatically scaled up or down. Platform as a Service typically addresses the need to scale as well as the need to separate concerns of access and data security for its customers.

Although this approach has many benefits for customers, it also has some disadvantages. The major drawback of Platform as a Service is that it may lock you in to the use of a particular development environment and stack of software components. Platform as a Service offerings usually have some proprietary elements (perhaps the development tools or even component libraries). Consequently, you may be wedded to the vendor's platform and unable to move your applications elsewhere without rewriting them to some degree. If you suddenly become dissatisfied with your Platform as a Service provider, you may face very high expenses when you suddenly need to rewrite the applications to satisfy the requirements of another PaaS vendor.

The fear of vendor lock-in has led to a new variety of Platform as a Service emerging: Open Platform as a Service. This would offer the same approach as Platform as a Service, except that there is no constraint on choice of development software. It avoids the possibility of lock-in.

Some examples of Platform as a Service include the Google App Engine, AppJet, Etelos, Qrimp, and Force.com, which is the official development environment for Salesforce.com. See the "Salesforce.com and automation application" sidebar elsewhere in this chapter for more on this pioneering example of Platform as a Service.

Seeing Software as a Service

One of the first implementations of cloud services was *Software as a Service (SaaS)* — business applications that are hosted by the provider and delivered as a service.

SaaS has its roots in an early kind of hosting operation carried out by *Application Service Providers (ASPs)*. The ASP business grew up soon after the Internet began to mushroom, with some companies offering to securely, privately host applications. Hosting of supply chain applications and *customer relationship management (CRM)* applications was particularly prominent, although some ASPs simply specialized in running email. Prior to the advent of this type of service, companies often spent huge amounts of money implementing and customizing these applications to satisfy internal business requirements. Many of these products weren't only difficult to implement but hard to learn and use. However, the most successful vendors were those who recognized that an application delivered as a service with a monthly fee based on the number of users had to be easy to use and easy to stay with.

CRM is one of the most common categories of Software as a Service; the most prominent vendor in this category is Salesforce.com, described in this chapter's sidebar. For a more extensive look at some of the other examples of Software as a Service, please refer to Chapter 12.

Buying Software as a Service offers a number of obvious advantages: While you can find a lot more information about these benefits in Chapter 12, the following provides some insight into why this approach to software delivery has gained so much traction with vendors and customers. The price of the software is on a *per-use* basis and involves no upfront costs from the service provider. (Of course, the reality is that your company may have some upfront work to do to get your data loaded into the Software as a Service application database and you may have to deal with ongoing data integration between your internal and cloud data stores.) Businesses get the immediate benefit of reducing capital expenditures. In addition, a business gains the flexibility to test new software on a rental basis and then can continue to use and adopt the software, if it proves suitable.

Salesforce.com and automation application

Salesforce.com built and delivered a *sales force automation application* (which automates sales functions such as tracking sales leads and prospects and forecasting sales) that was suitable for the typical salesperson and built a business around making that application available over the Internet through a browser.

The company then expanded by encouraging the growth of a software ecosystem around its extended set of customer relationship management (CRM) applications, prompting other companies to integrate their business applications with those of Salesforce.com (or build components to add to Salesforce.com). It began, for example, by allowing customers to change tabs and create their own database objects. Next, the company added what it called the AppExchange, which added published application programming interfaces (APIs) so that third-party software providers could integrate their applications into the Salesforce.com platform.

Most AppExchange applications are more like utilities than full-fledged packaged apps. Many of the packages sold through the AppExchange are for tracking. For example, one tracks information about commercial and residential prop-

erties; another optimizes the sales process for media/advertising companies; still another package analyzes sales data.

Salesforce.com took its offerings a step further by offering its own language called Apex. Apex is used only within the Salesforce.com platform and lets users build business applications and manage data and processes. A developer can use Apex to change the way the application looks. It is, in essence, the interface as a service.

With the advent of cloud computing, Salesforce.com has packaged these offerings into what it calls Force.com, which provides a set of common services its partners and customers can use to integrate into their own applications. Salesforce.com has thus started to also become a Platform as a Service vendor. Among the hundreds of applications that run on Force.com, it now offers a variety of HR software, and financial, supply chain, inventory, and risk management components. Just as Amazon is currently the trailblazer among the Infrastructure as a Service vendors, Salesforce.com is the trailblazer among the Software as a Service vendors. However, *many* vendors are now providing Applications as a Service. It has become a popular option for selling software.

Software as a Service modes

As a holdover from the traditional ASP model, Software as a Service comes in two distinct modes:

- ✔ **Simple multi-tenancy:** Each customer has its own resources that are segregated from those of other customers. It amounts to a relatively inefficient form of multi-tenancy.

- ✔ **Fine grain multi-tenancy:** This offers the same level of segregation but from a software engineering perspective, it's far more efficient. All resources are shared, but customer data and access capabilities are segregated within the application. This offers much superior economies of scale.

Initially, Software as a Service offerings were not simply implemented over the Internet. For the sake of security and reliability, these offerings would normally involve the use of *virtual private networks (VPNs)*. A VPN essentially makes the public network your own private network (by using some form of encryption) instead of having to purchase dedicated connectivity. This enables you to securely transmit data over a public network like the Internet.

Massively scaled Software as a Service

All as-a-service businesses are based on the service provider offering the service at a much lower cost than you providing it for yourself. If the price difference is large enough, assuming no other complications, it's a win-win — the provider grows a thriving business and the customers pay less to run their applications.

But some applications can be run *really* inexpensively in the cloud. When you have millions of users doing exactly the same thing — and we mean *exactly* the same thing (not similar things) — you can keep the cost per user very, very low. Enter *massively scaled Software as a Service.* One example is Yahoo Mail. Yahoo is the largest email provider, with approximately 260 million users.

This is possible because the provider can optimize all data center components including the hardware, communications, and software to support just one or two types of workloads.

Environments such as Facebook, eBay, Skype, Google Apps, and others are all designed for massive scaling. You may not think of many of these Web sites as being software applications at all. Nevertheless, all are used directly by businesses, for business purposes. For example, some companies use the social networking site Facebook as a free intranet for its employees. Online auctioneer eBay is the basis of more than 500,000 small businesses, Skype (free online calls and video) is used by small businesses the world over, and Google Apps (messaging and collaboration tools) has over a million different businesses enrolled. For more about this topic, take a look at Chapter 13.

Economies of scale

The companies that provide massively scaled Software as a Service achieve *dramatic economies of scale* — cost efficiencies gained from reducing per-unit costs when more of the same item is produced or more of the same workloads are processed.

It's worth listing all the reasons why:

- ✔ The standardized workloads can be executed on a highly integrated, massively replicable infrastructure stack. They don't have to support a wide array of workloads and a heterogeneous stack of hardware, middleware, OS, and so on.

- ✔ The computer hardware and network is highly streamlined and can be bought in bulk and configured to allow expansion. Often these companies require that hardware be engineered for their unique scaling requirements.

- ✔ All software can be stripped down so that only what is necessary is loaded.

- ✔ The service/software itself is written from scratch in a cloud-optimized way, tailored for efficiency at an instruction level.

- ✔ The provider may not offer or guarantee a specific service level.

- ✔ There is no need for virtualization technology to build virtual machines. The software can be engineered to the bare metal.

- ✔ The profile of the workload is measurable and predictable simply by numbers of users.

Management and Administration

If you refer to Figure 2-1, you will notice that the three layers are surrounded with an area called *Management and Administration*. This is where life in the cloud can get very complicated. It's simple enough to describe how to use some kind of cloud computing service, but you also have to integrate it into the IT operations of the organization, and that isn't necessarily a simple thing to do.

For example, because a cloud requires a self-service capability, it must be designed to manage not just provisioning customer requests but also issues such as workload management, security, metering, monitoring, and billing services. We provide much more detail on this topic in Chapters 21 and 22.

Many managers understand that for cloud services to be safe and effective, they must measure and monitor performance.

In fact, performance monitoring will become increasingly important as companies rely more on third-party services. And, from all indications, a typical company may use more than one cloud services provider. For example, a company may use one cloud provider for a platform such as collaboration and a completely different provider for compute services. They may use another provider for storage.

- ✔ How well does each cloud service perform?
- ✔ How are they performing together to support the business?
- ✔ Are the cloud services vendors adhering to governance rules that the company is required to follow?

Refer to Chapter 17 for more information on governance in the cloud.

Don't take a supplier's word that everything is working well. Although your company can save money in the data centers and on software licenses, you need to *spend* money and resources on service management to protect your business assets.

Chapter 3

Getting Inside the Cloud

· ·

In This Chapter

▶ Meeting organizational challenges

▶ Taking on administrative challenges

▶ Examining the technical interface

▶ Getting a handle on cloud resources

▶ Creating manageable services

· ·

At first glance, you might think that the cloud is a totally self-service environment. The reality is more complicated than that. The cloud, like every other computing platform, has to be managed. In this chapter, we discuss the overall cloud environment and the issues you need to consider, from organizational and administrative challenges to managing cloud resources.

Feeling Sensational about Organization

Cloud services impact your organization in subtle ways. The cloud impacts the whole company, not just the IT department:

✔ How do cloud services fit into your overall corporate and IT strategy? How will you manage cloud service providers along with your internal services? How will you make sure that your customers are well supported by services that are moving to a cloud?

✔ Does the cloud support your corporate and IT governance requirements?

✔ What are the important issues of emerging corporate and governmental standards, business process management, and the overall issues of managing costs?

Deciding on a strategy

Like any other technology strategy, a cloud strategy is considered in relationship to the following:

- ✔ Your IT organization's overall strategy
- ✔ Your company's overall strategy

You must make a complex evaluation of costs, benefits, business cultural issues, risks, and corporate and government standards before developing a *comprehensive* cloud strategy. Although very few organizations have tested cloud services in these heavy usage situations, a well-planned cloud service strategy has the potential to significantly reduce costs. Chapter 4 talks you through that strategizing.

Over time, however, as more well-tested commercial cloud services become available, companies will increasingly be able to rely on these services not just for IT cost savings, but also for delivering new value to the organization. The trend toward well-managed cloud services is especially important because of the increased automation across the organization. This may include the software embedded in everything from manufacturing systems to radio frequency identification tags that track inventory.

Cloud services can help organizations in steps. With *utility computing,* any customer can plug in an application or component because all the interfaces have been standardized between implementations. For companies to successfully use the cloud, management must decide what types of services they will begin deploying from the cloud.

One organization may decide that a Software as a Service approach is best, whereas another wants incremental capacity on demand. Before planning a usage strategy, consider what cloud services might be right for you. Most organizations adopt a hybrid strategy, combining internal managed services with cloud-based services. Chapter 9 details hybrid clouds.

Coping with governance issues

Four distinct cloud categories exist (and they're discussed at length in Chapter 2). Each approach presents different governance challenges:

- ✔ Infrastructure as a Service
- ✔ Platform as a Service
- ✔ Software as a Service
- ✔ Business Process as a Service

To make matters more complicated, these approaches have no clean dividing line. Emerging vendors often combine approaches into their offerings. In addition, in most instances, a hybrid situation develops where on-premise applications are used in collaboration with traditionally hosted services and cloud services.

Governing internally provided services and the externally provided cloud-based services introduces new challenges for a company's strategy:

- ✔ How do you manage the overall lifecycle of your IT resources, including software licensing, cost allocation, and charge backs?
- ✔ How to you protect the integrity of your information resources? How do you ensure that you're complying with data privacy rules and regulations?
- ✔ How do you make sure that all your service providers can prove and document that they're meeting governmental and corporate requirements?

IT governance issues are complicated by new suppliers and new capabilities. With governance, your company needs to prove that it's complying with rules set by both governmental agencies and the corporation. Ideally, service providers of all types will deliver the same levels of control that you would have with your own resources. However, when you don't control how that new supplier operates, governance gets more complicated. Cloud computing requires a higher level of oversight to ensure that governance standards are met.

Monitoring business processes

Most cloud services impact the way business processes are implemented within an organization. For example, your organization may be using a cloud-based service to check credit worthiness for potential customers. Therefore, you have to make sure that these services are linked back to your internal systems so things don't fall through the cracks.

Your business should standardize a way to monitor business processes that live entirely or partially in a cloud environment. An organization's important computer-dependent business processes need to be constantly monitored by software. Linking internal and external processes together in a seamless way is the best way to ensure customer satisfaction.

Many organizations already use third-party business process providers for things such as payment services. The importance of third-party providers continues to expand as more services are made available in the cloud — these services will be linked with a variety of internal and external providers. Software components of such business processes may migrate into the cloud, as long as this migration doesn't impede their monitoring. For that reason, you need to examine all cloud propositions to see if they impact business process monitoring.

Managing IT costs

All IT departments monitor costs, but few monitor them in terms of *asset performance* — the requirement to optimize the return on investments for both hardware and software. This is likely to change with the onset of cloud services. Unlike traditional licensing models, cloud propositions are based on rental arrangements.

You must compare two cost models:

- ✔ **Operating expenses** (paying per month, per user for each service)
- ✔ **Capital investments** (paying a purchase fee plus yearly maintenance for software that resides within your organization)

Evaluating the differences between the two cost models is a complex procedure for many companies. In some situations, the new cost models shift some responsibility away from IT to the business unit. For example, if a company's business unit hires 20 new employees and email is managed in the cloud, the business unit needs to budget for 20 more users. IT doesn't have to ensure that server capacity and IT staff are sufficient to support the additional users; that's now the responsibility of the cloud services provider. However, IT departments need to carefully monitor the effectiveness of the cloud environment to support the enterprise.

Administering Cloud Services

A company has to ask itself many questions:

- ✔ Are the cloud services doing what we want them to do?
- ✔ How do we know if the performance is at the right level?
- ✔ How can we judge whether the data that was deleted is really gone?

Solving these problems isn't easy. Investigating the reliability and viability of a cloud provider is one of the most complex areas faced when managing the cloud. The advent of cloud computing will be accompanied by disappointed customers and lawsuits for sure — some as a consequence of unrealistic expectations and some as a consequence of poor service.

It's particularly important for IT departments to enable administration systems that let them monitor every dimension of the service they're getting.

In theory, the cloud service provider can build and provide a very stable service that is less expensive than a customer can implement internally. However, there can be a serious gap between the actual service and the promises made in the provider's sales literature.

You have to do your homework when evaluating the providers. Evaluate their experience in the market, the type of partnerships they've established, and their reputation in the market. You can also talk to other customers that have used their services.

Here are some of the issues to consider:

- ✔ What vendors are available to solve your problem?
- ✔ How effective are the providers in managing their own environment?
- ✔ Do they provide repeatable services?
- ✔ How do these vendors handle an outage?
- ✔ What's their experience in dealing with customer issues?

In addition to finding a good partner, it's always a good idea to have more than one provider as an alternative.

Service level agreements and monitoring

Every company that buys any service from a cloud service provider must either accept a standard service level agreement (SLA) from the provider or negotiate such an agreement. A *service level agreement* is a contract that stipulates the type of service you need from providers and what type of penalties would result from an unexpected business interruption.

No organization should commit mission-critical systems to the cloud without negotiating an SLA that includes significant penalties for not delivering the promised service level. Management needs to know what service level is appropriate under changing business conditions. Management can't assume that the service provider will provide all the monitoring. Rather, the administrators must have their *own* ability to monitor service to satisfy the company's goals for performance.

Support

Support problems don't disappear when applications or infrastructures move to the cloud. You have to make sure that support targets are agreed on in advance with a cloud services provider. Therefore, your company must align its internal support team that deals with internal customers with the cloud provider.

What processes are in place to resolve problems when they arise? Just consider the situation where some important application has a performance problem. Especially in a hybrid environment, it's not always easy to tell if a problem resides within the cloud or outside of it. Such situations need to be prevented or at least dealt with very efficiently.

Billing and accounting

One cloud benefit is that, as a customer you can acquire just as much capability as needed. For this to work, billing and account management must be automated. Customers, therefore, need to be able to monitor what they're using and how much it costs.

Potential problems arise if service level penalties aren't clear and if the provider adds too many incidental charges. Customers can run up unexpected bills if they can't accurately track usage.

Looking at the Technical Interface

Because the cloud service market is so new, few applications have been built from the ground up for this new environment. So far, no corporate applications were built with this model in mind.

Organizations that already have well-designed interfaces between application and infrastructure components may find it easier to transition to the cloud. Companies that have moved to a *service-oriented architecture (SOA)* are well positioned to make the move. Chapter 19 talks about SOA in detail.

With SOA, organizations build modular business services that include standardized interfaces. This modular approach is needed when approaching the highly distributed cloud environment. SOA is a good start; however, a lot of standardized interfaces will need to be developed for cloud service platforms in the coming years. (For more on the topic of service-oriented architecture, see *Service Oriented Architecture For Dummies*, Second Edition, by Judith Hurwitz, Robin Bloor, Marcia Kaufman, and Fern Halper.)

APIs and data transformations

A cloud's *Application Programming Interface (API)* is the software interface that lets your company's infrastructure or applications plug in to the cloud. This is perhaps the most important place for standardization.

Many vendors in the cloud space would like to claim overall leadership and control over the interfaces. Therefore, many different vendors are developing their own interfaces. This, in turn, means that customers are likely to be forced to support multiple APIs. Managing multiple APIs means that when applications are changed, there's more programming involved; and there's more potential for errors when too many APIs are supported.

Even if vendors agree to a set of API standards, there will be data transformation issues (as data moves from one physical machine to another). These data transformations are the same as those required in projects such as building a data warehouse, with just one minor difference: The built-in software platform and Software as a Service environments must follow the data standards of the particular cloud service provider. For an organization to easily build connections between its internal data center and the cloud, it must use standardized APIs and data transformation capabilities.

Data and application architecture

New internally created services that support the changing business's changing demands must operate with cloud ecosystems. These services may need to migrate to and from the cloud. For example, a company might initiate a partnership that requires development and deployment in the cloud. This means that it will have to build an architecture that's modular enough to allow services to move between various cloud platforms.

The consistency and flexibility of an *SOA* approach makes it a good fit for the cloud. In an SOA environment, software components are put into services or containers. These containers hold software that executes a specific task. After software exists within a container, it can be ported from one environment to another, which makes it easier to port into and out of the cloud.

To be effective in a cloud environment, data also has to be packaged and managed. This isn't simple, but it's instrumental in making the cloud an effective business platform. The IT organization needs to manage data independently of the underlying packaged application, transactional system, or data environment such as a warehouse. Important data needs to easily move between internal data centers and external cloud-based environments. Your organization needs to start with consistent definitions of data elements to manage cloud-based information services.

Security in the cloud

Companies planning to use cloud services must be assured of tight, well-defined security services. Chapter 15 details security.

Many levels of security are required within a cloud environment:

- **Identity management:** For example, so that any application service or even hardware component can be authorized on a personal or group role basis.
- **Access control:** There also needs to be the right level of access control within the cloud environment to protect the security of resources.
- **Authorization and authentication:** There must be a mechanism so the right people can change applications and data.

A comprehensive security infrastructure must be provided at all levels and types of cloud services. Developers also need tools that allow them to secure the services they design to be delivered in the cloud. Organizations need consistent security across their own data center environments that intersect with a cloud service.

Managing Cloud Resources

In theory, cloud-services–based resources should be no different from the resources in your own environment, except that they live remotely. Ideally, you have a complete view of the resources you use today or may want to use in the future. Although this sounds straightforward, achieving it isn't that easy.

In most cloud environments, the customer is able to access only the services they're entitled to use. Entire applications may be used on a cloud services basis. Development tools are sometimes cloud based. In fact, testing and monitoring environments can be based on the cloud.

How should you, the cloud customer, approach managing cloud resources? Three aspects of cloud resource management apply:

- IT security
- Performance management
- Provisioning

IT security

IT security is a major concern for new adopters of cloud computing. Ideally, you want the IT security in the cloud to integrate seamlessly with the IT security in your own data center.

However, the cloud service provider implements its own IT security procedures

  ✔ To protect customers from external threats
  ✔ To ensure that individual customer environments are isolated from one another

For every type of cloud service, the provider delivers a good deal of the IT security. You may need to understand how the cloud provider handles issues such as patch management and configuration management as the provider upgrades to new tools and new operating systems.

As the customer, you should

  ✔ Understand the IT security software and hardware (firewalls, intrusion detection systems, virtual private networks [VPNs], and secure connections) that the cloud provider has in place.
  ✔ Know how the cloud providers are protecting the overall computing environment.

In the case of Infrastructure as a Service and Platform as a Service, cloud providers need to clarify the kind of IT security it expects the customer to put in place on its own behalf. With Software as a Service, the provider is responsible for all security except for access security — either an identity management system or at least a local access control application — through the customer's own systems.

Performance management

Performance management is all about how your software services run effectively inside your own environment and through the cloud.

If you start to connect software that runs in your own data center directly to software that runs in the cloud, you create a potential bottleneck at the point of connection.

When you move applications or services into the cloud, you change the basic data center network topology and some application configurations (and possibly some interfaces). This means that performance needs to be considered and designed in at the start for every type of cloud service: Infrastructure as a Service, Platform as a Service, and Software as a Service.

Services connected between the cloud and your computing environment can impact performance if they aren't well planned. This is especially likely to be the case if there are data translations or specific protocols to adhere to at the cloud gateway.

As a customer, your ability to directly control the resources will be much lower in the cloud. Therefore,

✔ The connection points between various services must be monitored in real time. A breakdown may impact your ability to provide a business process to your customers.

✔ There must be expanded bandwidth at connection points.

From the performance perspective, the situation is likely to be much less fragile if systems don't straddle the data center and the cloud.

In reality, many companies combine services in the cloud and services within their own data center. Therefore, monitoring across these environments prevents many problems.

Provisioning

With Software as a Service, a customer expects provisioning (to request a resource for immediate use) of extra services s to be immediate, automatic, and effortless. The cloud service provider is responsible for maintaining an agreed-on level of service and provisions resources accordingly.

The situation is similar with Platform as a Service or Infrastructure as a Service, but you may need to directly request additional resources — because in both cases you're directly managing the cloud resources instead of having them managed on your behalf.

The normal situation in a data center is that software workloads vary throughout the day, week, month, and year. So the data center has to be built for the maximum possible workload, with a little bit of extra capacity thrown in to cover unexpectedly high peaks. One of the immediate attractions of Infrastructure as a Service is that a data center could move its volatile workloads into the cloud and pay for additional resources on demand. In other words, hardware use in the data center is much more efficient.

Service management

Service management in this context covers all the data center operations activities. This broad discipline considers the necessary techniques and tools for managing services by both cloud providers and the internal data center managers across these environments:

- ✔ Physical
- ✔ IT
- ✔ Virtual

Service management encompasses many different disciplines, including

- ✔ Configuration management
- ✔ Asset management
- ✔ Network management
- ✔ Capacity planning
- ✔ Service desk
- ✔ Root cause analysis
- ✔ Workload management
- ✔ Patch and update management

The reality is that the cloud itself is a service management platform. Therefore, well-designed cloud service portfolios include a tight integration of the core service management capabilities and well-defined interfaces.

Untangling Software Dependencies

Perhaps the biggest problem that organizations face when they consider moving applications systems or whole collections of systems into the cloud is the issue of software dependencies. This is important because the cloud uses a service-oriented architecture approach where these services are loosely coupled (loosely linked) together. How do you deal with the dependencies between services? See Chapter 19 for more on loose coupling and service orientation.

In theory, all the applications running your data center share infrastructure and data. However, as companies begin migrating applications or capabilities (such as data or storage) into the cloud, these applications need to be designed to support technical independence.

Therefore, before any part of the data center moves to the cloud, it needs to be separated from dependencies that already exist. For a gradual move into the cloud, the full inventory of applications and systems needs to be considered in terms of which ones *must* — or at least *should* — move together. The interdependencies determine this, whatever their perspective:

- ✔ Hardware perspective (for example, a specific clustering of processors is required)
- ✔ Platform perspective (say, the provider must use a given OS and a given middleware product)
- ✔ Software perspective (maybe the specific services need to be closely coupled with related applications)
- ✔ From any mixture of these

Removing the dependencies among various applications and systems helps an organization evolve the data center into a more flexible, modular environment. Establishing this architectural approach, in effect, creates containers of functionality within the data center that ease the transition to the cloud.

Chapter 4

Developing Your Clo

. . . .

In This Chapter

▶ Knowing your company's strategy

▶ Assessing your environment

▶ Doing the math

▶ Weighing the risks

. . . .

*M*any companies think that the cloud has the potential to dramatically reduce the costs of managing their technology infrastructure. The situation isn't black and white. In some situations, cloud-based services are the right solution at the right time at the right price. In other circumstances, the cloud as a platform needs more investigation before applying it to a business problem. It is tempting to simply start using a variety of cloud services in response to an immediate problem. However, before you get too far down the road, you need to make sure that you have a strategy and road map for how and when you are going to use cloud services within your organization.

You need a strategy. Here, we list five key areas that should be part of your planning:

 ✔ When and how should you use a public, private, and hybrid cloud service?

 ✔ What is your company's strategy for managing capital and operational expenses over time?

 ✔ How do you plan to achieve the right level of service across the cloud and the data center?

 ✔ What are the rules and regulations that your cloud provider needs to adhere to, to keep your company safe and in compliance?

 ✔ How are you planning to control the data as it moves out of your data center into external clouds?

There is no *one* right path or strategy to leveraging cloud services within your business. The decision depends on your data center, your applications, your service portfolio, and your changing business requirements.

Seeing the Many Aspects of Your Cloud Strategy

You have to think about several issues before sending your organization into the cloud. There isn't just one approach. You might choose one or more of these approaches at different times for different reasons.

Consider a few simple examples:

- ✔ **Your company is building a new application that will change the way you sell products online.** You want to stress test this new application before releasing it to customers. Although you have a few extra resources inside your firewall, they aren't extensive enough to demonstrate if the new application will really scale. Using a cloud Infrastructure as a Service enables you to test the application effectively.

- ✔ **Your company has run its own email internally for more than 20 years.** It takes up a lot of space in the data center and requires a staff of ten people. Money is tight and the CIO must cut staff and capital expenses. The CIO finds a Software as a Service platform that can run the corporate email for a fraction of the cost of running email internally. Your company makes the move and the savings are dramatic.

- ✔ **Your company is building a new but highly experimental application that might transform its business model.** It might not be worth spending a lot of money on software and hardware upfront. In fact, if the project succeeds, the new application may be deployed in the cloud (and not within your company's own data center). Therefore, the company uses a *Platform as a Service (PaaS)* that includes its own well-designed and fully vetted development environment, new generation tools, and interfaces that allow it to connect to many different environments. No need to pretest all the components provided by the PaaS vendor — they're well designed and have been tested. The new application built on this platform is completed in record time and deployed to a test group of customers directly from the cloud service.

- ✔ **Your company has started using a third-party SaaS solution for its customer-management application.** It has successfully replaced the on-premise customer-relationship management package that you've been running in the data center for years. Now your company wonders what else could be moved out of the data center into the cloud. How about the mainframe transaction processing system that handles all orders worth more than $1 million? After some investigation, you realize that because the system is only used by a few individuals in the company and the information needs to be carefully governed, the cloud isn't a good choice.

✔ **Your CIO has seen some new software that could solve a serious problem, but you aren't convinced that the solution is right.** Instead of buying a license, your company decides to use it as a service. After six months, it proves valuable. The software company offers you the opportunity to use the Software as a Service or on premise.

As you can see, planning your cloud strategy has many different dimensions — maybe more than what you might have thought about in the past. You need a road map to think about how a cloud strategy can be used to support your company's business goals.

Questioning Your Company's Strategy

Deciding to investigate cloud computing is primarily a business decision. Therefore, start by evaluating these things:

✔ Your company's business strategy

✔ The role that your technology infrastructure plays in that strategy

Ask these questions:

✔ What type of business am I in?

✔ Is my industry highly regulated?

✔ How do I benefit my customers?

✔ How much value am I getting from my existing data center operations?

✔ What are my company's short-term and long-term goals?

✔ Am I under pressure to reduce capital expenses?

✔ Am I planning to develop new, untested technology-based offerings over the next 18–24 months?

✔ Am I looking to acquire complementary companies?

✔ How are my competitors dealing with their technology strategy?

✔ Are my competitors able to move more quickly than my company?

✔ What are my strategic advantages?

After you understand the company strategy, you can develop your own strategic plan.

'here You Are Today

 the curse of cloud computing is that it is actually quite
d. In many cases, you start with the cloud as a technical
 then move to a strategic approach over time. One of
ud computing is that for very low cost you can try out a
ow it works, and how it might benefit your company. You
-ly sign yourself up for a service.

And that might be a fine starting point. However, make sure that you're thinking strategically, not just about one or a series of cloud services; investigate
how these services fit into your overall computing strategy. You need to ask
yourself the following questions.

How tangled is my computing environment?

Whether you're a small or large company, you probably have a lot of applications. Some applications may have been developed internally, whereas
others may be packaged software. What makes a computing environment
complicated? There could be hundreds of these applications with thousands
of dependencies that are difficult to untangle. For example, your company
might have a single mortgage-management system that depends on ten other
accounting and customer-management systems. Your company might rely
on external services from a third party (a provider of payment services, for
example). Indeed, most data centers have evolved over time into a complex,
tangled web of applications, servers, and networks.

What's my data center environment?

When you consider peeling off some applications and moving them to the
cloud, think about the impact on your overall business. Many computing
environments aren't set up as a series of well-defined services.

Analyze your computing environment's current state. This type of analysis
gives you clues to possible cost savings. Instead of moving applications
directly to the cloud, you might actually have to start by simplifying your
internal computing environment.

Take a hard look at your data center:

- ✔ Is the architecture consistent or does each application have its own architecture?
- ✔ Are there common business services used by multiple applications?
- ✔ Are these common business services self-contained (or do they depend on other applications and services in your environment)?
- ✔ Has your organization implemented workload management?

The more service enabled your computing environment becomes, the better prepared your organization will be to take advantage of various cloud services. It's much harder to move components into the cloud if you can't separate applications or business services from your data center services.

What data supports my strategy?

Consider the information running in your data center. Before moving any data into the cloud, you need to think about

- ✔ Privacy and compliance issues
- ✔ Security issues
- ✔ Data management issues specific to your company

For example, if you're a financial services organization that moves your email into the cloud, email must be archived. After archiving the email, it must be easily accessible to meet regulatory considerations. Another example: A multinational company, before moving data into the cloud for marketing analysis, checks the laws regarding data access by different governments, cross-country data flow, and so on.

Data management and security are so important that we devote two separate chapters to each topic: See Chapters 8 and 15. In fact, your data may require reevaluation of a public cloud model to a private or hybrid model. Chapter 9 details private and hybrid clouds.

It might seem a lot of work to go through the exercise of understanding your current environment. It's crucial to helping you pick the right cloud strategy for your organization.

- ✔ You may think the best starting point is to implement Infrastructure as a Service to add incremental storage capacity to support a new business initiative.

✔ You might decide to use Platform as a Service to limit the capital expenses needed to develop a new application.

✔ Another starting point might be to add Software as a Service to analyze what the market is saying about your products and any possible acquisition targets.

✔ Some organizations might have the need for a Business Process as a Service (such as a supply chain service on demand) that could support testing a new line of business.

Assessing Your Expense Structure

One of the most important tasks when preparing for the cloud: Assessing your cost structure (for example, how much you're spending on supporting existing hardware, software, networking services). How can you determine the cost savings if you don't know what you're spending today? Also take potential future costs into account.

Things may get fuzzy. You may sometimes want to use business services offered by cloud application vendors. You may want to build some internal service oriented architecture-based services that can live inside a cloud environment. In some situations, it may save money to move a service such as email, software testing, or storage to a cloud, because the costs of performing the service internally are so much higher. In other situations, the costs for implementing a key application in the cloud may be much more expensive than running it internally.

Chapter 21 explains more about cloud economics.

Checking Up on Rules and Governances

We recommend assessing your current IT and business governance situation as you develop your cloud strategy. In some cases, governance and compliance prohibit certain types of information from leaving the organization's internal environment. How good is your internal security today? If you're considering a cloud service provider, you need to be confident that the company can support your security and governance needs with oversight and accountability. Examine the reports and documentation to support your oversight requirements. Talk to the provider's other customers to see how well it meets its customers governance requirements.

For example, you may want to leverage a third-party credit checking service from the cloud. How well constructed is it? Does it conform to your company's business rules?

Aside from security and privacy issues, you have a number of legal issues to consider as well. For example, what happens to your application and data if the cloud provider goes out of business? Who's liable for lost information? Does the provider guarantee uptime? What recourse do you have if the service level agreement isn't met?

Chapter 16 details governance issues.

Developing a Road Map

You must consider many things before developing a road map:

- The efficiency and effectiveness of your current data center
- Costs
- Risks
- Your organizational readiness

After you understand the issues and gaps, you can start designing your cloud plan — the road map that outlines the following:

- What are the services that you need to support your business growth?
- How you will roll them out?
- When you will roll them out (or *in,* as it were)?

Don't try to do everything at once with your cloud strategy. It probably makes sense to roll out these services gradually so you can see the benefits and get buy-in throughout your organization. Plus, starting cloud services step by step can help you react quickly to business needs.

Even if you figure out all the technical requirements for leveraging the cloud as part of your strategy, you still have to plan to communicate the action plan to the business and the IT communities. Some people might consider the cloud a threat because it will remove some tasks from the IT department. Business management will want to know that they have control over important business data. For more details on your strategy action plan see Chapter 22.

You need to understand how your vendors track performance and security. Don't simply take their word for it and assume that everything is perfectly fine. Even if the cloud vendor provides you with a slick dashboard, you should have your own means of monitoring your content. You're turning over some key responsibility to a cloud provider, but the buck still stops with your organization. Plan carefully for controlling your assets in the cloud. Chapter 20 talks more about management from a cloud customer perspective.

Part II
Understanding the Nature of the Cloud

The 5th Wave   By Rich Tennant

"We're still working out the kinks in our cloud computing environment."

In this part . . .

What's inside the cloud? In this part, we examine a highly scaled computing environment. Because that environment is front and center, we look at the technical foundation for this model, including workloads and data services.

Chapter 5

Seeing the Advantages of the Highly Scaled Data Center

In This Chapter

▶ Modeling a data center

▶ Location, location, location

▶ Powering things up

▶ Cooling things off

*A*s we discuss in Chapter 1, many company managers are demanding that IT management transform their data centers into platforms that can scale easily and effectively. Other managers are looking at the cloud platform as a way to eliminate the high costs of running traditional data centers.

If you're tasked with planning your cloud strategy, how do you do what's best for your organization? At first glance, it might seem obvious: Simply find a cloud services provider, analyze how much it charges for the services you need, and compare it to the costs of your own data center. It isn't that simple.

✔ It's unlikely that everything you do in your data center will be available as a cloud service.

✔ Even if it is, it might not meet your specific needs.

Ultimately, cloud services are attractive because the cost is likely to be far lower than providing the same service from your traditional data center, so we think it will help if you understand *why* cloud data center costs are lower. This economic factor applies to clouds whether they're private or public.

In fact, the cloud data center has two aspects:

✓ The costs of things that don't depend directly on technology

✓ The costs of things that do

In this chapter, we take an in-depth look at the things that don't depend on technology and explain why the cloud data center has a significant cost advantage.

Comparing Financial Damage: Traditional versus Cloud

How much does a data center cost to run? It depends on these things:

✓ **How big it is.** How many virtual servers? Is the data center massive? How much square footage; how many servers? Does it cost $5 million a year to run?

✓ **Where it is.** How much does office space cost. What about cost of staff? Is the data center close to inexpensive power sources?

✓ **What it's doing.** Does the data center protect sensitive data? What is its kind of business? What level of compliance must it adhere to?

Clearly, you have many ways to look at the situation.

Traditional data center

Although each data center is a little different, the average cost per year to operate a large data center is usually between $10 million to $25 million.

Stranger than fiction

We didn't make up the $10 million to $25 million number. In 2008, *BusinessWeek Magazine* published an article called "Computing Heads for the Clouds," by Rachael King (http://images.businessweek.com/ss/08/08/0804_cloudcomputing/1.htm). The magazine surveyed 11 different large data centers throughout the United States.

Where's the bulk of the money going? This might surprise you.

- ✔ **42 percent:** Hardware, software, disaster recovery arrangements, uninterrupted power supplies, and networking. (Costs are spread over time, *amortized,* because they are a combination of capital expenditures and regular payments.)

- ✔ **58 percent:** Heating, air conditioning, property and sales taxes, and labor costs. (In fact, as much as 40 percent of annual costs are labor alone.)

The reality of the traditional data center is further complicated because most of the costs maintain existing (and sometimes aging) applications and infrastructure. Some estimates show 80 percent of spending on maintenance.

Before you conclude that you need to throw out the data center and just move to the cloud, know the nature of the applications and the workloads at the core of data centers:

- ✔ Most data centers run a lot of different applications and have a wide variety of workloads.

- ✔ Many of the most important applications running in data centers are actually used by only a relatively few employees. For example, transaction management applications (which are critical to a company's relationship to customers and suppliers) might only be used by a few employees.

- ✔ Some applications that run on older systems are taken off the market (no longer sold) but are still necessary for business.

Because of the nature of these applications, it probably *wouldn't* be cost effective to move these environments to the cloud.

Cloud data center

In this case *cloud data centers* means data centers with 10,000 or more servers on site, all devoted to running very few applications that are built with consistent infrastructure components (such as racks, hardware, OS, networking, and so on).

What's the key difference in the cost structure of a traditional data center and a cloud data center? One of the most important factors is that cloud data centers aren't remodeled traditional data centers.

Cloud data centers are

- ✔ Constructed for a different purpose.
- ✔ Created at a different time than the traditional data center.
- ✔ Built to a different scale.
- ✔ Not constrained by the same limitations.
- ✔ Perform different workloads than traditional data centers.

Because of this design approach, the economics of a cloud data center are significantly different.

To create a basis for analyzing this, we used figures on the costs of creating a cloud data center described in a Microsoft paper titled "The Cost of a Cloud: Research Problems in Data Center Networks" by Albert Greenberg, James Hamilton, David A. Maltz, and Parveen Patel.

We took estimates for how much it cost to build a cloud data center and looked at three cost factors:

- ✔ **Labor** costs were 6 percent of the total costs of operating the cloud data center.
- ✔ **Power distribution and cooling** were 20 percent.
- ✔ **Computing** costs were 48 percent.

Of course, the cloud data center has some different costs than the traditional data center (such as buying land and construction).

This explanation of costs is designed to give you an idea of where the difference between the traditional data center and the cloud data center are. The upfront costs in constructing cloud data centers are actually spread across hundreds of thousands of individual users. Therefore, after they're constructed, these cloud data centers are well positioned to be profitable because they support so many customers with a large number of servers executing a single application.

Scaling the Cloud

From the provider's point of view, the whole point of cloud computing is to achieve economies of scale by managing a very large pool of computing resources in a highly economic and efficient fashion.

A picture makes it a little clearer. Figure 5-1 shows a graph of the cost per user of running just one software application using different kinds of computer resources; this is charted against the number of users. We need to emphasize that we're talking about just *one* application — not even two or three. In Figure 5-1, that one application runs in different computing environments, starting with inefficient dedicated servers all the way up to massively scaled grids.

An important point to note is that the Y-axis of user populations is logarithmic. That means that the curve is much less steep than if we drew it on a proportional scale of equal steps. If we drew it on a proportional scale, we'd need miles of paper.

We deliberately *didn't* put units on the X-axis. Instead, note the following:

✔ One end of the X-axis shows data center costs between $1–$50 per user per annum. That reflects, for example, the prices that Google charges for Google Apps or even the cost of providing free email (from Google, Microsoft, or Yahoo, which is paid for by ads). The cost per user is extremely low.

✔ The other end of the X-axis shows data center costs between $1,000–$5,000 per user per annum. That might be the cost of, for example, providing a print server that's almost always idle.

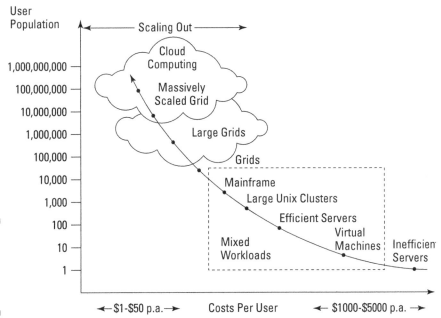

Figure 5-1:
Cloud computing economies of scale.

Basically, on the left in Figure 5-1 you have very efficient use of computer resources and, on the right, very *inefficient* use of resources.

Points on the line indicate the kind of computing resources that serve specific group sizes:

- ✔ **Inefficient servers:** This is a 1:1 user-to-server ratio (or close to 1). The cost of managing a single server in a data center will be thousands of dollars per year and this is as expensive as computing ever gets per user.

- ✔ **Virtual machines:** Applications and user numbers that can't use a whole server get *virtualized* (split among several virtual servers). This is efficient (making better use of underused servers), but also inefficient (virtualization requires significant overhead, as does running the multiple guest operating systems).

- ✔ **Efficient servers (and small clusters):** User populations from the hundreds to 1,000 can be served reasonably efficiently with a single or multiple servers if there's only one application being run on a server; servers can be highly efficient, yielding a relatively low cost per user.

- ✔ **Mainframe and large Unix clusters:** They're shown separately on the grid only for the sake of space. Both can handle very large database applications from thousands to tens of thousands of users.

- ✔ **Grids:** From the hundreds of thousands to a million users, you're in the area where *Software as a Service (SaaS)* vendors such as Salesforce.com operate. Business applications offered by SaaS vendors present a thorny scaling problem because it's a transactional database application. The main Salesforce.com CRM application runs on a grid of about 1,000 computers.

- ✔ **Large grids:** Concurrent users above one million. Still a very heavy workload and only possible via a *scale-out* (which lets a single workload expand by using more of the identical inexpensive resources) approach with a grid. Twitter and Linked-In are examples.

- ✔ **Massively scaled grid:** This is for user populations in the tens of millions. Example: Each query on Google search is resolved by a purpose-built grid of up to 1,000 servers; Google routes queries to many such grids. Yahoo also has a massively scaled-out email system. It caters to more than 260 million users, of which tens of millions must be active at a time.

The dotted box in Figure 5-1 indicates the *traditional* domain and kinds of resources of corporate computing. The same servers used in corporate environments could be used just as easily in scaled-out arrangements, where workloads aren't at all mixed. The reduction in per-user costs doesn't, at the moment, come from using different computer equipment or different operating systems: It comes from running a small number (or even just one) workload and scaling it up as much as possible. That's how cloud computing reduces costs dramatically.

No corporation that runs a mixed workload is ever going to achieve cloud computing's economies of scale.

But how do massively scaled data centers manage to get their per-user costs so very low? This becomes clear when you read about each area of data costs in Chapter 21.

Comparing Traditional and Cloud Data Center Costs

Before reading how to reduce data center costs, reread the *traditional* IT costs statistics:

- ✔ Portion of IT budget used to maintain and run existing systems: 70–80 percent
- ✔ Portion of IT budget used to build and implement new capabilities: 20–30 percent

Compare traditional and cloud data centers in Table 5-1.

Table 5-1 A Comparison of Corporate and Cloud Data Centers	
Traditional Corporate Data Center	*Cloud Data Center*
Thousands of different applications	Few applications (maybe even just one)
Mixed hardware environment	Homogeneous hardware environment
Multiple management tools	Standardized management tools
Frequent application patching and updating	Minimal application patching and updating
Complex workloads	Simple workloads
Multiple software architectures	Single standard software architecture

Looking at the table, it becomes clear that the cloud data center is much simpler to organize and operate and, because it is simple, it scales well. In other words, the larger you make it, the lower the costs per user are. In the next section, we examine some of these costs and see where the efficiencies arise.

Examining labor costs and productivity

Labor costs depend on several things:

- ✔ **Technology managing the data center:** Even improving that technology in a traditional corporate setting may reduce the cost of labor only a small amount.

- ✔ **In what environment someone works:** The labor cost per person is likely to be equivalent regardless of the data center type; the skills requirement is the same. But that person's *productivity* varies depending on the environment. Operating the scaled cloud data center is much simpler.

The impact of this set of differences on labor costs is dramatic. Corporate data centers usually have a ratio of operational staff to severs of around 1 person to 65 servers. In cloud data centers, that ratio is more like 1 person to 850 servers, and we've even come across better ratios than that. This is a 10-to-1 improvement in the productivity of labor (or possibly more — maybe going as high as 20 to 1).

Wondering where you are

The traditional setup's 58 percent costs depend a lot on location:

- ✔ Electricity fees
- ✔ Local taxes
- ✔ Labor costs

Compare a data center in North Carolina with one in New York (keeping in mind no two data centers have the same software workloads). Better to consider technology costs separately and see where economies arise, which we do in the following sections.

Electric power

Computers have been using more electricity in recent years and, at 7 percent of corporate data centers' costs (including heating and cooling), the cost is significant. Cloud data centers use even more: Electricity costs hover around 12 percent.

Cloud data centers can do the following:

✔ **Put the data center where the cheap power is.** Electricity fluctuates in price from year to year and costs are difficult to control.

✔ **Negotiate a discounted power contract with its power company.** Cloud data centers, by their level of usage, fall into the least expensive category.

If a cloud data center is contemplating building a data center, it can negotiate a long-term deal for an even deeper discount than industrial usage gives them. Put the data center very close to the power plant and bargain for a lower cost supply based on these points:

- Distance from the power station (because less electrical power is lost in transit).

- Minimal power interruption from electrical storms (if you have a private circuit direct to the power station).

Outsourcing

Because power is so critical to the cloud data center, organizations have to consider the availability and cost of energy sources as they would any primary data center resource.

Electricity sources include the following:

✔ Hydroelectric is generally expensive when it has to travel far to customers, but otherwise it's usually cheap and can be the ideal source of power for a data center.

✔ Oil prices change, which can cause cost fluctuation.

✔ Liquified natural gas (LNG) suffers from the same changing fuel prices as oil.

✔ Coal is more stable in price, but not green.

✔ Nuclear is inexpensive to run but expensive to build and gain approval

---

Other location costs

Other location related costs when building a new data center include the following:

✔ **Land costs:** The days of siting data centers in skyscrapers in Manhattan are over. Better to use cheap land with low property taxes. There are exceptions, of course. For example, in algorithmic financial trading, latency lost due to networking (communications) distance directly impacts revenue.

✔ **Building costs:** A designed-entirely-as-a-data-center building is a must.

- *Heat management* is the overriding priority, so building *out* almost certainly makes more sense than building *up.* Cool geographical areas may make more sense than hotter ones.

- *Safety* is another important consideration. Data centers need to be electrically safe, secure, and fireproof.

✔ **Staff:** Although staff costs are very low for the cloud data center, as a percentage of the whole, location in areas (or even countries) where staff costs are low can further reduce staff costs.

✔ **Investment incentives and taxation:** Many areas of the world, including states in the United States, welcome inward investment and help finance it with very generous tax exemptions and cash incentives. Take advantage of these opportunities when you find them.

In the next chapter, we examine technology costs, which also favor the cloud data center in many ways. The simple fact is that data centers as they exist now, in the enterprise, are a cottage industry that's going to change in the coming years by the mass-production efficiencies of cloud data centers.

Chapter 6

Exploring the Technical Foundation for Scaling Computer Systems

In This Chapter

▶ Comparing traditional data centers to clouds

▶ Achieving economies of scale

▶ Saving money via the bottom line

*I*n Chapter 5, we contrast the non-technology operational costs of the traditional data center with those of the cloud data center (electricity, cooling, space, and so on). In this chapter, we contrast technology costs between the traditional data center and the cloud data center.

We divided into four areas the places where IT spends money:

✓ **Hardware,** including servers, storage, and so on

✓ **A power supply** for those systems and how to keep them from overheating

✓ **Networking and communications equipment** so the systems can interoperate

✓ **Electricity** to support the overall data center

Some elements are more expensive than others. In Chapter 5, we look at two reports that detail the costs of running traditional and cloud data centers. Using this same set of numbers, we calculated the costs of the areas. The results are quite interesting. The greatest expense in the traditional data center is server and storage hardware, which accounts for 36 percent of the amortized costs. The second biggest expense? Power distribution and cooling. Amortized over a year, power and cooling are 20 percent of the total expenses. Both networking and electricity each add 12 percent to the total expense number per year. Add hardware and its supporting power and cooling, and you have 56 percent of the technology related costs.

We discuss electricity costs in the previous chapter, but only from the perspective of arranging for an inexpensive supply. In this chapter, we take on the issue of using that electricity efficiently.

Server-ing Up Some Hardware

Although we'd like to tell you that costs are static, clearly they aren't. Costs for your data center hardware will vary dramatically depending on the type of workloads you support.

Data storage is an excellent example of this variation. If a data center is feeding video to the Internet from a vast video library (like YouTube does) the storage requirements are huge. However, storing short text messages (as Twitter does) doesn't require a lot of space. Indeed, Twitter doesn't even store its billions of messages indefinitely. The YouTube library, on the other hand, just keeps on growing.

Tradition! versus clouds

What does this mean when you look at the differences in the costs of hardware between the traditional data center and the cloud data center? Look at a snapshot of each:

- ✔ **Tradition:** In a traditional data center, IT management has a structured process for purchasing hardware. Each year they talk to business units, determine what new applications to add or expand, and work with vendors on the procurement process. In addition, most IT organizations refresh their hardware on a regular basis to make sure that things run smoothly and old systems are retired before they cause problems.

- ✔ **Cloud:** When a business is creating a cloud data center (either a private one inside the firewall or a service provider) the process of procuring systems is very different. Because the cloud supports very different workloads, IT management doesn't buy traditional hardware. Rather, IT management might go directly to an engineering company that designs the system boards and networking switches for them, and then take the contract to a manufacturer to have them build the precise hardware that they want.

The bottom line is that the cloud data center is well suited to buying precisely what you need in a very economical manner. In contrast, the traditional data center doesn't have the same economies of scale.

We aren't being critical of the server products that are built and delivered by big computer manufacturers. Such engineering is difficult to criticize in its natural context. All such servers, whether mainframes or cheap commodity server boards, are designed for general circumstances of typical customers. It's just really unlikely that the requirements of a cloud center are anywhere close to typical.

Considering cloud hardware

When your company is establishing a cloud data center, think about the hardware elements in a different way. The following sections summarize considerations.

Cooling

Cloud data centers have the luxury of being able to engineer the way systems (boards, chips, and more) are cooled. When systems are cooled via air conditioning, they require tremendous amounts of power. However, purpose-built cloud data centers can be engineered to be cooled by water, for example (which is 3,000 times more efficient than air in cooling equipment).

CPU, memory, and local disk

Traditional data tends to be filled with a lot of surplus equipment (either to support unanticipated workloads or because an application or process wasn't engineered to be efficient). Surplus memory, CPUs, and disks take up valuable space and, of course, they need to be cooled. The cloud data center typically supports self-service provisioning of resources so capacity is added only when you need it.

Data storage and networking

Data storage and networking need to be managed collectively if they're going to be efficient. This problem has complicated the way the traditional data centers have been managed, and has forced organizations to buy a lot of additional hardware and software. The cloud data center can be engineered to overcome this problem. The cloud knows where its data needs to be because it is so efficient in the way it manages workloads. The cloud actually is engineered to manage data efficiently.

Redundancy

Data centers must always move data around the network for backup and disaster recovery. Traditional data centers support so many different workloads that many approaches to backup and recovery have to be taken. This makes backing up and recovering data complicated and expensive. The cloud, in contrast, is designed to handle data workloads consistently. For example, in a cloud data center you can establish a global policy about how and when backups will be handled. This can be then handled in an automated manner, reducing the cost of handling backup and recovery.

Software embedded within the data center

We talk a lot about software in the context of applications, but a considerable amount of software is linked at a systems level. This type of system level software is a big cost in the traditional data center simply because there are so many more workloads with so many operating systems and related software elements.

As you know, cloud data centers have fewer elements because they have simpler workloads. There are some differences in how software costs are managed depending on the type of cloud model. Cloud providers understand these costs well and design their offerings to maximize revenue. It will help you understand pricing by understanding the cost factors for each of the models.

The following gives you a sense of the difference between IaaS, PaaS, and SaaS when it comes to embedded software costs:

- ✔ An **Infrastructure as a Service (IaaS)** operation is likely to have higher software costs because although it provides only an *environment* for running applications, it has to build that environment according to equivalent environments in corporate data centers. Therefore, the IaaS vendor has to spend a lot of resources on management and security software in addition to the operating systems. See Chapter 10 for more about IaaS.

- ✔ With a **Platform as a Service (PaaS)** operation, the provider delivers a full software stack. To reduce cost, the PaaS vendor is likely to provide a software stack consisting of proprietary components. The licensing costs may be lower for IaaS than the PaaS environment because the operator is likely to force the use of specific software products. However, the PaaS vendor must maintain and support the software stack it provides. See Chapter 11 for more about PaaS.

✔ With **Software as a Service (SaaS),** the SaaS vendor provides a proprietary application as its value to customers. While the vendor invests in this software, it typically relies on partners to support many of the other functions. These vendors also take advantage of open-source components. See Chapter 12 for more about SaaS.

Open-source dynamic

The cloud is an economic and business model as much as a technology model.

It isn't surprising, then, that open-source software is an important element for almost all cloud providers. Some of it is very high quality and nearly all of it can be used for no license fee, as long as you obey the restrictions of the associated license.

Open-source software has already become a business factor in the *Internet service provider (ISP)* business, with most ISPs providing an easily installed, highly functional software stack for building Web sites. Many cloud providers take open-source software as a foundation and customize it to optimize support for their workloads.

The other software area that impacts costs is the way operating systems are handled in the data center. Under traditional operation, an OS has many background processes running. All such processes have a function and quite a few of them run by default, whether you need them or not. Some of them are keeping logs, some are handling messages from the network, some fire off scheduled jobs, some handle printing, some provide directory services, and so on. They all sit there happily chewing up CPU cycles. None of them should be there unless they have a specific role to play.

In a traditional environment, no one would think of deleting useful background processes, but nothing superfluous should run in an environment that prizes efficient resource usage. Not only that, but if you're running a cloud data center, you may be interested in rewriting some of these tasks because you need them to run slightly differently. That's why open source plays a large role in cloud operations.

Economies of Scale

We spend a lot of time in this chapter saying why the economics of the cloud are so different than that of the traditional data center. Of course, not every workload is right for the cloud.

Benefitting enormously

However, when the workload is right for the cloud there are many economic benefits:

- ✔ **Better communications prices:** Very large data centers can negotiate with their communications provider. They may buy a great deal of bandwidth, but they won't be paying such a high rate per gigabyte for a guaranteed service.

- ✔ **Predictable network traffic:** It's tougher to do if the scaled data center is IaaS or PaaS, because the overall workload is less homogeneous.

- ✔ **Network virtualization:** You can gain economies of scale if a network is tailored to support the networking hardware. Google, for example, designs its own switches.

Very application-specific scaled data centers are designed to be much more efficient. The important point here is this: Executing CPU instructions is what a data center does. That's why it's there. Efficient software is the primary optimization the cloud data center should be concerned with.

Optimizing otherwise

A company builds a cloud data center (or several) with the goal of keeping throughput costs as low as possible. It doesn't matter whether it's IaaS, PaaS, or SaaS — the metric that matters is the cost of executing each task. (Well, other metrics do matter — the cost of managing each byte of data stored and the cost of each byte of information transmitted or received by the data center — but they're the same kind of metric.)

Backup and disaster recovery

The three-data-center strategy with mirroring looks promising as a means of never needing to have backups (or UPS). It's really inexpensive for disaster recovery and, if you have a global business, you may even be able to load balance across three data centers in the United States, Europe, and the Far East. In many instances, the workload will follow the sun, which may also help reduce costs.

System management

There's a potentially big win in the system management area. Part of root cause analysis and maintenance can be carried out preemptively by service management processors designed for the job. Because you control the OS,

you can also insert an agent (that gathers the d.
data) in every instance of the OS. You will end up
Configuration Management Database (CMDB) that
ensure purity of software across the data center an
whole environment only every 18 months, say.

Security

You can bolt down the whole data center with a set of ch
permissions. The main worry is that someone (external o.
to run a rogue process that does something nasty. But if th
closely controlled mechanism for loading any executable, th   .s
to happen. You can even design that into both the OS and the   ..ian-
agement capabilities. Security is often an afterthought in corpe ..ce IT, but it
may be possible to write it into the application in PaaS and SaaS operations.

Client caching

Put as much processing as possible on the customer's client device (PC, Mac,
or Smartphone) so it isn't executed in the data center. Naturally, you put the
interface on the client, but you can design the architecture to maximize the
client. The beauty is that the customer probably won't mind because most
client devices have CPU cycles to spare.

Keeping the Bottom Line in Mind

We want you to take away two things from this chapter:

- ✔ **The traditional data center isn't designed for single workloads and is therefore more expensive to operate.** In situations where complex, mixed workloads are demanded, the cloud data center will not be more economical. However, when a workload can be optimized, the cloud center is the most efficient and cost-effective model.

- ✔ **The various kinds of cloud data centers have different cost profiles.** The more complex the cloud environment, the more expensive it is to operate; therefore, customers will pay more. IaaS and PaaS both have mixed workloads that increase the cost. A SaaS model consisting of a single workload will be the most cost effective for the provider to manage and therefore is the most economical model.

Chapter 7

Checking the Cloud's Workload Strategy

In This Chapter

▶ Getting ahold of workloads

▶ Putting risks on the sale to weigh

▶ Putting workloads to the real-world test

*L*ots of hardware, software, networking, and services have to be brought together to make a cloud environment into a reality. Clearly, making a cloud work means that workloads have to be managed efficiently. How does this happen? You can't simply take all the data and all the services and put them into a big cloud in the sky. In fact, for a cloud to work well, it must be well architected and well organized. In this chapter, we take a look at what happens with workloads in the cloud — how they're managed and how they're orchestrated.

Managing Workloads in the Cloud

How do you organize the cloud? The basic requirement is that workloads need to be organized. A *workload* is an independent service or collection of code that can be executed. Therefore, a workload doesn't depend on outside elements. A workload can be a small or complete application.

You must be able to balance two things:

- ✔ The applications or components running in the cloud
- ✔ The needs of the business to perform predictably, especially during peak loads

Organizations have to actively manage workloads so they know

- How their applications are running
- What they're doing
- How much an individual department should be charged for its use of services

A business needs to plan for their workloads, even when they're using an external cloud provider. Management needs to understand the types of workloads they're putting into a cloud. Workloads can be everything from a data-intensive workload to a storage or a transaction processing workload.

Thinking of workloads as well-planned services

The cloud requires that workloads have to be handled in a very abstracted manner. The *abstraction* is a way to keep the technical details away from the user. The result of this abstraction is a type of service that makes it easier to have a well-defined function with a defined purpose. This service lives inside a container with an *Application Programming Interface (API)* so it can be easily moved from one place to another.

If you're familiar with a service-oriented architecture, you probably recognize that this might sound a lot like a business service. A *business service* is a function or process designed to include well-defined Web services interfaces. Therefore, this type of service is designed for many different situations, which is an important concept for the cloud.

A brief history of workload management

The function of managing workloads isn't a new concept. It's been around for decades, first in the mainframe market and then in Unix and Linux. Life was a lot easier in the mainframe era where there were defined techniques for managing a more unified workload. Things changed dramatically in a more chaotic, heterogeneous computing environment. Companies had to provide components that allowed processes to run across unrelated systems. They needed to

be able to make changes to configurations in near real time. For example, companies had to take into account managing workloads related to CPU, memory, storage I/O, and networking foundations. They also had to take into account rebalancing workloads when new applications were added or when new business processes were implemented.

Different workload types

Two types of workloads exist:

- ✔ Workloads that can be executed at any time in batch mode
- ✔ Workloads that need to be executed in real time

For example, an insurance company is likely to have a workload that calculates interest rate. This doesn't have to happen immediately. In contrast, an online retail system that calculates taxes on a purchase needs to be executed in real time. Many business information systems that help management understand the status of their business are batch workloads. A credit card payment system is a real-time workload.

You might have a single workload that's an entire application used by a group of customers. In other situations, a smaller service may be used in many different contexts. There might be a workload that's a payment service platform. This payment service might be live in a cloud and may be used by many different software developers who all need a payment engine (so they can collect payments from their customers without building their own engine). Many Platform as a Service vendors offer workloads or services like them to their partners.

Workloads as self-contained entities

If workloads are self-contained entities, what are the characteristics of these services?

- ✔ **A workload has no dependencies.** It's a discrete set of application logic that can be executed independently of a specific application.

- ✔ **The workload interface must be consistent.** Currently, the most pragmatic, well-accepted interfaces are based on XML(eXtensible Markup Language). XML-based interfaces can keep the data independent of each implementation; the process understands how a service is used. For example, the bill payment service with an XML interface knows that it calculates a bill based on usage.

- ✔ **A workload may have rules or policies that apply in specific situations.** There may be authorization and security policies associated with using a service for a particular function. There may be a rule about when to use a specific workload. For example, a workload such as an accounting process might need to be executed at the end of a specific cycle. Therefore, although a workload can be thought of as a container or service, it will be used in conjunction with both simple and very complex processes.

Creating interfaces between containers

Providing interfaces such as XML-based or APIs is a key factor in ensuring that workloads can be managed effectively in the cloud. With a well-defined interface, a developer has a method of cleanly linking one service to another. If you have a series of workloads placed in neat containers without dependencies to other services, you have a better chance of ensuring a flexible environment that can support changing workloads.

Therefore, one of the imperatives of the cloud is that workloads be dynamic.

These workloads don't serve a single master. They're used by many different customers in many different situations. This type of flexibility is the reason many companies are moving to the cloud (or considering the cloud's ability to solve business problems).

Workloads *can* be combined. This has the impact of creating dependencies between these workloads, but in a controlled manner. Two workloads might be linked together to fulfill a task. As long as this link is documented, it can be done safely. Why is creating a dependency such a potential problem? If you have a service that expects to use a particular operating system, you can't use that service in an environment that uses another operating system.

Workloads live in a container that perform a definitive function without dependencies. A workload also needs to have well-defined interfaces if they're to be used in many combinations.

You know that within the cloud it's important to have specific containers that support workloads. But how do the interfaces between containers work so you can optimize their use? To understand this, it is important to understand XML a little more.

Discovering how XML fits in

We think that XML-based web services interfaces are going to become the primary way that the cloud connects containers.

XML stands for *eXtensible Markup Language*. To understand its value, break it into parts:

- ✔ **A set of instructions** that you add to a collection of words, pictures, and so on, that controls their on-screen appearance, formatting, and behavior.

- ✔ **Tags** that you define and embed in the content, and then write programs that write programs that agree on how data is defined within the context of your container.

If many different containers or services all use the same language to explain to each other what they do and how they can be used, these services can much more easily talk, connect, and send messages to each other.

Using container workloads: Case study

How do containers or services work in a cloud-based environment? Imagine that you have many functions within a cloud. If you place traditional programs in the cloud without any structure, all you have is one big workload that can typically conduct a single business function. Most organizations wouldn't get economic value.

Here's a real-world company that did get economic value: Intuit is a well-established software company that sells a product called QuickBooks — it's the most popular accounting software for small and medium businesses.

The cloud hides a lot of infrastructure and complexity away from the end customer, but there are, in fact, a lot of moving parts. The company decided to provide other services, including Platform as a Service and Software as a Service; customers could use the workload of a business invoice that they create online and transmit electrically to customers.

However, Inuit didn't stop there. The company went on to create a series of services or workloads with which its partners could easily enhance their service delivery to customers. For example, Intuit designed a payment system to bill its customers for products and services. It put this service into a well-defined container with XML-based interfaces and let its partners use that service as part of their own product (offered within the Inuit platform as a service environment). Therefore, the software partner didn't have to write its own complex payment software. It could rely on the workload that Intuit designed and tested.

The bottom line is that creating workloads with well-defined interfaces makes delivery software in the cloud a pragmatic and cost-effective way to work with customers.

Balancing Risk and Practical Models

Workloads can be very complicated to manage. In the traditional data center, workloads tend to be thought of as full applications rather than individual workloads. Typically, when the application is complex and very expensive to run, expenses tend to be divided across the departments that use that application.

Now companies look at other factors, such as the level of service required by that department. For example, what happens if the system is unavailable for two hours a day? If that system produces monthly research reports, the company's business isn't at risk. However, if the system is responsible for real-time security monitoring, two hours of downtime could severely impact the company.

Creating a more rigorous *service level agreement (SLA)* for the security monitoring system is going to be money well spent.

This type of balancing of risks and service level agreements are well understood in the traditional data center. However, when you introduce a cloud infrastructure into the mix, the level of risk changes dramatically. What is the nature of your cloud provider? Does the organization you have selected provide the type of SLAs that match your level of risk? What does the workload actually look like? If it is a distinct workload, it may be easy to pick up that workload and move it to another location — either another cloud provider or back into your own data center if things don't work out.

If you're dealing with a brand-new service that isn't critical to the company's well-being, it is probably cost effective to trust the cloud provider to deliver the level of service that you need. You might not need to verify it on a consistent basis. You're storing information that isn't mission critical. You are required to store that data and you know that the cloud service provider has a proven track record. Of course, no matter what you are moving to the cloud, the security and protection of that data is still your responsibility.

However, you might have a very different situation. What if you're considering moving to the cloud an existing workload that has run in your data center for years. It is a high-risk service. Few companies run a similar service. A cloud vendor approaches you with an offer to take over this workload. Although it seems like the right thing to do initially, you might be surprised if you dig a little deeper. By the time you add the required service levels and the added security, the cost combined with the risk may change your thinking. Because this particular workload has been optimized to run effectively in the existing data center, it may actually cost a lot more to run the workload in the cloud.

Do your homework before you reach conclusions about the best and safest approach for your company.

Testing Workloads in the Real World

After you and your partners in the cloud business have created standardized workloads, you can reuse them in different situations. Companies that are part of your cloud infrastructure can help you move quickly with the cloud as the scalable platform. But you aren't done just because you have created workloads.

The key to a well-functioning infrastructure is that workloads in both clouds and within your own environment have to be linked *together* based on the business process you're trying to achieve.

What does this mean in the real world? Take the example of the company that has started using the cloud to manage a sales management system for its sales force, which is spread across 100 countries. When a salesperson makes a sale, he needs to send that transaction outside the cloud to an internally run system that takes the order, checks the customer credit through a third party, and confirms that transaction. But it doesn't end there. Now that the customer has been cleared, the inventory system needs to be notified and a product is shipped through another partner that manages transportation for goods and services.

Workload management isn't complete unless it's in context with *asset management* (how organizations manage the hardware, software, and services lifecycles). Asset management in this context needs to embrace

 ✔ License management

 ✔ Technology evaluation

 ✔ Capability planning

Runbook

Ironically, this approach to linking workloads together is based on an age-old function called Runbook automation. Runbook automation started in the mainframe era when companies needed to consistently automate processes to do everything from executing and verifying a transaction to ensuring that a print job was processed on the right printer at the right time. Today, Runbook automation is the technique used in the process of integrating, orchestrating, and initiating tasks between service components that need to run between systems, applications, and platforms.

What services are going to live in the cloud? Do you need to account for any licenses in the cloud?

When you're adding new services, you have to understand

- ✔ Their component parts
- ✔ Where they live
- ✔ How they relate to other services

For example, you might have an important workload moved to a cloud. Which internal applications and groups use that service? If that workload is changed, are the right departments alerted? In managing a cloud-based workload or even hybrid workloads (that live in both the cloud and on premise), you have to make sure that you're managing the configuration data efficiently. *Configuration management software* (an application that tracks and controls changes to software code) helps define workloads and tracks changes to those workloads.

Company management must look at these series of workloads and test them as though they were an integrated system. For example, you might have workloads running across many different cloud environments and within data centers. You might use a Software as a Service application that needs to send data to your internal accounts receivable system. You might have a business process that requires that a new customer receive an email confirming receipt of an order. You therefore need to think holistically about how your workloads will work together.

What are the requirements for companies dealing with workloads that incorporate security, coordination, workflow, and dependency tracking? Companies need to clearly test these scenarios before attempting to put this into practice in the real world.

Chapter 8

Managing Data

. . . .

In This Chapter

▶ Ensuring security and privacy

▶ Recognizing management resources

▶ Discussing questions with your cloud vendor

. . . .

*T*here is no way around it: The issues surrounding data in a cloud environment is a big and complicated topic. The reality is that data is the lifeblood of organizations. Therefore, how you manage data, regardless of where it lives, is critical to the health of your business. Data has an entire lifecycle: It's created, changed, secured, stored (or destroyed), and governed. Although this is the normal process *within* the data center, forgetting management elements is easy when an outside service manages that data.

In this chapter, we discuss the key aspects of managing data in the cloud, including

✔ Data security and privacy (including data controls and managing the movement of data from point A to point B)

✔ Managing the resources for large-scale data processing

✔ Data storage

Declaring Data Types

The amount of data available for company use is exploding. In fact, the very nature of data is changing:

✔ **Data diversity is increasing.** Data in the cloud is becoming more diverse. In addition to traditional structured data (revenue, name, and so on), it includes emails, contracts, images, blogs, and more.

✔ **The amount of data is increasing.** Just think of how many videos YouTube manages or all the images Facebook handles. Even in the traditional data realm, organizations are starting to aggregate huge amounts of data (to solve problems that they could never have imagined tackling in the past decade). These might be one-time efforts or ongoing research projects that require massive amounts of computing resources under very controlled circumstances.

✔ **Latency requirements are becoming more demanding.** Companies are increasingly demanding lower latency (for instance, the time for data to get from one point to another) for many applications. Think real-time data for Radio Frequency ID tags (RFID) as one example. This requires a powerful management environment.

Even in the traditional data realm, organizations are starting to aggregate huge amounts of data to solve problems that they could never have imagined tackling in the past decade. The cloud can

✔ Provide resources to access data on demand and at a much lower price point than the company can.

✔ Help businesses looking to support the use of data collaboratively across their employees, customers, and business partners.

The cost associated with managing data on demand is a controversial topic in cloud circles. It's one thing to access data stored in the cloud. Using data across applications that are in two different clouds can get expensive; it might involve real-time synchronization or permanent cloud-hosted data, regardless of the current application demand.

Securing Data in the Cloud

There are three key areas of concern related to security and privacy of data:

✔ Location of your data

✔ Control of your data

✔ Secure transfer of your data

Each of these areas is discussed in this section.

Because security is such a big issue, we've devoted all of Chapter 15 to it. In addition, if you want to find out more about security in the cloud, we point you to the Cloud Security Alliance (www.cloudsecurityalliance.org) for more information.

In the cloud, company data that was previously secured inside of the firewall may now move outside to feed any number of business applications and processes.

Cloud providers must ensure the security and privacy of your data, but *you* are ultimately responsible for your company's data. This means that industry and government regulations created to protect personal and business information still apply even if the data is managed or stored by an outside vendor.

For example, the European Union has implemented a complex set of data protection laws for its member states. In addition, industry regulations (such as the Health Insurance Portability and Accountability Act [HIPAA]) must be followed whether or not your data is in the cloud.

Data privacy and security issues are overriding concerns for companies evaluating a cloud services strategy. For this reason, many companies are testing public cloud environments with smaller, more-contained implementations that don't rely on data subject to compliance regulations.

Data location in the cloud

After data goes into the cloud, you may not have control over where it's stored geographically. Consider these issues:

- ✔ **Specific country laws:** Laws governing data differ across geographic boundaries. Your own country's legal protections may not apply if your data is located outside of the country. A foreign government may be able to access your data or keep you from fully controlling your data when you need it.

- ✔ **Data transfer across country borders:** A global company with subsidiaries or partners (or clients for that matter) in other countries may be concerned about cross-border transfer of data due to local laws. Virtualization makes this an especially tough problem because the cloud provider might not know where the data is at any particular moment. For more about virtualization, see Chapter 17.

- ✔ **Co-mingling of data:** Even if your data is in a country that has laws you're comfortable with, your data may be physically stored in a database along with data from other companies. This raises concerns about virus attacks or hackers trying to get at another company's data.

- ✔ **Secondary data use:** In public cloud situations, your data or metadata may be vulnerable to alternative or secondary uses by the cloud service provider.

  - • Without proper controls or service level agreements, your data may be used for marketing purposes (and merged with data from other organizations for these alternative uses). The recent uproar about Facebook mining data from its network is an example.

  - • The service provider may own any metadata (see the "Sorting Out Metadata Matters" section later in this chapter for a description of metadata) it has created to help manage your data, lessening your ability to maintain control over your data.

Data control in the cloud

Controls include the governance policies set in place to make sure that your data can be trusted. The integrity, reliability, and confidentiality of your data must be beyond reproach. And this holds for cloud providers too.

For example, assume that you're using a cloud service for word processing. The documents you create are stored with the cloud provider. These documents belong to your company and you expect to control access to those documents. No one should be able to get them without your permission, but perhaps a software bug lets other users access the documents. This privacy violation resulted from a malfunctioning access control. This is an example of the type of slip-up that you want to make sure doesn't happen.

You must understand what level of controls will be maintained by your cloud provider and consider how these controls can be audited.

Here is a sampling of the different types of controls designed to ensure the completeness and accuracy of data input, output, and processing:

- ✔ Input validation controls to ensure that all data input to any system or application are complete, accurate, and reasonable.

- ✔ Processing controls to ensure that data are processed completely and accurately in an application.

- ✔ File controls to make sure that data are manipulated accurately in any type of file (structured and unstructured).

- ✔ Output reconciliation controls to ensure that data can be reconciled from input to output.

- ✔ Access controls to ensure that only those who are authorized to access the data can do so. Sensitive data must also be protected in storage and transfer. Encrypting the data can help to do this.

- ✔ Change management controls to ensure that data can't be changed without proper authorization.

- ✔ Backup and recovery controls. Many security breaches come from problems in data backup. It is important to maintain physical and logical controls over data backup. For example, what mechanisms are in place to ensure that no one can physically get into a facility?

✔ Data destruction controls to ensure that when data is permanently deleted it is deleted from everywhere — including all backup and redundant storage sites.

Securing data for transport in the cloud

Regarding data transport, keep two things in mind:

✔ Make sure that no one can intercept your data as it moves from point A to point B in the cloud.

✔ Make sure that no data leaks (malicious or otherwise) from any storage in the cloud.

None of these concepts are new; the goal of securely transporting data has been around as long as the Internet.

In the cloud, the journey from point A to point B might take on three different forms:

✔ Within a cloud environment

✔ Over the public Internet between an enterprise and a cloud provider

✔ Between clouds

The security process may include segregating your data from other companies' data and then encrypting it by using an approved method. In addition, you may want to ensure the security of older data that remains with a cloud vendor after you no longer need it.

A *virtual private network (VPN)* is one way to manage the security of data during its transport in a cloud environment. A VPN essentially makes the public network your own private network instead of using dedicated connectivity. A well-designed VPN needs to incorporate two things:

✔ A *firewall* to act as a barrier to between the public Internet and any private network (like at your enterprise).

✔ *Encryption* to protect your sensitive data from hackers; only the computer that you send it to should have the key to decode the data.

Decoding encryption

Encryption comes in many forms:

✔ In symmetric key encryption, each computer has a secret code that it uses to encrypt data. Only these computers know the code. The code also contains the key to decoding the message.

✔ In public key encryption, there are two keys: a public key and a private key. The private key is known only to one computer; the public key is given by the computer to any other computer that wants to communicate with it. To decode a message, the computer uses the public key and its own private key. There are definitely some challenges to utilizing private keys in the cloud. The benefit of the cloud includes the ability to add capacity on demand and any additional security steps may slow down some of the processes.

This gives you a taste of some of the pressing security and privacy issues surrounding data. The key point here is that no matter which cloud vendor you choose, there are no hard-and-fast rules surrounding security. You really can't assume anything.

Your level of concern about security may vary, depending on the governance requirements for your data. In some situations, such as with a test environment processing test data, you may have limited concerns about some of these security and privacy issues. In other situations where you may have a lot at risk if the security and privacy of your data is compromised, you need to evaluate how your cloud vendor treats the security issues.

In addition, you will need to determine how you can audit the ongoing security processes to make sure that your data *remains* secure.

Concerns about privacy and security of data have contributed to many companies' interest in developing private cloud environments — where company data remains inside the firewall — and to consider hybrid cloud environments — which incorporate some elements of a private cloud and some elements of a public cloud. Please refer to Chapter 15 for more information on security in the cloud.

Looking at Data, Scalability, and Cloud Services

The need to process continually increasing amounts of data is one of the key factors driving the demand for cloud services.

For example, until YouTube, virtually all public video was stored by TV networks. The explosive amount of video (a type of data) currently available through YouTube was unimaginable prior to its creation in 1995. Today, you store videos, watch videos, and search for videos by using YouTube as your video provider (to handle the streaming of the video to your Web site).

A number of emerging technologies for managing these increasing volumes and diversity of data are worth mentioning:

- **Resources to support large-scale processing and data mining in the cloud:** One example of this type of computing-intensive application is scientific research for computational genomics. Other examples include business services for tracking and analyzing radio frequency identification tags, analyzing news feeds in real time, providing real-time stock quotes to trading floors, and analyzing product data to provide real-time pricing promotions. Organizations supporting these types of applications are often in critical need of more IT infrastructure, computing power, and data management capabilities than they have internally.

- **Databases and data stores in the cloud:** New databases are being created for the cloud environment. Some companies may just want to store their data there; others may be building services on top of the data.

- **Data archiving in the cloud:** Archiving data offsite has been popular for a number of years. Some cloud providers are trying to put a new spin on this.

In the following sections, we examine each of these technologies.

Large-scale data processing

The lure of cloud computing is its elasticity: You can add as much capacity as you need to process and analyze your data. The data might be processed on clusters of computers. This means that the analysis is occurring across machines.

Companies are considering this approach to help them manage their supply chains and inventory control. Or, consider the case of a company processing product data, from across the country, to determine when to change a price or introduce a promotion. This data might come from the point-of-sale (POS) systems across multiple stores in multiple states. POS systems generate a lot of data, and the company might need to add computing capacity to meet demand.

This model is large-scale, distributed computing and a number of frameworks are emerging to support this model, including

✔ **MapReduce**, a software framework introduced by Google to support distributed computing on large sets of data. It is designed to take advantage of cloud resources. This computing is done across large numbers of computers, called *clusters*. Each cluster is referred to as a node. MapReduce can deal with both structured and unstructured data. Users specify a map function that processes a key/value pair to generate a set of intermediate pairs and a reduction function that merges these pairs.

✔ **Apache Hadoop**, an open-source distributed computing platform written in Java and inspired by MapReduce. It creates a computer pool, each with a Hadoop file system. It then uses a hash algorithm to cluster data elements that are similar. Hadoop can create a map function of organized key/value pairs that can be output to a table, to memory, or to a temporary file to be analyzed. Three copies of the data exist so that nothing gets lost.

Databases and data stores in the cloud

Given the scale of some of these applications, it isn't surprising that new database technologies are being developed to support this kind of computing.

Some database experts believe that relational database models may have difficulty processing data across large numbers of servers — in other words, when the data is distributed across multiple machines. Performance can be slow when you're executing complex queries that involve a join across a distributed environment. Additionally, in an old-style database cluster, data must either be replicated across the boxes in the cluster or partitioned between them. According to other database experts, this makes it hard to provision servers on demand.

In response, some large cloud providers have developed their own databases. Here's a sample listing:

✔ **Google Bigtable:** This hybrid is sort of like one big table. Because tables can be large, they're split at row boundaries into tablets, which might be 100 megabytes or so. MapReduce is often used for generating and modifying data stored in Bigtable. Bigtable is also the data storage vehicle behind Google's App Engine (a platform for developing applications).

✔ **Amazon SimpleDB:** This Web service is for indexing and querying data. It's used with two other Amazon products to store, process, and query data sets in the cloud. Amazon likens the database to a spreadsheet in that it has columns and rows with attributes and items stored in each. Unlike a spreadsheet, however, each cell can have multiple values and each item can have its own set of associated attributes. Amazon then automatically indexes the data.

✔ **Cloud-based SQL:** Microsoft has introduced a cloud-based SQL relational database called SQL Database (SDS). SDS provides data storage by using a relational model in the cloud and access to that data from cloud and client applications. It runs on the Microsoft Azure services platform. The Azure platform is an Internet-scale cloud-services platform hosted in Microsoft data centers; the platform provides an operating system and a set of developer services.

Numerous open-source databases are also being developed:

✔ MongoDB (schema-free, document-oriented data store written in C++)

✔ CouchDB (Apache open-source database)

✔ LucidDB (Java/C++ open-source data warehouse)

It's a matter of semantics

Lot of terms are floating around out there when it comes to databases in the cloud. Some possible terms you'll hear include *database as a service* and *cloud databases*. What's the difference?

Some experts use *database as a service* to describe vendors that offer clients a hosted database solution. The database is in the cloud, but you know that the cloud provider is managing it and you know where the data center is physically located. You don't pay for the hardware and you can run your analysis on this data and pay on a pay-per-use basis.

The term *cloud database* is used when the database is in the cloud, meaning that you may not know where the data physically resides.

There is also the situation where your database vendor (such as Oracle) might host its database in a cloud service, such as Amazon, and your contract is with the cloud vendor, not the database vendor.

Data archiving

Data backup and archiving is nothing new. In fact, many companies are used to archiving static, seldom-used data offsite. Much of this is driven by compliance regulations that require companies to archive records for a number of years.

The cloud has different data archiving models. In some models, the archive may be available on demand. In others, this may not be the case.

Sorting Out Metadata Matters

Metadata is of critical importance to the ongoing reliability and integrity of your data in cloud environments. This is because metadata provides the means for your data to be understood in context with its intended use or meaning. *Metadata* is defined as the definitions, mappings, and other characteristics used to describe how to find, access, and use a company's data (and software) components.

One example of metadata is data related to an account number. This might include the number, description, data type, name, address, phone number, and privacy level. The term *account number* may be defined differently depending on the application, and it may be interpreted differently across multiple end-user companies or cloud service providers.

Metadata helps make sense of the varied definitions and creates a consistent level of understanding about the data. Metadata — whether supplied and maintained by your company or your cloud service provider — can be used as the traffic cop to ensure that the data traffic is directed to the appropriate location at the right time.

Talking to Your Cloud Vendor about Data

You're thinking about using some of the data services in the cloud. Before you sign the contract, remember that data (especially your company's data) is a precious asset and you need to treat it as such.

In addition to issues surrounding security and privacy of your data that we cover earlier in the chapter, we recommend asking your potential vendor about the following topics:

✔ **Data integrity:** What controls do you have to ensure the integrity of my data? For example, are there controls to make sure that all data input to any system or application is complete, accurate, and reasonable? What about any processing controls to make sure that data processing is accurate? And, there also need to be output controls in place to ensure that any output from any system, application, or process can be verified and trusted. This dovetails with the next bullet about any specific compliance issues that your particular industry might have.

✔ **Compliance:** You are probably aware of any compliance issues particular to your industry. Obviously, you need to make sure that your provider can comply with these regulations.

✔ **Loss of data:** What provisions are in the contract if the provider does something to your data (loses it because of improper backup and recovery procedures, for instance)? If the contract says that your monthly fee is simply waived, you need to ask some more questions.

✔ **Business continuity plans:** What happens if your cloud vendor's data center goes down? What business continuity plans does your provider have in place: How long will it take the provider to get your data back up and running? For example, a SaaS vendor might tell you that they back up data every day, but it might take several days to get the backup onto systems in another facility. Does this meet your business imperatives?

✔ **Uptime:** Your provider might tell you that you will be able to access your data 99.999 percent of the time — however, read the contract. Does this uptime include scheduled maintenance?

✔ **Data storage costs:** Pay-as-you-go and no-capital-purchase options sound great, but read the fine print. For example, how much will it cost to move your data into the cloud? What about other hidden integration costs? How much will it cost to store your data? You should do your own calculations so you're not caught off guard. Find out how the provider charges for data storage. Some providers offer a tiered pricing structure. Others offer pricing based on server capacity.

✔ **Contract termination:** How will data be returned if the contract is terminated? If you're using a SaaS provider and it has created data for you too, will any of that get turned over to you? You need to ask yourself if this is an issue. Some companies just want the data destroyed. Understand how your provider would destroy your data to make sure that it isn't floating around in the cloud.

✔ **Data ownership:** Who owns your data after it goes into the cloud? Some service providers might want to take your data, merge it with other data, and do some analysis.

✔ **Switching vendors:** If you create applications with one cloud vendor and then decide to move to another vendor, how difficult will it be to move your data? In other words, how interoperable are the services? Some of these vendors may have proprietary APIs and it might be costly to switch. You need to know this before you enter into an agreement.

Chapter 9

Discovering Private and Hybrid Clouds

In This Chapter

▶ Defining a private cloud

▶ Choosing between public, private, and hybrid cloud environments

▶ Investigating private cloud economics

▶ Looking at vendor solutions for private and hybrid

*W*hile many business executives are attracted to the idea of the public cloud, just as many are interested in achieving the benefits of the cloud but on an internal basis. There are different reasons why companies investigating a cloud might want a private cloud instead of using a public one. The most obvious reason is privacy and security of data. Another reason that some companies are considering the private cloud is that they have already invested in a lot of hardware, software, and space and would like to be able to leverage their investments, but in a more efficient manner.

What if you could avoid the security issue by keeping your data *inside* your firewall and still gain public cloud benefits? Then consider a private or a hybrid cloud. Many companies are looking at a situation where they actually see the benefits of using a public cloud for some services, a private cloud for others, a hybrid cloud for some situations, and their traditional data center for the rest. Indeed, the world of IT is complicated. We suspect that most organizations will have a combination of approaches — a hybrid of public and private clouds with traditional data centers included.

In this chapter, we explain what a private cloud is and how it can work in tandem with public clouds. We explain the technology and services vendors are offering, and what happens when companies implement a strategy that combines a private cloud behind the firewall or a virtual private network with public cloud services.

Pining for Privacy

While it may be clear that a private cloud is private and a public cloud is open to anyone, there are nuances that help make the differences evident.

Here are a few examples that might help:

- ✓ You're a company selling a service to retailers that helps them manage their digital gift cards. You might use a public cloud service to enable the retailers to submit information to you, but you want to make sure that the data you're collecting for them remains confidential and safe. You would, therefore, put that important data in a private cloud behind your company's firewall.

- ✓ You're a healthcare company in France. Your government requires that your patients' data be stored within the country. You'd probably want to keep that data in a private cloud.

- ✓ You're a financial services company that has selected a sales management system based on SaaS. However, you're concerned about the security of your customer data. The SaaS company offers a private cloud version of its service by adding a virtual private network that adds a second layer of security.

Defining a private cloud

There's confusion — as well as passionate debate — over the definition of a private cloud. When we say *private cloud,* we mean a highly virtualized cloud data center located inside your company's firewall. It may also be a private space dedicated to your company within a cloud vendor data center designed to handle your company's workloads.

The characteristics of the private cloud are as follows:

- ✓ Allows IT to provision services and compute capability to internal users in a self-service manner

- ✓ Automates management tasks and lets you bill business units for the services they consume

- ✓ Provides a well-managed environment

- ✓ Optimizes the use of computing resources such as servers

✔ Supports specific workloads

✔ Provides self-service based provisioning of hardware and software resources

You might think this sounds a lot like a public cloud! A private cloud exhibits the key characteristics of a public cloud, including elasticity, scalability, and self-service provisioning. (Please refer to Chapter 1 for detailed information on cloud characteristics.) The major difference is *control* over the environment. In a private cloud, you (or a trusted partner) control the service management.

It might help to think of the public cloud as the Internet and the private cloud as the intranet.

If private and public clouds are so similar, why would you develop a private cloud instead of ordering capacity on demand from an Infrastructure as a Service provider or using Software as a Service? Here are several good reasons companies are using a private rather than a public cloud:

✔ Your organization has a huge, well-run data center with a lot of spare capacity. It would be more expensive to use a public cloud even if you have to add new software to transform that data center into a cloud.

✔ Your organization offers IT services to a large ecosystem of partners as part of your core business. Therefore, a private cloud could be a revenue source.

✔ Your company's data is its lifeblood. You feel that to keep control you must keep your information behind your own firewall.

✔ You need to keep your data center running in accordance with rules of governance and compliance.

✔ You have critical performance requirements, meaning you need 99.9999 percent availability. Therefore, a private cloud may be your only option. This higher level of service is more expensive, but is a business requirement.

Some early adopters of private cloud technology have experienced server use rates of up to 90 percent. This is a real breakthrough, particularly in challenging economic times.

Comparing public, private, and hybrid

We wish we could tell you that there are clear distinctions between private and public clouds. Unfortunately, the lines are blurring between these two approaches. Hybrid approaches also are starting to take hold. For example, some public cloud companies are now offering private versions of their public clouds. Some companies that only offered private cloud technologies are now offering public versions of those same capabilities.

In this section we offer some issues to consider when you're making your business decision.

Going public

When is a public cloud the obvious choice? Here are some examples:

- ✔ Your standardized workload for applications is used by lots of people. Email is an excellent example.
- ✔ You need to test and develop application code.
- ✔ You have SaaS (Software as a Service) applications from a vendor who has a well-implemented security strategy.
- ✔ You need incremental capacity (to add compute capacity for peak times).
- ✔ You're doing collaboration projects.
- ✔ You're doing an ad-hoc software development project using a Platform as a Service (PaaS) offering.

Many IT department executives are concerned about public cloud security and reliability. You need to get security right and handle any legal and governance issues, or the short-term cost savings could turn into a long-term nightmare. For more details on security, read Chapter 15; for more on governance, read Chapter 16.

Keeping things private

In contrast, when would a private cloud be the obvious choice? Here are some examples:

- ✔ Your business is your data and your applications. Therefore, control and security are paramount.
- ✔ Your business is part of an industry that must conform to strict security and data privacy issues. A private cloud will meet those requirements. (See Chapter 16 for more on Governance).
- ✔ Your company is large enough that you have the economies of scale to run a next generation cloud data center efficiently and effectively.

Amazon and Salesforce.com offer private cloud services

Just as we were finalizing this chapter, both Amazon (see Chapter 10 for more on Amazon's offerings) and Salesforce.com (see Chapter 12 for more on Salesforce.com's SaaS platform) announced that they would be offering private cloud implementations of their public cloud-based services. Both companies are using a VPN, which uses encryption to make the public network or a public cloud work as though it were private.

Amazon has announced what it calls Amazon Virtual Private Cloud (Amazon VPC), which will provide customers with isolated AWS (Amazon Work Space) compute resources protected by VPN connections. Therefore, customers can use enhanced security features such as multi-factor authentication to protect data. See Chapter 15 for more on security in the cloud.

Salesforce.com is partnering with NTT to offer a VPN to customers that want additional security for their CRM applications. Salesforce.com uses NTT's Comm Network, which incorporates a VPN for enhanced security.

Driving a hybrid

Now add one more choice into the mix: the hybrid cloud. When would you use it? It isn't about making an either/or choice between a public or private cloud. In most situations, we think a hybrid environment will satisfy many business needs. Here are a few examples:

✔ Your company likes a SaaS application and wants to use it as a standard throughout the company; you're concerned about security. To solve this problem, your SaaS vendor creates a private cloud just for your company inside their firewall. They provide you with a *virtual private network (VPN)* for additional security. Now you have both public and private cloud ingredients.

✔ Your company offers services that are tailored for different vertical markets. For example, you might offer to handle claims payments for insurance agents, shipping services for manufacturers, or credit checking services for local banks. You may want to use a public cloud to create an online environment so each of your customers can send you requests and review their account status. However, you might want to keep the data that you manage for these customers within your own private cloud.

Although private and public cloud environments each have management requirements by themselves, these requirements become much more complex when you need to manage private, public, and traditional data centers all together. You need to add capabilities for *federating* (linking distributed resources) these environments. In addition, your service levels need to focus on how a *service* is working rather than how a *server* is working.

Examining the Economics of the Private Cloud

There isn't one right way to evaluate the economic benefits of public or private clouds. There may be some expenses in the public cloud that only become apparent after you're already in your project.

Before getting started, figure out which option is the most appropriate for

- ✔ Your company's information technology strategy
- ✔ Your security strategy
- ✔ Your budgeting strategy

The economics of cloud computing are complicated. (For more details on the economics of the cloud, see Chapters 5, 6, and 21.)

Assessing capital expenditures

What are your data center and IT operations actually costing you? It isn't a simple question to answer. Most companies divide the area of expenses for IT into two buckets:

- ✔ Capital expenditures are spent on buying equipment (servers, networks, storage systems).
- ✔ Operating expenditures are the normal costs of operating a business day to day (salaries, system maintenance, and research and development).

Sometimes management likes the idea of not paying for equipment or a software package upfront. They may either want to pay in smaller, incremental payments. In this case, they might prefer a cloud platform.

✔ **Example 1:** You anticipate some big IT investment expenditures. Public cloud offerings may look economically very attractive (so you can avoid those purchases).

✔ **Example 2:** Your very large company has an excess of IT resources. You may want to work with what you have and re-architect as modular services. (For more on service orientation, see Chapter 19.) In addition, you might also want to add service management to support the automation of internal customers' changing workloads. (For additional insight into service management and provisioning, take a look at Chapters 7 and 20.)

Take a look at Chapters 10 through 12 to read how to assess the costs of different types of cloud models.

Vendor private cloud offerings

Understanding what each vendor offers and how they compare can be confusing.

Most of the technology vendors are still working on their cloud strategy as they firm up new products and develop partnerships. In fact, the competitive landscape for the private cloud market is a moving target at this point.

One thing we can say with certainty is that the vendor offerings for private and hybrid clouds will have evolved between the time this book is written and its publication date.

With that caveat, we have organized the vendors into three categories to give you a sense of how different types of companies are approaching the market.

Services-led technology

The services components (internal or partners) of these vendors have developed best practices over thousands of engagements and all this experience is brought to the forefront of each company's cloud strategy.

If your company lacks internal expertise on clouds and needs to implement a specialized set of solutions, a services-led engagement might be a good approach for you. In addition, a services company may have direct experience in your industry that may save you time.

The vendors in this category all have

✔ Large customer bases

✔ Years of experience working with customers on implementations

    ✔ Service teams working with customers to answer the tough questions around security, governance, cost, and business objectives

    ✔ Enough size to develop a partner ecosystem to deliver on a comprehensive vision for private, public, and hybrid clouds across services, software, hardware, and storage

    ✔ A lot of their own sophisticated technology to use in private clouds (maybe servers, storage systems, service management software, service oriented architecture frameworks and services, security software, and middleware)

Systems integrators

Creating a cloud strategy is a complicated process. A cloud infrastructure needs a well-defined architecture or it can't scale and won't be manageable.

Do you need lots of help with cloud strategy development and implementation, as well as integration services? Systems integrators handle those kinds of customers.

Many systems integrators

    ✔ Have deep knowledge of data center creation

    ✔ Partner closely with technology providers to create practices focused on private and hybrid cloud creation

    ✔ Have specialized knowledge in areas such as security and service orientation

Technology enablers

Just about any technology company that offers solutions for service-oriented architecture (SOA), service management, security, testing, storage, virtualization, and network management (to name but a few) are revamping their offerings so they can be sold for the cloud. Some cynics call this *cloud washing*. The reality is that cloud computing needs all these technologies.

Offering Up Key Vendors

We can't cover all vendors, but in the next section we look at the private (and hybrid) cloud strategies and offerings of some of the key vendors in each category. This should get you started in understanding what's available. The companies we include are IBM, HP, EMC, Unisys, Computer Sciences Corporation, Accenture, VMware, CA, Platform, Rackspace, 3Tera, and Eucalyptus.

Services-led technology companies

All the following vendors are delivering private cloud offerings via an ecosystem of partners. However, services companies' offerings are based on their intellectual property. For example, IBM is focused on specialized software and best practices services, whereas EMC is focused on virtualization and the impact of the cloud on storage requirements. HP, on the other hand, is very focused on implementation services.

IBM

With many of its large enterprise customers determined to transform their data centers to become more efficient, IBM has already done a lot of private and hybrid cloud implementations. While the majority of IBM's initial efforts have been directed toward packaging private and hybrid solutions for enterprise data centers, in the longer term we expect to see a much broader strategy that includes all aspects of the cloud, including public clouds for SaaS, IaaS, and PaaS. IBM has created a centralized cloud computing organization with a goal of creating offerings that encompass software, hardware, and services.

IBM anticipates a lot of demand for solutions to manage the interface between public and private clouds. For example, IBM's Blue Business platform supports both public and private cloud interfaces. In this scenario, the customer has a physical box on-site in the data center. This way the customer can have a private cloud inside the firewall that also supports the ability to burst out into the public cloud when they need additional compute capacity or storage.

A key element of the IBM private and hybrid cloud strategy is to offer solutions based on varying customer-driven workloads. These solutions are organized together as IBM Smart Business Cloud. IBM private and public cloud strategies offer solutions based on varying customer-centric workloads.

These solutions are delivered via three consumption models:

- ✔ Smart Business on the IBM Cloud (public cloud) is a set of standardized services delivered by IBM on the IBM cloud.

- ✔ Smart Business Cloud (private cloud) provides private cloud services, behind the client's firewall, built and/or managed by IBM.

- ✔ Smart Business Systems (cloud in a box) are preintegrated, workload-optimized systems for clients who want to build their own cloud with hardware and software.

In addition, IBM has a packaged private cloud offering. IBM combines the hardware, software, storage, virtualization, networking, and service management components in one package and adds options for services and financing. This package can include some preestablished connections to public cloud services.

As of August 2009, several categories of workload solutions are available for private cloud implementations, including the IBM Smart Analytics System. The following workloads are currently available:

- ✔ **Development and test:** Many organizations have a lot of variation in the demand for test and development resources, making these types of workloads a very practical first step for companies looking to improve data center and IT efficiency and cost-effectiveness. This offering is a private cloud implementation that provides customers with a self-service portal to develop and test on their own. This same service can be implemented inside a customer's firewall. IBM also has a public cloud offering for this area.

- ✔ **Desktop and devices:** End-user connections to desktops and mobile devices are another workload type that IBM has identified as a requirement for private clouds. Companies want their users to access applications from anywhere (at any time) by using thin clients or other Internet-connected devices. This cloud service provides the technology infrastructure for these user environments.

- ✔ **Infrastructure storage:** IBM is offering access to storage on demand in various ways. Customers can install the IBM Smart Business Storage Cloud behind the firewall in the data center. Customers can also buy hardware with the virtual image of hardware and software required for additional storage. IBM also has an option for customers to buy on-demand storage on the IBM public cloud.

- ✔ **Infrastructure compute:** This offering is IBM's version of computing power on demand. This large enterprise offering has shared virtual images on the IBM cloud. IBM has partnered with Amazon and Google to add its middleware Software as a Service model in the Amazon and Google cloud environments.

In keeping with its strategy of providing packaged solutions to help companies get up to speed quickly, IBM also offers its IBM Cloudburst appliance, a family of preintegrated hardware, storage, virtualization, and networking with built-in service management.

Hewlett-Packard

HP has been working on cloudlike implementations with its customers since 2001. These implementations have typically included consulting and integration support and have leveraged HP's extensive collection of technology management products.

Based on experiences in these customer engagements, HP has put a special emphasis on helping customers who want to create hybrid cloud environments. The company is leveraging its extensive services teams (including the EDS division) to help educate and lead their customers down an appropriate path to the cloud. EDS has significant experience with vertical *market-managed services* (hosted services specialized for different industries) and HP will leverage this knowledge and *intellectual property (IP)* in its evolving cloud strategy.

HP's teams of business and IT consultants and engineers get involved with the design and implementation of many different types of cloud environments. For example, HP's Infrastructure Design Service will help you design compute, storage, data center, and Infrastructure as a Service implementations. Other teams provide management consulting, business technology optimization, and testing services.

While companies can easily incorporate a CRM software as a service implementation into its IT environment, large-scale adoption of cloud computing requires IT to adopt a services focus; HP is designing some of its consulting services with this in mind. In addition, HP has expanded its cloud environment consulting teams to help companies focus in on the quality of service delivered across all business lines.

HP is packaging its hardware for private cloud implementations. Two key examples:

- ✔ Proliant SL, a scale-out server environment based on commodity servers

- ✔ Blade Matrix, a *cloud in a box* that includes the preintegration of networks, servers, storage, and automation capabilities

EMC

EMC has developed a shared vision for the private cloud along with its key partners like VMware, Cisco, and AT&T. This group sees lots of opportunity in providing technology and services to companies looking for a better approach to managing IT infrastructure.

And although some companies may use private clouds as an entry point and then transition to public clouds, EMC sees the private cloud as much more than just a staging ground for public clouds. EMC and partners want to help you create a flexible set of IT resources by federating your private clouds with external infrastructures provided by third-party providers.

Not surprisingly, EMC's contribution is concentrated on providing storage, backup, archiving, and security (from RSA) to support the data centers in a private cloud environment. When all IT resources (servers, network, and storage) are pooled in the virtualized data center model, many things need to change.

Storage must be designed and managed differently. For example, many EMC products require a dedicated pair of servers, and this requirement won't fly in a virtualized environment. New tools and processes are required to plan and manage IT resources and ensure information security. For example, your company can use EMC's Atmos cloud storage service to build a scalable internal storage cloud, and then tie it to an external cloud storage service. Cisco brings the network and capability of building a scalable network to the mix. VMware's vSphere, as described later in this section, is the cloud operating system.

Systems integrators companies

There is no one answer to the best way to gain data center efficiency and leverage cloud benefits such as elasticity and self-service. Clouds don't come in boxes, so you'll need to work with providers and consultants. This is why companies like IBM and HP lead cloud service engagements with their own internal services teams.

However, there's a lot more work to go around, and companies like Unisys and CSC focus on security and governance. Other integrators, such as Accenture, are transforming their existing knowledge of managed services and hosting to provide cloud assistance to customers.

Clearly, it's early for the systems integrators. They will find techniques for participating in this new market, but their service offerings are still emerging.

Unisys

Unisys, a veteran computing company, has focused its cloud strategy on security. Its primary offering is the Unisys Secure Cloud Solution, which is a hosted managed cloud service. Unisys intends to have a version of this available by the end of the year that it will call Cloud-in-a-box. The objective is to make it easier for you to create your own private cloud. The company also intends to offer a hybrid cloud service in 2010. This offering will enable you to have your own private cloud and combine that with hosted cloud services from Unisys.

Computer Sciences Corporation

Computer Sciences is focusing on IT security and reliability for its cloud strategy. While CSC has offered security services on a hosting basis, the company is now launching an Infrastructure as a Service version. CSC will try to differentiate itself by taking into account the physical location of a company (because different countries have regulations regarding the movement of data). A future service will help these companies securely connect to third-party clouds. CSC intends to build its services on top of Cisco's Unified Computing System.

Accenture

Accenture offers what it calls its Cloud Computing Suite, which includes the following services:

- ✔ Accenture Cloud Computing Accelerator
- ✔ Accenture Cloud Opportunity Assessment Tool
- ✔ Accenture Cloud Computing Data Processing Solution

Accenture is leveraging its experience with managed services and hosting to move into the cloud market. It also is partnering with many of the software and hardware providers (including EMC, Microsoft, and HP) to provide cloud solutions for its customers.

Savvis, Inc.

Savvis is primarily an outsourced infrastructure service provider for enterprises. Over the past several years the company has begun providing private cloud solutions for its customers. The company is leveraging its 29 data centers to create cloud services, such as providing virtual lab services for developers and a platform for independent software vendors (ISVs) to offer their SaaS applications. In addition, the company is offering a hybrid cloud service so customers can establish a private cloud environment without one of the Savvis data centers.

Technology enabler companies

We put these companies together because their cloud offerings are focused on hardware and/or software technology and less on implementation services. For the most part, they have one or more of the key technology components required to build a cloud.

However, as of August 2009, you can't get all the technology you need to build a private cloud from any one of these vendors except Platform. Partnership relationships are understandably very important to these companies to make sure that customers get the most value from the technology they provide.

VMware

VMware's cloud strategy and technology road map is focused on private clouds and providing a way to bridge to external clouds through private clouds. With virtualization as the key underpinning technology enabling cloud infrastructures, VMware has identified three key building blocks for the private cloud:

- ✔ The cloud operating system
- ✔ Service level management
- ✔ Federation and standards

The company can provide a portion of these requirements and relies on partners for the remainder.

VMware provides the cloud operating system for private clouds through its software solution called vSphere. The company refers to this solution as a *cloud operating system* because it manages the data center infrastructure components (CPUs, storage, and networking), just as a computer operating system (like Linux or Windows) manages the components of a computer.

vSphere has two main components:

- ✔ Infrastructure services that transform server, storage, and network hardware into a shared resource
- ✔ Application services that provide built-in service level controls

VMware's acquisition of SpringSource (in August of 2009) lets the company fill in more of these private cloud building blocks with its own technology. SpringSource brings development tools and a management platform to the product mix, moving VMware toward a Platform as a Service offering. Partners like EMC and Cisco provide solutions for the additional critical components of a private cloud. EMC brings storage, management, and security (from RSA) to the mix, while Cisco brings network and scalable network business to the VMware cloud offering.

CA

CA is well positioned to help companies manage the mediation layer between private and public clouds. CA expects that your company will want to take advantage of public cloud services for a portion of your workload, but need to manage these public services into connection with private cloud implementations.

Your company will need a way to manage the combined services from public and private sources in order to take advantage of hybrid cloud services and deliver higher quality IT services at a lower cost.

For example, if you're using a lot of virtualized servers, you need a way to make sure that they're operating efficiently. Also, you must make sure that you can treat internal and external resources as though they were an integrated environment. This requires sophisticated service management. (For more on service management, see Chapter 20.)

CA's strategy is to provide services that help you understand where specific workloads are running (public versus private cloud) and where they should be running for optimal performance and productivity gains. CA can help your company understand and manage the security and provision requirements between private and public cloud workloads. In addition, CA expects to offer its cloud services to service providers as well as directly to businesses, but doesn't plan to be a provider of public clouds like Google or Amazon.

CA has a lot of infrastructure management software that can be applied to cloud environments.

A number of CA's products have been adapted to support VMware's private cloud operating system, vSphere:

- ✔ Spectrum Infrastructure Manager
- ✔ eHealth Performance Manager
- ✔ Spectrum Automation Manager

The solutions all have a common focus: to help you manage private cloud environments with a unified information model and a single-user interface.

Platform Computing, Inc.

Platform Computing is an independent cloud management software company that is well known in the industry for its clusters and grids. With a strong background in high-performance computing, the company has developed all the components required for building a private cloud. Platform's approach is to work with partners to help your company deliver IT as a service by implementing private clouds.

To deliver on this cloud strategy, Platform has developed a close relationship with an ecosystem of partners. Platform is already partnered with system management and virtualization vendors (such as HP, IBM, VMware, RedHat). Other partnerships, such as those with CA and BMC, are in the planning process.

The company's offering for the cloud, Platform ISF, creates a shared computing infrastructure from physical and virtual resources. This shared infrastructure delivers application environments according to specific policies that take into account the various workloads, available resources, and the relationship between them. Platform ISF helps you manage this workload across virtual and physical environments because it looks at the relationship between workloads and resources. For example, because Platform ISF is aware of workload and resource usage, it can help balance resource use among different business units in your company.

Rackspace

Rackspace is an enterprise-hosting provider with the majority of its customer base in the cloud. The company has three core products that all deliver computing as a service:

- ✔ Rackspace Managed Hosting
- ✔ Rackspace Cloud
- ✔ Rackspace Email and Apps

Rackspace Cloud focuses on hosting Web sites for its customers. It provides storage space, bandwidth usage, and compute cycles. It also has a service for companies that want to gradually move their whole operation into the cloud.

The Rackspace private cloud offering enables your company to run the centrally managed VMware virtualization platform on private dedicated hardware environments in its own data center. It is designed with single-tenant architecture because Rackspace feels that this approach will provide its customers with the level of control and security they demand from the cloud. Companies want control, but they don't want to give up on the scalability, flexibility, and resource optimization they can get from a public cloud. Rackspace's customers are able to quickly provision virtualized server instances and use only what they need.

3Tera

3Tera's AppLogic is a grid operating system (supporting platform) designed to support cloud computing. It supports middleware and Web applications under this operating system. Therefore, AppLogic is used by 3Tera partners to help virtualize software, which makes for easier management in a cloud environment.

AppLogic works by allowing an application to be put into a "container" as though it were a business service. (See Chapter 19 for more on service orientation.) In this way, an application designed for use on a traditional data center can act as though it were designed for the cloud.

In addition, 3Tera has announced a new offering called Cloudware that's based on AppLogic but expands operating system support to Windows and Solaris. It also adds services to support a service catalog and other service management capabilities. Because it can virtualize traditional applications, it is used in many private cloud implementations.

Eucalyptus

Eucalyptus Systems is an open-source software infrastructure for implementing cloud computing on clusters — a group of computers linked together in a way that allows the group to work as one computer. (And just in case you're wondering where the company got its name, it is the combination of the first letters from the phrase "Elastic Utility Computing Architecture for Linking Your Programs to Useful Systems".) Companies use software from Eucalyptus to build private, public, or hybrid clouds.

You can use Eucalyptus software along with IT resources (servers, networks, storage) to form your own data center into a private cloud. Many companies building private clouds are concerned about the lack of standards in this emerging area. They don't want to make a choice now that will lock them in to a specific vendor and make it hard to switch in the future.

Eucalyptus provides an integrated set of *application programming interfaces (APIs)* that are compatible with Amazon Web Services, including Amazon's Elastic Compute Cloud (EC2), Amazon Simple Storage Service (S3), and Amazon Elastic Block Store (EBS).

Eucalyptus Systems understands it needs to develop a large ecosystem of third-party software solutions to help increase demand for its private cloud platform. So far, Eucalyptus has partnered with some key cloud companies including AppScale, Canonical, CohesiveFT, Rightscale, rPath and Ylastic, providing solutions that extend the usability and accessibility of Eucalyptus. The company's partnership with Canonical has led to some interesting developments with Ubuntu — a community based open-source Linux-based operating system for servers, laptops, and desktops). As we mention earlier in the chapter, many companies begin looking at private clouds because they want to bring the public cloud qualities of elasticity and self-service inside the firewall. The Ubuntu Enterprise Cloud (which is powered by Eucalyptus) allows companies using Amazon's EC2 platform to extend these compute services for use in a private cloud.

Part III
Examining the Cloud Elements

The 5th Wave   By Rich Tennant

"I assume everyone on your team is on board with the proposed changes to the system architecture."

In this part . . .

The *as a Service* model is a fundamental cloud concept. In this part, we dive headfirst into these services: software, platform, and infrastructure. This dive includes examining the massive scalability required to support cloud services.

Chapter 10

Seeing Infrastructure as a Service

In This Chapter

▶ Comparing ISPs and IaaS

▶ Looking at Amazon's EC2

▶ Checking out the IaaS competitive landscape

▶ Enabling technology for IaaS

▶ Trusting the trusted cloud

*I*n this chapter, we investigate *Infrastructure as a Service (IaaS)* in a little more depth.

IaaS is the delivery of computer hardware (servers, networking technology, storage, and data center space) as a service. You also can expect it to include the delivery of operating systems and virtualization technology to manage the resources. The IaaS customers rent computing resources instead of buying and installing them in their own data center.

Tracing IaaS to ISP

Most commentators place the dawn of IaaS when Amazon launched its Electric Cloud Computing (EC2) service in 2006. Amazon's move into the market was definitely a step forward. But long before then, *Internet service providers (ISPs)* were happily renting out servers to companies.

Why are we talking about ISPs in terms of IaaS? If you look at the ISP business model and technology infrastructure, you see a lot of similarities to the IaaS model. In fact, if you compare what customers get from an ISP to what they get from an IaaS vendor, you see that it's pretty much the same capability. Both rent infrastructure for the purpose of running applications.

Therefore, the good news is that infrastructure as a service is actually the maturation of the ISP model. The key difference is the addition of new technologies such as virtualization and well-defined self-service management interfaces.

Renting (but not to own)

Why do companies rent external infrastructure to run their Web sites? All reasons are related to four motivations:

✔ Price

✔ Aggregation of resources

✔ Speed to deployment

✔ Security

ISPs are particularly useful for small companies that want to set up a Web site that won't attract a large amount of traffic. But ISPs are also capable of running large Web sites. In most cases, organizations choose to run their own Web sites only when traffic becomes very heavy.

Taking price beyond hardware

At the time of this writing, you can rent a Quad Core Xeon server running at 2.4 GHz with 8GB of memory and 250GB of disk space for about $300 per month. That's $3,600 per year. A server of this kind doesn't cost a great deal (say $2,000–$3,000), but if you're going to use it as a Web server, the cost of ownership will most likely be significantly more than $3,600 per year when you take into account the networking, Internet connections, server management, and everything else the ISP provides.

Managing traffic

The ISP not only aggregates server resources but also networking resources, disk space, and bandwidth. Consequently, the ISP customer no longer needs to be concerned about these resources as long as the contract indicates adequate resources to handle spikes in demand. This can be a particular concern for Web sites, which are sometimes subjected to flash floods of traffic; an ISP may not be prepared to scale on demand to meet additional demand for network bandwidth and computer capacity.

Deploying quickly

The ISP and its successor in the IaaS market typically allocate resources from a pool and therefore it's usually fast to make new resources available. Normally, when you buy a service or more capacity, it's available almost instantly (within hours). Because these providers aggregate homogeneous resources across large numbers of customers, it can normally make new resources available faster than the typical data center can. This includes providing a ready-to-run server (or virtual server) that is normally created from a standard software image suitable for a Web server.

Security is variable depending on provider

Service providers may vary in the actual level of security they provide. However, they will know about Internet security, and larger ISPs may be prepared for and able to deal with Internet-specific threats such as denial of service attacks.

Following the ISP pattern

Much of the IaaS market will likely follow in the path of the ISP market. The ISP model has been proven and some large ISPs (GoDaddy at www.godaddy.com and inMotion Hosting at www.inmotionhosting.com) run millions of Web sites.

The ISP service is typically paid for based on the amount of resources used over time. This can include *dynamic scaling* so that if more resources are required than expected, they will be provided immediately (up to a given limit). The arrangement involves an agreed-upon service level — normally 99.9 percent availability or better, with limits set on CPU usage, memory, disk space, and Internet bandwidth.

No one will object if you want to rent a server or a virtual server from an ISP and you run a data mart (instead of running a Web site). Nothing in the customer agreement stops you from using the resources in that way. It wouldn't make much sense, however, because you probably wouldn't get the service level agreement you wanted or the support you needed.

IaaS takes the ISP model to a new level. If your infrastructure (including computer hardware, operating systems, and virtualization technology) is delivered as a service, then you will expect the service delivery level to be synchronized with all the variations in your demand for those services.

Exploring Amazon EC2: Case Study

Currently the highest profile IaaS operation is Amazon's Elastic Compute Cloud, which is generally known as Amazon EC2. Ironically, Amazon didn't start out to build a big infrastructure services business. Instead, the company built a massive infrastructure to support its retail business and discovered that it was underused.

It decided to leverage this asset while adding to the bottom line. A funny thing happened after this modest plan was put in place: Customers began to find that this could mushroom into something big. Fast-forward a few years: Today, Amazon has established itself as the guerrilla in the market. Amazon's EC2 was launched in August 2006 and has evolved since then by adding different services and support for different operating systems.

What does Amazon offer today? Customers can rent computers or virtual instances to run their own computer applications. EC2 provides a Web services interface through which a customer can create virtual machines and load and run any software. The customer has control of a virtual operating environment and so can create, launch, and terminate server instances as needed, which is why Amazon describes it as *elastic*. The customer can set up server instances in zones that are insulated from each other (regarding the failure of any component) and thus can set up a server instance that backs up another server instance.

EC2 Compute Units

EC2 uses Xen virtualization to create and manage its virtual machines. (Xen is a popular, proven open-source *hypervisor* — a thin layer of software that allows other operating systems to run on the same system.) The Amazon service allows the creation of virtual servers in one of three sizes: small, large, or extra large.

Currently Amazon sizes these instances by using EC2 Compute Units based on the approximate equivalent CPU capacity of physical hardware. One EC2 Compute Unit equals a 1.0–1.2 GHz 2007 AMD Opteron or 2007 Intel Xeon processor. Using that as a basis, Table 10-1 shows the allocations of resources. The first three table entries are the common instances that EC2 offers. Amazon also provides two other alternatives for compute-intensive applications, which it refers to as High-CPU Instances. Those are the last two entries.

Platforms and storage

Amazon EC2 supports the following operating systems:

- Linux
- Sun Microsystems' OpenSolaris and Solaris Express Community Edition
- Microsoft's Windows Server 2003

This covers most of the common operating systems that companies might want to use, other than those from IBM and Hewlett-Packard, both of which provide their own cloud services (both alone and through partnerships).

The storage offered with the various instances persists only as long as the instance is in use. Amazon also provides persistent storage for those who want it, in the form of *Elastic Block Storage (EBS)*. Users can set up and manage storage volumes of anything from 1GB to 1TB (terabyte). You can connect these EBSs to servers, so the data is attached to the server instance while it exists.

Storage needs can also be met by Amazon's *Simple Storage Service (S3)*, which is available independently to EC2 because its goal is simply to provide storage space that is accessible via the Internet at any time. With S3, storage items (called *objects*) can be any size from 1 byte to 5 gigabytes, and there's no limit of the number of items that can be stored. Each object is stored in a "bucket" and retrieved via a unique, user-assigned key. Full authentication security is provided.

Table 10-1	Resource Allocation Based on EC2 Compute Units			
Instance	*System*	*Compute Units*	*Instance Storage*	*Platform*
EC2 Small Instance[*]	1.7GB of memory	1 EC2 Compute Unit (i.e. 1 virtual core with 1 EC2 Compute Unit)	160GB	32-bit platform
Large Instance[*]	7.5GB of memory	4 EC2 Compute Units (i.e. 2 virtual cores with 2 EC2 Compute Units each)	850GB	64-bit platform
Extra Large Instance[*]	15GB of memory	8 EC2 Compute Units (4 virtual cores with 2 EC2 Compute Units each)	1690GB	64-bit platform
High-CPU Medium Instance[*]	1.7GB of memory	5 EC2 Compute Units (2 virtual cores with 2.5 EC2 Compute Units each)	350GB	Moderate I/O usage, 32-bit platform
High-CPU Extra Large Instance[*]	7GB of memory	20 EC2 Compute Units (8 virtual cores with 2.5 EC2 Compute Units each)	1690GB	High I/O usage, 64-bit platform

Alternatives for compute-intensive applications (known as High-CPU Instances).

EC2 pricing

Amazon's primary charges are of two types:

- ✔ Hourly charge per virtual machine
- ✔ Data transfer charge

Amazon's EC2 hourly charges are counted from the moment a virtual machine is created to the time it's taken down (rounding up to the next hour). The charge applies whether the resources are fully used or lying idle.

The data transfer charges are for data in and out, not for data retained. There are increased rates for running Windows and some small charges for data transfer between instances.

If you compare resource for resource, the ISP offering of a Quad Core Xeon server running at 2.4 GHz with 8 gigabytes of memory and 250GB of disk space for about $300 per month is clearly a better deal than Amazon offers, but that tells you that the Amazon's IaaS business has a completely different character than an ISP business. Amazon sells by the hour and ISPs don't — that's the major difference.

EC2 customers

Many activities that occur in a data center are temporary. Consider these examples:

- ✔ End-of-month and end-of-year workloads
- ✔ Ad-hoc workloads (such as creating a temporary data mart to analyze a data set)
- ✔ System testing

You either cater for these workloads by putting something permanent in place, or you have to commission resources for them. It's really unlikely that your data center has the ability to set up and take down virtual servers under user control.

That's what Amazon provides. If you make efficient use of the capability, it's likely to be less expensive than trying to achieve something similar in your own data center. Amazon provides the capability to remove some of the peak demands on the data center. For most companies that's a win all the way around: for the systems users, for developers for operational staff, and for the company itself in terms of cost and service levels.

Checking Out Other IaaS Companies

We spend a good deal of time in this chapter describing Amazon's EC2 because it's the best known of the IaaS operations. However, it's by no means the only one. Companies that have entered the IaaS market include Rackspace Cloud, GoGrid, MediaTemple, GridLayer, Flexiscale, and Joyent. All of these, like Amazon, offer a pay-per-use arrangement, with the prices, capabilities, and terms of usage varying.

The services they provide are similar to EC2 as well in that they provide access to a resource pool and enable the configuration of virtual servers and the installation of platform software and Web server software in a simple way. Their approaches vary.

These companies (and others not mentioned) will inevitably be joined by major IT companies such as IBM, Hewlett-Packard, Cisco, EMC, Microsoft, Oracle, CSC, and Accenture, all of whom are strategizing and some of whom are building data centers and preparing to enter the market.

Rackspace

Rackspace Cloud, a spinoff from Rackspace, for example, entered the market in 2005 before Amazon did and offers a service that is much closer to an ISP service than Amazon's.

It focuses primarily on attracting customers that want to host Web sites and its charges are more oriented to Web site usage. It charges for

- ✔ Storage space
- ✔ Bandwidth usage
- ✔ Compute cycles (which constitute its own measure of CPU and memory usage)

However, it also offers "instant servers" that can be bought on an hourly basis with prices based on memory used and instant storage.

This service is for companies that might want to gradually move their whole operation into the cloud (assuming that all their software can run on *commodity servers* — no-frills servers designed for basic workloads or servers grouped in clusters to provide lots of computing power through virtualization). Refer to Chapter 6 for more information.

GoGrid

GoGrid has similar pricing to Rackspace, charging for

- ✔ Storage space (more than 10GB)
- ✔ Outbound data transfer
- ✔ Server RAM hours (with different prices for different combinations of memory and CPU)

GoGrid emphasizes ease of use and offers a greater level of technical control (including load balancing) than either the Amazon EC2 or Rackspace cloud.

Others

Many other companies are entering the IaaS market. Here are a few:

- ✔ **MediaTemple** is a highly successful ISP that's turning its hand to IaaS, but continuing with ISP-type pricing.
- ✔ **Gridlayer** is a grid computing company that has more than 12,000 servers deployed. It offers virtual private servers, storage, and virtual private data centers. The *virtual private data center* is what it sounds like — a collection of server resources that can be configured according to need.
- ✔ **Flexiscale** is like most of the IaaS companies already described, although it distinguishes itself by providing an API to its environmental software (which most companies don't). It also provides a *virtual LAN (VLAN)* to each customer. It claims to be significantly less expensive than Amazon EC2, although it's clear from the pricing that other IaaS companies may come in less expensive than Amazon EC2, depending on your needs.
- ✔ **Joyent Accelerator** is an ISP that has moved into the IaaS market and its pricing (based on a monthly fee for specific levels of hardware) reflects that. Its Zeus Accelerator is a virtual appliance that manages Web applications to guarantee performance. Joyent also has specific expertise in most Web platforms, including Ruby on Rails.

Examining IaaS-Enabling Technology

The ability to offer IaaS requires software that can manage the infrastructure that's being shared. In this area, two technologies are worth drawing attention to:

✔ AppLogic from 3Tera

✔ Eucalyptus, an open source initiative

AppLogic

3Tera, Inc., was founded in 2004 to develop system software for utility computing and cloud computing. In February 2006, it launched its AppLogic product, which has since been taken up by many service providers and cloud computing vendors.

You can think of AppLogic as management software that converts arrays of servers into virtualized resource pools that can be shared among multiple users.

The software enables users to create and retire virtual machines but also to define necessary infrastructure such as firewalls, VPNs, load balancers, and storage by using a browser interface. AppLogic enables the configuration of

✔ Virtual private servers

✔ Virtual private data centers (involving complex configuration of application infrastructure)

✔ Cloud data storage

✔ Software as a Service (SaaS) applications

AppLogic is sold either on a usage basis or by software license, so it can be used in house for private clouds. The product has been so successful among service providers that it enables hybrid situations where a customer uses more than one provider. It's also useful in migrating from a private cloud to a public cloud.

Eucalyptus

Eucalyptus is a rather forced acronym standing for Elastic Utility Computing Architecture for Linking Your Programs To Useful Systems. Unfortunately the name doesn't give a reasonable description of what the software does.

Eucalyptus is a system for implementing on-premise private and hybrid clouds, using the hardware and software infrastructure that's in place, without modification. In effect, it's an add-on capability for data center virtualization to create genuine cloud capability such as self-service provisioning, security, performance management, and end-user customization.

Eucalyptus is open source, so the software can be downloaded free and it is also shipped with the Ubuntu 9.04 (and later) distribution of Linux. It is thus becoming the default open-source cloud capability. It is implemented by using commonly available Linux tools and basic Web service technologies. The current interface to Eucalyptus is compatible with Amazon's EC2, S3, and *Elastic Block Store (EBS)* — a *storage area network (SAN)* in the cloud — interfaces, so it is possible to create a private cloud by using Eucalyptus with the intention of moving some or all of it onto EC2.

Trusting the Cloud

A significant amount of nervousness surrounds the prospect of using cloud services. Part of this can be chalked up to unfamiliarity with using cloud-based capability, but some of it is goes much deeper than that.

CSC, the global systems integration company, was quick to recognize this issue and first used the term *trusted cloud* to define the kind of environment that many organizations would want and expect from a cloud service provider.

The *trusted cloud* includes services that are

✔ Secure

✔ Transparent of control and result (whether it provides a full customer interface so that you can see how everything functions)

✔ Able to provide evidence that systems operate as advertised (whether it definitely meets the services levels it is supposed to be providing)

An organization might have many concerns in moving systems into an IaaS environment, but these are the primary ones.

Although companies clearly trust their Web sites to cloud providers, they're much less likely to trust their mission-critical systems to the cloud. Secure cloud data centers exist. In a way, this type of trusted cloud is similar to what outsourcing specialists and managed service providers offer (plus a cloud customer interface that puts the customer directly in control).

We discuss cloud standards in Chapter 14, and clearly standards will emerge in time so customers can select cloud services without making significant technical changes to either software or data. At the moment, however, no established standards exist, so those organizations moving systems into the cloud need to be concerned not just about the preceding points, but also about overall control of their systems.

The IaaS customer needs to be able to integrate all systems and software running in the cloud with other corporate systems and manage the whole as a single unit. This kind of orchestration of systems is a new challenge in many areas, particularly in managing performance and managing security in a coherent way.

What Infrastructure as a Service Means to You

More and more companies are looking to defray costs and gain flexibility by leveraging infrastructure that can be used on demand. What does this mean to you?

✔ Think about how you're getting your services.

✔ Understand which services include a set of well-defined interfaces and which ones will lock you in to a complex set of services that will be difficult to move away from.

✔ Know why you're using a cloud service. For example, if you need some temporary capacity to test a new application, your requirements will be very different than if you're creating an application that will operate in a cloud.

In addition to understanding potential cloud gains, get familiar with how your infrastructure service provider handles the following capabilities:

✔ Explicitly defines service level agreements for availability, support, and performance (of provisioning more resource)

✔ A utility computing billing arrangement, relating cost to actual resource usage in a measured way

✔ A virtualization environment that enables the configuration of systems (for compute power, bandwidth, and storage) as well as the creation individual virtual machines (all to be available on an ad-hoc basis)

✔ A flexible, extensible, resource-rich environment that's engineered for secure *multi-tenancy* (multiple users or tenants running the software in a shared environment on its servers)

✔ Internet connectivity, including a Web services interface to the customer's management environment

Chapter 11

Exploring Platform as a Service

In This Chapter

▶ Examining integrated lifecycle platform as a service

▶ Exploring anchored lifecycle platform as a service

▶ Enabling platforms as a service

*T*here are many ways to approach cloud computing, depending on what business problem you're trying to solve. When organizations are looking for capacity on demand, they often look to *Infrastructure as a Service (IaaS)*. However, when an organization is looking for a deeper set of capabilities, they look at *Platform as a Service (PaaS)*.

Of course, like everything in life, there are shades of gray. In fact, many companies that fit into the IaaS category offer platform services as well. But to keep things a little simpler, we focus on the technologies and companies that provide infrastructure and various development and deployment services for the cloud.

Although PaaS has many definitions, we'd like you to think about it as a computing platform that includes a set of development, middleware, and deployment capabilities. A key vendor characteristic is creating and encouraging a deep ecosystem of partners who all commit to this environment for the future.

In this chapter, we discuss what types of services are included in a Platform as a Service, the variety of approaches, and the considerations that you should take into account. We provide examples of several key platforms emerging on the PaaS market.

Putting Platform as a Service on a Pedestal

There isn't only one approach to PaaS. In fact, the lines between Platform as a Service and Infrastructure as a Service can blur as well. But for purposes of getting your head around platforms that help you develop applications in the cloud, we separated Infrastructure as a Service. (See Chapter 10 for more on it.) Platform as a Service has many characteristics worth mentioning.

Consider what all PaaS solutions have in common:

- ✔ PaaS has to leverage the Internet.

- ✔ PaaS must offer some type of development language so professional developers (and in some cases users) can add value.

- ✔ These environments need a way to monitor and measure resource use and to track overall performance of the vendor's platform.

- ✔ Almost all PaaS platforms are based on a *multi-tenancy architecture* (which lets multiple clients run their copy separately from each other through virtualization) so that each customer's code or data is isolated from others. See Chapter 12 for more on multi-tenancy.

- ✔ A PaaS environment needs to support the development lifecycle and the team development process, including testing.

- ✔ A PaaS platform needs to include services interfaces such as SOAP (Simple Object Access Protocol) and XML (eXtensible Markup Language), among others.

- ✔ A PaaS platform must be able to deploy, manage, test, and maintain the developed applications.

- ✔ A PaaS platform must support well-defined and well-documented interfaces so elements and components can be used in the following:

  - • *Composite applications* are created by combining services to create an enterprise application based on orchestration of business logic and rules.

  - • *Portals,* which are an organized environment that organizes application components for the customer.

  - • *Mashups,* which let end users easily bring together two or more business services that can communicate and exchange data.

NIST PaaS

The National Institute of Standards and Technology (NIST), a U.S. federal government agency established to design technology standards, has come up with one definition of PaaS worth noting:

"Platform as a Service is the ability to provide a computing environment and the related development and deployment stack needed to deliver a solution to the consuming customer."

Although PaaS platforms have some common characteristics, we think there are some different approaches that are appropriate for different needs. We have divided the environments into three categories:

✔ Integrated lifecycle platform

✔ Anchored lifecycle platform

✔ Enabling technologies as a platform

Integrated lifecycle platforms

Several emerging key platforms provide the developer with a full environment for creating an application without buying any individual tools. For example, the platform provider will provide the developer with a full stack including an operating system, a programming language, security, storage, version control, collaborative tools, as well as tools to build Web interaction.

These integrated PaaS companies often include the following:

✔ A workflow engine

✔ Development tools

✔ A testing environment

✔ An ability to integrate databases

✔ Third-party tools and services

These platforms provide services as a well-integrated and well-tuned stack with its own middleware and often its own programming interfaces.

Two prominent examples of integrated lifecycle platforms are Google App Engine and Microsoft's Azure, which we discuss in the section "Getting Inside the Integrated Lifecycle Platform," later in this chapter.

Anchored lifecycle platforms

Although anchored platforms have most of the same characteristics as the integrated lifecycle platform, there is one key difference: These environments have a packaged business software at the core.

The most prominent example of an anchored platform is Salesforce.com and its Force.com platform. Likewise, Intuit is leveraging its QuickBooks financial software environment to create an anchored platform.

Enabling technologies as a platform

Not all platforms in the cloud include a full lifecycle environment. Some platforms are focused on providing specialized capabilities. Some of these capabilities may be a specific tool.

For example, although Amazon.com provides a comprehensive IaaS platform, it also offers platform tools such as SimpleDB and Simple Query Service (SQS). Other enabling technology environments (such as Rightscale) provide an integrated management platform designed for the cloud. Hyperic, a division of Springsource (recently acquired by VMWare), offers a cloud-based monitoring environment. WaveMaker lets users customize their platform and allows developers to reuse existing code within the PaaS environment. There are testing-based and social networking-based services as well.

The following sections in this chapter take a closer look at these three types of PaaS. To do this, we look at some of the key vendors that provide these capabilities. Clearly, there are many other players besides the ones we list here, and there will be even more before this book is even published. Our goal is to give you an understanding of how each of these PaaS approaches works.

Getting Inside the Integrated Lifecycle Platform

To really get a good understanding of what it means to have a lifecycle platform as a service, we thought it would be helpful to give you an in-depth look at two of the most important PaaS vendors: Google with its App Engine and Microsoft with its Azure platform.

Google App Engine

When you visit the Google App Engine Web site at `http://code.google.com/appengine`, you will notice four phrases:

- ✔ No assembly is required.
- ✔ Google App Engine exposes a fully integrated development environment.
- ✔ It's easy to scale.
- ✔ It's free to get started.

That really sums up Google's strategy for PaaS. Google isn't trying to help customers create every application to run on every platform. It is actually quite focused, helping customers build Web-based applications. The platform is for development and deployment.

In essence, the developer provides the Google App Engine with a URL (Web address) for the application it's building and the engine maps that code to Google's development platform. The App Engine handles the Web application lifecycle, including routine tasks such as request logs, checking the application status, updating the application version, operating the underlying database, and handling workflow.

Google has integrated all the development tools into a single integrated environment. When customers tie their development into the lifecycle environment provided by Google, they also gain access to Google's IaaS. In this way, customers can add more capacity on demand.

Other Google infrastructure services

In addition to development services, Google also provides other integrated platform services, including but not limited to the following:

- ✔ Google Accounts for authentication
- ✔ Google native file system called GFS (Google File System)
- ✔ BigTable platform (for data management), a distributed storage system that manages very large-scale structured data

It also includes infrastructure services such as

- ✔ Load balancing
- ✔ Persistent storage with queries
- ✔ Sorting and transactions

✔ Programming interfaces to support authenticating users and sending email by using Google Accounts

✔ Scheduled tasks for triggering events at specified times and regular intervals

This is essentially the same platform that Google uses to build its own software.

Google development stack

In addition to these infrastructure tools, Google App Engine also includes a development stack. Google calls this a *scalable serving infrastructure* that connects the Web application code to the Google environment.

It does this by integrating with the following tools:

✔ **Python runtime:** To create an application for the platform requires a programming language. The first one that Google supported was Python, a high-level programming language that makes it easier to rapidly build complex applications with minimal programming. Python includes models and packages and supports code reuse.

✔ **Java runtime:** Google added Java as a second supported programming language platform. This runtime is integrated with Google's toolkits and is intended to be used for AJAX (asynchronous JavaScript and XML) or interactive Web applications.

✔ **A Software Development Kit (SDK):** This set of development tools enables developers to write application code.

✔ **A Web-based administration console:** The console helps developers manage their applications.

✔ **Datastore:** A *datastore* is a software layer that stores a Web application's data. It is built on the Bigtable (a high-performance database) structure. (For more details on data in the cloud, see Chapter 8).

Google fees

Google has set up Google App Engine to encourage its wide adoption. As with other cloud platforms, customers pay based on usage, so there's no set-up cost or other maintenance fees. For example, there is no charge for a developer to build an application. After a customer deploys that application, however, the charges begin to add up. The customer pays for storage and bandwidth. Each of these applications can use up to 500MB of storage, up to 5 million page views each month without an additional fee. A customer is allowed to register up to ten applications per developer account.

When developers create an application, they're granted a quota of resources that they can use without paying anything. This includes 6.5 hours of CPU time per day and 1 gigabyte of data transferred in and out of the application per day.

When additional resources are required, costs are as follows:

- $0.10–$0.12 per CPU core-hour
- $0.15– $0.18 per GB per month of storage
- $0.11– $0.13 per GB outgoing bandwidth
- $0.09– $0.11 per GB incoming bandwidth
- $0.15 per GB per month for stored data
- $0.0001 per recipients emailed

Microsoft Azure

Microsoft, the incumbent in the application development and deployment market, has taken its .Net platform into the cloud. Azure is Microsoft's PaaS strategy that was announced in 2008. Microsoft defines the Azure platform as "an Internet-scale cloud services platform hosted in Microsoft data centers, which provides an operating system and a set of developer services that can be used individually or together."

Microsoft's overall strategy is a combination of on-premise computing with cloud-based services. The idea is that developers want to build some applications that live on-site, while other components will live in the cloud. Microsoft calls this strategy *software plus services.* The heart of Microsoft's strategy is to allow developers to use the same underlying technology and enablers to build both on-premise applications and cloud applications.

While the main focus of the Azure platform is to bring Microsoft's familiar programming model to the cloud, Microsoft also intends to support other programming models, including Ruby on Rails and Python. For interoperability, Microsoft supports various Internet protocols, including HTTP, REST, SOAP, and XML.

Azure platform

The Azure platform is composed of four different components:

- **Windows Azure:** This Windows environment runs applications locally and stores the related data on servers inside the Microsoft data center.

✔ **Microsoft .NET Services:** These are the same .Net services that Microsoft has in its Windows environment. It has been extended to support cloud-based as well as on-premise applications.

✔ **Microsoft SQL Services:** These are the same data services Microsoft offers on premise that have been extended to the cloud. However, if you want to take advantage of Azure's scaling capability, you must rewrite the SQL code. The goal of SQL services is to provide an asset of cloud-based approaches for storing the data in the cloud. The data services expose both SOAP and REST interfaces as data access methods. For data storage, Azure doesn't use a relational model.

✔ **Live Services:** This set of services allows developers to connect code developed in the Windows Live platform into the cloud. These services include a framework intended to integrate, connect, and synchronize code. The platform also includes support for different programming languages and allows all resources to include a URL address.

When you put the pieces together, Microsoft has created a platform that allows developers to use familiar tools such as Microsoft's Visual Studio and .Net services and then store the data in a Microsoft-owned cloud platform. Therefore, developers familiar with building .Net applications will be comfortable with Microsoft's cloud approach.

Like Google, Microsoft has a pay-as-you-go consumption model for its PaaS offering. And like Google, Microsoft doesn't charge for development and testing phases. It begins charging customers when the applications are deployed.

Azure fees

The following is a list of the pricing Microsoft has released:

Windows Azure:

✔ Compute at $0.12 per hour

✔ Storage at $0.15 per GB stored

✔ Storage transactions at $0.01 per 10K

SQL Azure:

✔ Web Edition: Up to 1GB relational database at $9.99

✔ Business Edition: Up to 10GB relational database at $99.99

.NET Services:

✔ Messages at $0.15 per 100K message operations (including Service Bus messages and Access Control tokens)

✔ Bandwidth across all three services will be charged at $0.10 in and $0.15 out per GB

Getting Inside Anchored Lifecycle Platform as a Service

Why did we distinguish between integrated lifecycle platforms and anchored lifecycle platforms? It is simple, really. Anchored platform as a service is a business application-centric approach to development in the cloud. Therefore, anchored Platform as a Service vendors started out in life as Software as a Service vendors, for the most part.

Because of their heritage, vendors in this space have several characteristics in common:

 ✔ A large customer base

 ✔ Defined services such as billing

 ✔ Security and authentication

 ✔ Programming languages

 ✔ Integration services

These services are the same ones the company used to create its own SaaS offerings.

In the next section, we focus on two of the anchored Platform as a Service vendors and how they structure their offerings.

Salesforce.com's Force.com platform

Salesforce.com initiated a platform called Force.com as its foray into the cloud platform market. It helps commercial software developers create cloud-based applications based on Salesforce.com's development environment. In addition, applications built with Force.com's tools can also take advantage of the CRM applications.

At the heart of this platform is the *multi-tenancy* architecture. This means that applications designed with Force.com assume that users will share a single physical instance. However, those instances and the application code built in those instances are isolated from each other. In addition, this type of multi-tenancy also means that customizations designed by one user will be isolated from customized designs built by any other user.

History.com on Salesforce.com

We need to give credit to Salesforce.com for being the innovator in this space. A little history lesson will help put the anchored PaaS area into perspective. When Salesforce.com first came to market in 1999, the objective was to provide a packaged *Customer Relationship Management (CRM)* as a service. No matter how many customers asked the company to provide them with an on-premise version of the product, the answer was always no. In the beginning, customers were a little wary of having this upstart control their customer application. But after a couple of years, companies started to like what they saw. With this Software as a Service, platform customers could have their cake and eat it too. They didn't have to manage or update the application. Over time, Salesforce.com grew until it had thousands of customers and plenty of individual users.

Now here is when things changed. Instead of stopping with a nice, neat CRM application, Salesforce.com decided that it could leverage this platform and create a broader community of software vendors that might like to build their applications on top of their environment. The company therefore took its own programming environment that it had used to create its CRM application and made it available to third-party software developers. In this regard, anchored PaaS isn't that much different than integrated PaaS. The difference is the ecosystem. When vendors began to write their applications to take advantage of Salesforce.com's platform, they could now market and sell their software to the growing Salesforce.com customer base. That is the real difference between integrated lifecycle platform and an anchored platform. (For more details on Salesforce.com, see Chapter 12).

Force.com platform

The Force.com platform is centered around a development stack that includes the following components:

- ✔ **Metadata architecture:** Salesforce.com needed a metadata architecture to support its multi-tenancy approach. Salesforce.com considers this metadata stack as the core of its differentiation in the market. The metadata layer is complex and includes an application server called Resin. The Resin Application Server is a high-performance XML application server for use with Java server pages (JSPs), servlets, JavaBeans, XML, and a host of other technologies.

  On top of this metadata layer is an authorization server. The metadata layer is structured so that each organization has unique access to the stack. Therefore, two companies could be physically connected to the same server but there would be no way for them to access each other's data. The metadata layer will only point to the data that is specific to a user. The environment is designed so that each customer has a specific Web Service Description Language-based API. In fact, the architecture includes the approach of access APIs through the WSDL interface. There are two versions of WSDL: one general and one for a specific customer implementation. If a customer wants to share data, for example, they have to go through the general WSDL interface.

✔ **Service delivery infrastructure:** Salesforce.com's cloud delivery infrastructure is based on its managed and secure data center environment. This is the same infrastructure used to manage its CRM customers.

✔ **Database as a service:** The database is built on top of the metadata services. The data services provide data security by enabling customers to declare validation rules (such as confirming that an account number is valid). It enables customers to build customized objects and fields. The customer isn't responsible for database tuning, backup, or upgrades, because of the cloud infrastructure.

✔ **Integration as a service:** At the center of Force.com's integration capabilities is a Web services *Application Programming Interface (API)*. This API allows customers to access data stored in a Force.com application because it supports industry-standard SOAP Web services. Salesforce. com partners use this API to create connectors to packaged applications such as SAP R/3 and Oracle Financials. In addition, there are prebuilt integrations to services such as Amazon's Web services, Facebook, and Google App Engine. Force.com also supports Web services standards including Java, .NET, PHP, and Perl.

✔ **Logic as a service:** This is a set of automated workflow services. A built-in workflow engine includes services such as task creation, record assignment, and other event-triggered services. Customers can use a Salesforce.com programming language (called Apex) as a way to extend the application by writing new code.

✔ **User interface as a service:** Force.com provides two ways of building or customizing user interfaces:

  • A builder to change the application layout and Visualforce

  • A framework for building user interfaces for both private and public clouds

Developers can use standard Web development tools including HTML, AJAX, and Adobe Flex.

✔ **Development as a service:** Development tools include the Metadata API, an IDE (Integrated Development Environment), a *development sandbox* (a separate development space for developers), and a service called Code Share for building cloud-based applications.

✔ **AppExchange marketplace:** This site enables vendors that have used the Salesforce.com interfaces. It is, in essence, a channel for partners to sell into the installed base.

Like many Platform as a Service providers, Salesforce.com allows *independent software vendors (ISVs)* and commercial developers to join their Force.com program without any start-up fees. If a developer is selling to existing Salesforce.com customers via AppExchange, there's no cost to the ISV. However, if an ISV sells a stand-alone application to a new customer that isn't using Salesforce.com, there is an embedded license charge of $15 per user per month.

Force.com fees

In addition, developers building Force.com-based sites have the following costs:

- ✔ **Force.com Free Edition** includes up to 250,000 monthly page views. (Customers can build one custom application supporting 100 users.) Customers needing more access can purchase additional Force.com subscriptions for $50 per user per month.

- ✔ **Force.com Enterprise Edition** includes up to 500,000 monthly page views.

- ✔ **Force.com Unlimited Edition** includes up to one million monthly page views.

- ✔ **Additional monthly pages** are available for $1,000 per month for up to one million additional page views (regardless of edition).

Intuit

Intuit's target market is the small- and medium-sized businesses that use its popular QuickBooks application to run their day-to-day financial operations. Intuit has used this foundation combined with a series of acquisitions to create a PaaS model. More than 80,000 developers and about four million customers are part of the company's ecosystem.

Federated Applications

Intuit's new cloud-based Platform as a Service is called Federated Applications. In essence, the developers can write their application with any programming language, use any database or cloud computing resource, and then connect this code to the Intuit platform via XML-based interfaces and configuration files. These developers can then create cloud-based applications by leveraging the same development platform that Intuit created to build its own packaged applications.

These components include user interface services, billing services, account management, and permissions, data and single sign-on services. Therefore, a software developer can use the billing service that Intuit has built instead of building one from scratch. These services are federated together through Intuit's Workplace portal environment. Intuit uses a *service-oriented architecture (SOA)* to build its platform. For more on SOA, see Chapter 19.

After linking an application to the Intuit Workplace portal, a customer is essentially published into Intuit's cloud marketplace. Therefore, a QuickBooks customer can go to the portal and buy an application designed to work with QuickBooks. The user interface, account management, security, and billing are the same. Integration with QuickBooks is automatic.

Intuit's Partner Platform

What are the components of Intuit's Partner Platform? They are as follows:

- ✔ **QuickBase:** This Web infrastructure is for small business applications. The foundation of the QuickBase platform is a database that includes team workflow, communications, and task management. QuickBase provides partners with support for multi-tenancy. It is used as a collaboration platform by partners.

- ✔ **Workplace:** This is a portal environment for customers. It can either be used as a stand-alone environment or can be integrated with QuickBooks. Customers can use a QuickBase application within the workplace to control how the application will be presented to individual users. In addition, the Workplace also provides services that track subscriptions and revenue.

- ✔ **Federated Applications model:** With the federated application services, developers can integrate existing code through a configuration service. There are four integration methods:

  - **Data integration:** To integrate at the data level, the partner must program to a set of Application Programming Interfaces (APIs) that enable data synchronization. This allows developers to take advantage of the platform's common cloud data *schema* (which defines the relationships between data elements). For more on data in the cloud, see Chapter 8.

  - **Login integration:** To integrate at login, the partner uses a Federated Identity Web API. After the developer has used this API, customers can use their Intuit Workplace login credentials to access the partner application that they bought.

  - **User management and permissions integration:** Intuit provides developers with a Web API so their application can handle processes such as adding more users.

  - **Navigation-based integration:** A developer who has built a Software as a Service–based application can use this tool to provide the Intuit Workplace toolbar. This allows the customer to have common integration.

Unlike many of the companies in the PaaS market, Intuit charges between 14–20 percent of revenue to partners who sell through Intuit's Workplace. The exact percentage depends on the volume sold. If the vendor is offering a free application via the Workplace, there is a utility fee. While the customer buys the application directly from the vendor, the transaction is handled directly by Intuit. There are no fees for page views or data storage.

LongJump

LongJump is a division of Relationals, Inc., a privately held provider of SaaS *Customer Relationship Management (CRM)* and Sales Force Automation (SFA) business applications to more than 150 enterprise companies. The company is leveraging its platform to move into the platform as a service market — specifically for companies who are building private clouds. Therefore, it assumes that development will take place inside a private data center or inside one of the Infrastructure as a Service environments (Amazon, RackSpace, and so on).

The company offers a Java-based development suite that includes a plug-in to the Eclipse *Integrated Development Environment (IDE)*. LongJump's PaaS environment enables developers to use services that it calls Building Blocks. These services include objects, scripts, component extensions, business logic, data policies, and workflows.

A developer uses LongJump's platform to create Building Blocks that can then be reused for other purposes. For example, a single contract object and its records can be created and reused by business teams such as sales, business development, compliance, legal, and finance by simply modifying data policies and workflows.

LongJump Development Suite

The new LongJump Development Suite includes the following components:

- A visual browser-based user interface for data and process modeling, as well as advanced coding and scripting features for developers who are familiar with Java. That way they can enhance and extend applications or completely create new data models and processes from scratch.

- LongJump provides a set of Web services as a technique to allow services to communicate and pass data from one to the other (using SOAP and REST APIs to connect to external systems or platforms). When LongJump objects are extended, those fields are immediately available for integration with SOAP and REST APIs, workflow processes, and the built-in report creation wizard.

✔ Development Suite features include Java development tools (including JSP and HTML-based code), AJAX library, and data model definitions. It includes plug-in to a standard Eclipse IDE.

LongJump fees

LongJump offers its development platform free to existing customers of its packaged applications. After an application is built on the platform, LongJump has a three-tiered pricing model. For premium telephone support, call 800-886-9028. The cost is $50 for a 30-minute call, billed prior to the call. Additional time is available at $50 for every 30 minutes.

LongJump offers a free evaluation version.

Table 11-1 outlines the pricing model for LongJump.

Table 11-1	LongJump Three-Tiered Pricing Model		
	Bronze	*Silver*	*Gold*
Price per user per month	$30	$60	$90
User Limit	Unlimited	Unlimited	Unlimited
Objects	Up to 10	Up to 200	Up to 2,000
Prebuilt Objects	Not included	Not included	Not included
Data Storage per Account	5MB	10MB	20MB
Document Storage per Account	25MB	50MB	100MB

Notes: Three-user minimum required. Data storage includes the actual records of information within the application, as well as all related records. For example, 20MB equals approximately 20,000 records in most situations. Document storage includes uploaded files and images that are stored as attachments to records or in the document library.

LongJump charges for migration service and storage, for adding 50MB of data storage, and adding 250MB of document storage per account. (Note that 50MB of data storage is enough for 50,000 records.)

Enabling Technologies as a Platform

No matter what type of Platform as a Service you're investigating, some technologies are needed to supplement these platforms. We can't possibly mention all the emerging technologies or vendors. Instead, we give you a taste of three companies and how they help enable PaaS.

There are hundreds of different players in different areas. For example, some companies provide testing capabilities for PaaS vendors; some companies provide management frameworks. Other platforms help customers move data and code from on premise to the cloud.

Testing in the cloud

Testing in the cloud is a very critical; however, most platforms don't provide their own testing environment. Therefore, you might want to look at the various options on the market.

Hundreds of vendors, big and small, provide services to test cloud-based platforms. They include HP, IBM, and independent companies such as iTKO and SOASTA. All have one common capability: They integrate with the platform and enable customers to test their applications before deploying them to a public or private cloud. While the platform vendors themselves offer their own testing tied to their platform, many customers and developers need testing for their own code and for integration testing.

Service management for the cloud

Managing applications created in clouds is a complex area and few platform vendors provide their own management services. Therefore, a range of companies are emerging to fill the gap, including companies like RightScale. In fact, RightScale is the primary management platform for Amazon.com EC2 offering. (See Chapter 10 for more on Infrastructure as a Service.) Companies including HP, IBM, CA, and others also provide service management offerings that are sold independently.

Integration and configuration platforms

For cloud development to flourish, you need enabling tools that make it easy to customize cloud applications for different end-user needs. A variety of platforms provide capabilities for this need.

For example, WaveMaker is a cloud-development platform based on Java. It's intended to make it easier for developers to customize and extend Web applications from a Web browser. It can also integrate existing data and logic into a cloud platform.

Gigaspaces is another enabling platform. The Gigaspaces XAP cloud PaaS is tightly integrated with Amazon EC2's infrastructure. It allows customers to build Web applications for the cloud by migrating existing enterprise applications. It does this by providing a development platform that supports major frameworks, languages, and management environments.

Social network, framework, and portal platforms

We could write a whole book on social networks, frameworks, and portals, but we want to give you an idea of the type of enabling technology that is a natural part of enablement of Platform as a Service. Customers are taking advantage of platforms for blogging like Wordpress; they're using open-source environments like Joomla to create cloud-based applications. Even social networking environments like Facebook and Twitter are becoming a part of enablement of the cloud.

Chapter 12

Using Software as a Service

In This Chapter

▶ Looking at the origins of SaaS: Salesforce.com

▶ Understanding how the SaaS model works

▶ Understanding the economics and the ecosystem

*"W*hen did Software as a Service get its start?" might sound like a straightforward question, but it isn't. In one way, you could say that when time-sharing systems were all the rage more than 30 years ago, all software was delivered to customers as a service.

Mainframe systems were simply too expensive for most companies to buy their own systems. A couple of decades later, minicomputers, servers, and personal computers changed the dynamics of the market. Economically, it was feasible for any Tom, Dick, and Harriet to own their own systems and the software. Not all software moved to an internal model however. (Software such as ADP's payroll system, for example, remained Software as a Service.)

Two key events converged to create the model that we now call *Software as a Service (SaaS):*

✔ First, the Internet became a commercial platform.

✔ Second, software costs and complexities became so difficult that running, upgrading, and managing software become too complex for many companies to manage. This was especially true for small- and medium-sized companies that didn't want the expenses of managingall the components. These companies were the first to embrace this new generation of SaaS.

Today, SaaS is the most mature area of cloud computing. SaaS gained initial traction with the *customer relationship management (CRM)* market and has expanded into others — particularly the collaboration market and the enabling tools and management environments. In this chapter, we explain what SaaS is, talk about its business model, and discuss the types of vendors that are in the market today.

SalesForce.com's Approach to Evolving Software as a Service

What's inside the development environment? And why are we talking about this now? SalesForce.com's approach to its platform is similar to many of the platforms on the market. Therefore, understanding what a platform is built on will help you make decisions.

You may not see how the product is made, but you're still responsible for the integrity and security of your data and how well the application works.

Salesforce.com software environment

Here is a list of the components of the Salesforce.com software environment:

- **Multi-tenancy foundation:** Within a *multi-tenant architecture,* each user's private code is stored in a separate container and is isolated from other containers.

- **Metadata:** *Metadata* is an architectural approach that allows each user's customized logic and data to be managed separately.

- **Infrastructure:** This data center environment underlies the Salesforce. com application environment. It includes capabilities such as middleware, security, and database management. It also includes performance management and monitoring.

- **Database:** There is a set of database services that sits on top of an Oracle database. It includes ways to manage data objects and fields, as well as documents that are used by the Salesforce.com application.

- **Integration:** This set of standardized Web services APIs enables applications to have a common approach to access information from one application to another (as well as data from other enterprise applications). If there's a standardized way to link one SaaS application to another service, customers or implementers don't have to resort to custom coding.

- **Logic:** This component includes services that create business processes (such as workflow, approval processes, and so on) that the application uses.

- **User Interface:** This includes a framework and tools to build the way the application appears to the customer.

Digging into the origins of SaaS

You could probably find many examples over the years of companies that offered their software products as a service. But to keep things simple, we start with the company that really put Software as a Service as we know it today on the map — Salesforce.com. We think that the story of how SalesForce.com started and how it has evolved says a lot about this market.

Marc Benioff, the founder of SalesForce.com, had been a marketing executive for Oracle for many years. After leaving and going off on his own, he started Salesforce.com. Being a marketing executive, Marc had a bold marketing moniker for his fledgling company: No software. The plan was quite simple: Create a way to allow customers to use a popular application — *customer relationship management (CRM)* over the Internet. Customers would purchase a seat and could use the application over the Web. The customer never had to update the software, didn't have to store data on a server, and never had to worry about maintenance fees. If that customer was traveling to a remote location, he could access his sales leads from any PC. There were no capital expenses, with the exception of a PC and an Internet connection.

Initial Salesforce.com customers were small businesses that had no problem with a company managing its customer data. These customers were willing to take a risk in exchange for not having to buy hardware or hire staff. And because there was only a one-month commitment, they knew they could simply take their customer data and go home if it didn't work out for them.

Larger companies, on the other hand, were wary. What was this company? Was it financially viable; was the software any good? Would it be in business very long? If they liked the application, could they have the code and put it on their own server? SalesForce.com was able to convince at least some early customers that the company was well financed and safe to do business with. However, it refused to make its code available to companies to run on premise. Salesforce.com was able to break out of the small companies by selling directly to departments of large companies. These sales and marketing departments were able to put the fees to run Salesforce.com on their expense reports. Slowly but surely, Salesforce.com made inroads into large companies that appreciated the ability to avoid buying equipment.

What was behind Salesforce.com that customers did not see? Software, and plenty of it. The typical customer doesn't have to and doesn't want to understand the inner workings of Salesforce.com to use it. However, as you see later in this chapter, the underlying software that developed the offering has become the foundation of the company's partner ecosystem.

Like everything in cloud, there are overlaps between SaaS and the other areas of cloud computing. For example, Salesforce.com has a large partnering program for Platform as a Service called Force.com. (See Chapter 11 for more details on Platform as a Service). The foundation of Force.com as a development environment for partners is based on its own software development platform.

SalesForce.com ecosystem

Why are we telling you about what is inside the Salesforce.com software environment? We think it's important to understand that SaaS is a special instance of an enterprise application designed to support many different customers safely and securely with enough scalability to support changing situations.

In addition, this foundation then becomes the anchor for a rich partner ecosystem. Salesforce.com's partner ecosystem is called Force.com. It is a Platform as a Service (see Chapter 11) that allows complementary software companies to use this infrastructure and a set of tools developed by Salesforce.com to build on top of this CRM platform.

This isn't a new phenomenon. Companies have built partner ecosystems for decades. These leading vendors have encouraged independent software vendors to build their applications on top of their enabling software. Companies including IBM, HP, Microsoft, and VMware — to name a few — have used this approach to build success in the market. The difference with SaaS is that the ecosystems of partners are an essential part of the business model.

Today, Salesforce.com has revenues of more than $1 billion with a broad ecosystem of partners. Its brand is well regarded and large companies no longer ask the company to let them run the software in-house. A strong brand is essential to the success of SaaS and any cloud computing environment. But Salesforce.com isn't alone in the market. Companies such as Netsuite, Oracle, IBM, HP, Microsoft, Intuit, and hundreds of others have all entered the market.

But before we give you an idea of what types of products are out there, you should understand the economics of Software as a Service. While you will be reviewing the technical capabilities of solutions, you need to have a clear understanding of the economic implications.

Characterizing Software as a Service

What characteristics have to be in place for an SaaS to be commercially viable? Here's what we think is necessary:

>   ✓ **The SaaS application needs to be generalized enough so that lots of customers will be interested in the service.** Here are some examples of these types of applications: accounting, collaboration, project management,

testing, analytics, content management, Internet marketing, risk management and of course, CRM. What doesn't work as SaaS? A specialized one-of-a-kind application with a small number of potential customers.

✔ **SaaS applications need sophisticated navigation and ease of use.** If an SaaS application isn't easy to use, customers will simply stop subscribing. Most SaaS vendors offer prospective customers a free trial for a month or so. If the customer doesn't start using the application during that first month, it's likely that the customer won't sign a contract. This is really important because it has been reported that less than 20 percent of users remain customers after the first month or so.

✔ **The SaaS application needs be modular and service oriented.** Without this modular approach, it will be hard to change and difficult to have third-party independent companies join the ecosystem.

✔ **An SaaS application needs to include measuring and monitoring so customers can be charged actual usage.**

✔ **An SaaS application must have a built-in billing service.**

✔ **SaaS applications need published interfaces and an ecosystem of partners who can expand the company's customer base and market reach.**

✔ **SaaS applications have to ensure that each customer's data and specialized configurations are separate and secure from other customers' data and configurations.**

✔ **SaaS applications need to provide sophisticated business process configurators for customers.** Each customer can change the process within the standardized SaaS application. For example, a company might want to add a process so a manager has to approve the price being offered to a new customer. A built-in configuration tool enables this to be done on an ad hoc basis without programming.

✔ **SaaS applications need to constantly provide fast releases of new features and new capabilities.** This must be done without impacting the customer's ability to continue business as usual.

✔ **SaaS applications have to protect the integrity of customer data.** That includes providing techniques for allowing data to migrate either to a private database inside the firewall or to a third-party storage capability.

What about the traditional on-premise software model?

The traditional way companies used software was to buy a *perpetual license,* because it doesn't end, and implement that software on their own systems internally. You pay once for the software and continue to pay a maintenance fee. This is quite different than the newer model of Software as a Service. A company offers to sell you a CRM capability. You decide on how many users will need the software and you pay on a per-month, per-user fee. The company takes care of all the maintenance of the software, the data center, the backup, and the support of the system.

Clearly, this varies from the perpetual license model of software acquisition. A perpetual license model means that the customer pays once for a license to the software. In the old days, you purchased a server, an operating system, a database license, and a license to the CRM system. You also probably needed some systems management and security software and needed to buy a backup drive and assorted other components. Every year, you paid a fee of between 10–25 percent of the purchase price of the software to get updates and software patches. Many companies still buy many products this way and we don't expect that to change any time soon. Some products are too specialized to be sold as SaaS anytime soon.

Understanding the Economics and the Ecosystem

The economics of the SaaS market are different than the traditional perpetual license software model. In the perpetual license model, the customer pays for the total cost of licensing the software and agrees to pay a per-year additional cost to cover maintenance and support. Maintenance can be as low as 10 percent or as high as 25 percent of the purchase price. One of the key differences with the SaaS model is that the economics are entirely different. The most important difference is that there is actually a lower barrier to entry when a company is trying to sell you a SaaS product.

Pretending you're a customer

Say you're a customer who's looking for a CRM product. If you decide that SaaS might be the way to go, you can shop around at various vendor Web sites, find a product that looks promising, and try it out for free for 30 days.

If at the end of that trial you decide that this product is really good, the company may decide that it is time to buy. Even though you might eventually want to have the product used by 50 people in the company, you might actually buy an entry-level configuration like a 5-user pack to get started. If the individuals in the company really like the product, you can add packages until you support all 50 users.

Determining the right revenue model costs

What does this mean in terms of the revenue model for vendors and how customers should think about weighing the costs between traditional perpetual licenses and SaaS-based license? Look at these numbers over a five-year period. It can be complex to work out all the details, but here is a general rule:

- ✔ Take the initial cost for the traditional software purchase.

- ✔ Add an annual fee of 20 percent for maintenance and support.

- ✔ Consider IT costs (including support services and hardware renewal, and so on. (For example, does your data center have enough room for the new CRM application? Will you need to add support staff or new management software?)

The other factor to consider is that the vendor might do everything it can to make you a customer. They might have some special incentives. For example, many SaaS vendors offer packaged deals. (An instance is if you decide to pay for a full year upfront, the price will be less; if you purchase large numbers of licenses, the costs will also be less.)

Calculating two examples

If you buy a traditional software product, it will cost you a one-time fee of $100,000. Now you have to add an annual fee of 20 percent for maintenance and support. If you look at the costs over five years, for example, you may determine the following: Software will cost $100,000; maintenance expenses will add another $100,000 over five years, for a total five-year cost of $200,000.

You have to consider all the related infrastructure costs. (Take a look at Chapter 21 for a full discussion on the economics of the cloud.) We can't begin to give you a sense of what that will cost you because every situation is different. For example, you might already have a sophisticated data center with excess capacity and sufficient staff to support an additional application. Or you might have to add everything from new hardware to networking to backup and support personnel. Do you charge each department based on their percentage usage of data center resources? Do you divide costs evenly between all departments as you would utilities such as electricity? No matter how your organization calculates expenses, that must be taken into account.

Many small- and medium-sized businesses lack or don't want the data centers that their larger counterparts have. Larger companies that can calculate the long-term impact of adding applications are also looking seriously at the SaaS cloud model.

If you go the SaaS route, here's what you're looking at: You determine that to support 50 users, it will cost you between $10 and $150 per user, per month. That figure includes support, general training, and data center services. Even if you take the high-end estimate of $150 per user, the cost of using the CRM SaaS application for those 50 users for 5 years will run about $37,500 — far less than the $200,000 cost of on-premise software, even when you add other costs (such as customization of business processes within the application and personnel training).

We can't give you an absolute figure; do your homework and compare all aspects of running software before you decide which approach is best for you. Prices can vary widely from an open-source version that offers support for a price to vendors that provide the software plus full integration services.

For example, you might look at an open-source CRM product. Although the basic product is free, you get no support or software upgrades, and must rely on finding patches and bug fixes from the community. If you're very technical, that might be a fine choice, but many customers want to pay for support to avoid a lot of headaches.

The value of the ecosystem

When SaaS vendors become well-established brands in the market, they attract an *ecosystem* (a set of partners that works directly with a key vendor, both in technical and go-to-market terms) that sees the value of linkage.

This is how it works: A SaaS vendor with thousands of paying customers opens up its programming interfaces to other independent software vendors. These vendors create software that sits on top of the infrastructure of the SaaS vendor. Therefore, they can get to market quickly because they only have to write their industry-specific code. They don't worry about messaging middleware, or business process services, or other complex programming. In addition, they can market their software to the SaaS vendor's happy customers (either through the SaaS vendor's portal or through the partner's direct sales force). This has become a standard model used by SaaS vendors to build their brand and power in the market.

If you're a customer who has licensed an SaaS application, you'll probably find another application that's built on the same infrastructure that easily integrates with what you already have.

Building an app on top of Salesforce.com

CODA is a software company that has been in the financial services packaged software market since the 1970s. The company had always partnered with on-premise software vendors such as HP, Digital Equipment Corporation, and IBM. In addition, the company liked to move to new platforms as they emerged (including the mainframe, the minicomputer, and client/server).

There came a time when CODA wanted to move quickly to take advantage of the movement to Software as a Service. Moving to a new platform was based on the ambitious plan to do for financial products what Salesforce.com has done for CRM. Needless to say, it was an ambitious goal. CODA management began to appreciate the potential for SaaS as a way to build customers faster than the sales process of on-premise software. Before deciding to use sForce (Salesforce.com's development platform), the company performed a return-on-investment analysis.

The challenge was the cost of writing the code from scratch internally. Basically, development management realized that they would have to write for a multi-tenancy environment that would have required several years of work to get the right infrastructure services in place. They simply couldn't justify the expense or the time required for development. Without worrying about any specific software infrastructure, CODA's developers focused on customer-facing features such as specialized processes for different industries.

Unlike some of the smaller companies that have built on top of sForce, CODA is a large company that serves mid-market companies. Salesforce.com needs CODA as much as CODA needs them. Salesforce.com needed to prove to the market that its platform could support a major application. CODA's application is happy with its relationship and is saving time and money. The test will be if customers adopt its new SaaS platform.

CODA wrote its application with Salesforce.com's Java-like language called APEX. Therefore, the company's locked into the Salesforce.com platform. From a go-to-market perspective, however, this is a plus because Salesforce.com will help CODA sell into its customer base.

Examining Types of SaaS Platforms

Because SaaS has been around longer than most other types of cloud computing, hundreds — if not thousands — of companies are trying to become leaders. It isn't easy. They face many obstacles. For example, it costs a lot of money initially to build the type of data center and the applications that can scale to support thousands of companies (and potentially millions of individual users). It takes time to turn a one-month free trial into a long-term contract. Despite these obstacles, some very successful SaaS companies exist, ranging from emerging players to the big IT companies.

We don't have the room to give you an exhaustive list of every company you might find, but we plan to give you a taste of what is out there. (In Chapter 23, we list resources that will help you identify even more players.)

It can be overwhelming when you look at how many companies have created SaaS versions of their products — even companies whoseprimary focus is the on-premise model feel compelled to offer customers a SaaS version of their offerings.

To help you make sense of this complicated world, we divide SaaS into three categories:

- ✔ **Packaged software:** This is the biggest area of the SaaS market. Packaged software comes in many different flavors: customer relationship management, supply chain management, financial management, and human resources, to name the most common. These integrated offers focus on a specific process, such as managing employees' benefits, salaries, and annual performance reviews. These products tend to have several characteristics in common: They're designed with specific business processes built in that customers can modify. They have moved in great numbers to the cloud because customers were finding the platforms too hard to manage.

- ✔ **Collaborative software:** This increasingly vibrant area of the market is driven by the ubiquitous availability of the Internet, combined with the fact that teams are located all over the world. This area is dominated by software that focuses on all sorts of collaborative efforts including Web conferencing, document collaboration, project planning, instant messaging, and even email. In a sense, it was inevitable that these platforms would move to the cloud: These tasks occur throughout the organization and need to be easily accessed from many locations.

- ✔ **Enabling and management tools:** We brought these two areas together because they support the development and the deployment of SaaS. What's in this category? Think about the development tools that developers need when creating and extending a SaaS platform; also think about the testing, monitoring, and measuring that a customer and the developer need. Also consider the compliance issues related to the use of this type of software in the real world. These issues are included in this third category.

In the next section, we give you a taste for the vendors in each of these categories, what they offer customers, and the issues you should consider. We can't possibly do this topic justice, but we give you a road map for how to understand the offerings and issues.

Packaged Software as a Service

We write a lot about how Salesforce.com created *customer relationship management (CRM)* as a service. It took a few years, but the company invested in its infrastructure, built a flexible and modular application, and made the navigation easier. But as with any successful venture, Salesforce.com competitors soon began entering the market in droves.

What companies are out in the market today that you should look at? It isn't as straightforward as it might sound. This is a dynamic market, so whatever company looks promising today could be gone tomorrow. On the other hand, the small emerging company that looks too new to consider could become a major force. Likewise, companies that have been successful as on-premise software providers are streaming into the SaaS market and could become viable competitors.

Companies in the packaged software market include the following:

- ✔ **Netsuite**, like Salesforce.com, offers a CRM foundation. Since its founding in 1998, Netsuite has added a number of modules for *enterprise resource planning (ERP)* application including financial capabilities, e-commerce, and business intelligence.

- ✔ **Intuit** provides a Financial Services Suite of products that support accounting services for small- and medium-sized businesses. The company provides a rich set of interfaces that enables partners to connect their services and applications into its environment.

- ✔ **RightNow** provides a CRM suite of products that includes marketing, sales, and various industry solutions.

- ✔ **Concur** focuses on employees spend management. It automates costs control via automated processes.

- ✔ **Taleo** focuses on talent management tasks.

- ✔ **SugarCRM** is a CRM platform built on an open-source platform. The company offers support for a fee.

- ✔ **Constant Contact** is a marketing automation platform that partners directly with Salesforce.com and other CRM platforms. They automate the process of sending emails and other marketing efforts.

Some of the traditional on-premise software companies have also moved into the packaged SaaS market, including

- ✔ Microsoft with its Dynamics package

- ✔ SAP with its By Design offering for the small- to medium-sized business market

- ✔ Oracle with its On Demand offering based on its acquisition of Siebel Software

Collaboration as a Service

Collaboration is one of the natural markets for SaaS. There's enough bandwidth and all companies are connecting to the Internet. In addition, more companies than ever have remote offices and workers across the globe. A team may be easily be spread across 100 locations in 40 different countries!

With the availability of SaaS-based collaboration services, things have changed dramatically. Although it hasn't yet surfaced as a major market, we expect that there will be companies that offer *unified communications* (an integration of telephony, instant messaging, and email) as a service. These offerings will come from the large telecommunications companies in partnerships with companies like HP and IBM. GoogleVoice could emerge as an important player in the future.

What companies are focused on collaboration as a service today? The following is a list to get you started:

- ✔ **MicrosoftLive** has made its first foray into collaboration as a service with its Meeting Live offering. Today Microsoft offers Meeting Live and live messaging services. In addition, Microsoft offers the ability to run its email server (Exchange as a Service). In the future, the company will have online versions of many of its collaborative applications.

- ✔ **LotusLive** is IBM's collaborative environment that includes a set of tools including social networking, instant messaging, and the ability to share files and conduct online meetings. IBM is publishing interfaces to allow other collaborative tools to be integrated into the platform.

- ✔ **GoogleApps** from Google, which has as many as 1.5 million businesses that use its various collaborative applications including e-mail, document management, and instant messaging. It publishes APIs so third-party software developers can integrate with the platform.

- ✔ **Cisco Webex Collaboration** platform comes from Cisco (which bought Webex in 2007) and it has become the centerpiece of its collaboration SaaS platform. It will probably use this platform to add unified communications as a service.

- ✔ **Zoho**, an open-source collaboration platform, includes email, document management, project management, and invoice management. It offers APIs to its environment and has begun to integrate its collaboration tools with other companies, such as Microsoft. Zoho offers support for a fee.

- ✔ **Citrix GotoMeeting** offers an online meeting service as part of its larger suite of virtualization products. See Chapter 17 for more about virtualization.

Enabling and management tools

How you use all sorts of software in your organization is changing dramatically — whether you're considering a supply chain as a service or a word processor as a service. As we discuss in Chapters 10 and 11, many companies are looking to service providers for needed functionality.

Underneath many of these environments is the open-source Eclipse framework. A set of enabling and management tools is being offered on a service basis. Although some of these services might actually be delivered within a private cloud in your own data center, many vendors will enable you to use their data center services. In this section, we talk about the enabling technologies that are being offered as services.

Over time, a lot more software and capabilities will be offered as a service, but we talk about five different areas in this section, including

- ✔ Testing as a service
- ✔ Monitoring and management as a service
- ✔ Development as a service
- ✔ Security as a service
- ✔ Compliance and governance as a service

Testing as a service

Testing is one of the biggest uses for cloud computing. Even when a company moves to using a public or private cloud, it still needs to conduct the same testing it would need in an on-premise data center , including

- ✔ Functional testing
- ✔ Unit testing
- ✔ Stress testing
- ✔ Compatibility testing
- ✔ Performance testing
- ✔ Requirements management
- ✔ Integration testing

One of the biggest problems for developers is accurately simulating the conditions (expected and unexpected) when software is deployed.

In addition, more companies are looking at testing as a service and development as a service as a way to keep track of development teams that are often distributed across the globe.

Having developers rely on SaaS-based services for testing can save tremendous amounts of time and money. When developers embark on testing, they often ask for hardware and software to get the task done. Typically, these organizations can't recoup the systems they hand over to developers. Many vendors produce testing as a service platforms, including HP, IBM, Sogeti (a United Kingdom–based IT services firm), Compuware, as well as smaller companies such as iTKO and SOASTA. We could actually name hundreds that are pouring into the testing-as-a-service space.

Monitoring and management as a service

Is what you see what you get? Maybe. That's why companies using SaaS need to do some of their own monitoring to determine if their service levels have been met by their SaaS providers. Even more complicated is when companies are using more than one SaaS application. And to complicate things even further, you must monitor not just a single application but also the *combination* of applications.

Companies in the systems management space are positioning themselves for this world. Vendors come at this market from two different perspectives:

- ✔ From the top down, large telecommunications are packaging their capabilities so they can help provide cloud management and monitoring.

- ✔ You also see traditional Web services monitoring companies offering services that will tell you if your Web site has added new services to support the cloud.

Development tooling as a service

Developers beginning to create new software are increasingly turning to development as a service. (In other words, development is done in a cloud-based environment instead of implementing development within a single internal-development environment.) This delivery model of development infrastructure can be done through one of the Platform as a Service vendors such as Google, Intuit, Microsoft, Force.com, and Bungee Labs. (See Chapter 11 for more on Platform as a Service.) Likewise, Infrastructure as a Service vendors such as Amazon.com offer support services for developers. (See Chapter 10 on Infrastructure as a Service.)

Security as a service

Almost without exception, vendors providing antivirus software are offering their products as a service. These vendors include Symantec, McAfee, CA, and Kapersky Labs. In addition, companies such as Hewlett-Packard and IBM have tools that scan environments for vulnerability scanning and testing.

Identity management is an important aspect of on premise as well as cloud services. Lots of companies in this market will begin offering identity management as a service.

Compliance and governance as a service

Compliance and governance tasks are time consuming and complicated tasks that large companies are required to do. Therefore, offering these capabilities as a service is critical.

Not surprisingly, hundreds of companies are moving into this market. Services that are becoming SaaS include the following:

- ✔ Patch management
- ✔ Business continuity planning
- ✔ Discovery of records and messages
- ✔ Various governance requirements such as SOX (Sarbanes-Oxley) in the United States and SaS 70 (Statement of Audit Standard) controls for data

For more on governance, see Chapter 16.

Chapter 13

Understanding Massively Scaled Applications and Business Processes

In This Chapter

▶ Defining massively scaled applications and business process

▶ Exploring current massively scaled applications

▶ Delivering business processes in a massive way

*Y*ou can gain cost efficiencies by provisioning capacity on demand from a cloud provider. Or you can increase the overall efficiency of your data center with a private cloud; see Chapter 9. Bearing all that in mind, cloud providers have a unique sweet spot based on their use of massively scaled applications. In this chapter, we describe how companies use massively scaled cloud applications to offer highly cost-effective business processes and services.

What do we mean by *massively scaled?* Millions of users doing exactly the same thing. When you do that, you drastically reduce the cost per user.

Most businesses require their data centers to facilitate the operation of many different types of workloads — such as compute-intensive analytics, collaboration capabilities for employees, virtualized desktop management, or business services like billing. Your typical IT infrastructure needs to be flexible enough to support lots of change and you need to build in redundancy to make sure that each workload has the capacity it needs when necessary.

But just imagine building a large data center with only one or two transactions in mind. You can make decisions about software architecture, hardware, and communications that enable a very efficient data center when you're designing for massive repetitions of a single type of workload.

Naming Names: Companies with Massively Scaled Applications

We use Amazon as an example because it's both an online retailer and a cloud services provider. (We provide more details about Amazon's IaaS offerings in Chapter 10.) Most of the companies offering massively scaled applications are either online retailers or cloud providers, but not both. Many of the companies in this space deliver a low-cost (or free) business process as a service.

In general these businesses have very high user populations allowing them to drive per-user costs of software down to record low levels. When a business process such as email management is delivered from a massively scaled data center, your own data center can't come close to matching the cloud center's price.

Massive data centers evolved with Internet growth. Internet-based businesses like Amazon probably didn't realize they'd be assembling such large data centers. Their business grew and they expanded into their massive data center as the Internet evolved. Companies like this may have predicted the future, but they can't have known for sure that their Web traffic was going to be so high.

Listing the companies

It's worth describing some of the businesses that deliver massively scaled cloud applications and business processes. You may not have thought of some of these companies as providing a business process as a service.

Most of the businesses listed here covered uncharted business territory when they developed their service. For this reason, the services they offer may not traditionally be thought of as businesses services — but that is really what they are.

Here's a list of companies in this field and the business processes they deliver:

- **eBay** at www.ebay.com provides an electronic auction service.
- **PayPal** at www.paypal.com is owned by eBay. PayPal operates independently. It provides an Internet payment capability as a service.
- **Skype** at www.skype.com also is partially owned by eBay and a private equity firm. It provides *Voice over IP (VoIP)* telephone calls as a service, most of which are free.

✔ **Google** at www.google.com provides an Internet search capability as a service. (This service is free when you have access to the Internet.) Additionally, Google provides an Internet email service, Gmail. There are quite a few other Google services including maps, news aggregation, Google apps, and so on.

✔ **YouTube** at www.youtube.com was acquired by Google. YouTube provides video self-publishing as a service.

✔ **Yahoo!** at www.yahoo.com is like Google, providing an Internet search service and email service. Yahoo's email service is the most widely used in the world.

✔ **Flickr** at www.flickr.com provides photo publishing as a service.

✔ **Wikipedia** at www.wikipedia.org is an encyclopedia as a service.

✔ **Craigslist** at www.craigslist.org offers small ads as a service.

✔ **WordPress** at www.wordpress.org does blog hosting as a service.

✔ **Twitter** at www.twitter.com offers microblogging, or short messages, as a service. It can be used in several useful ways by companies and individuals.

✔ **Internet Movie Database** at www.imdb.com was acquired by Amazon. IMDB provides information about movies as a service.

✔ **Digg** at www.digg.com offers news aggregation as a service.

✔ **Facebook** at www.facebook.com is personal information, social networking, and email combined as a service.

✔ **LinkedIn** at www.linkedin.com is business contacts and networking as a service.

Defining business process as a service

Business processes are the steps you take or the activities you perform to facilitate the delivery of products or services to your customers or stakeholders. These business processes (such as managing email, shipping packages, or writing a marketing document) are delivered as a service when they're delivered to you in an automated, standardized, and repeatable way from a cloud service provider.

This is by no means an exhaustive list and the services aren't only useful to consumers. For example, many businesses use eBay to sell things that they want to dispose of and some businesses are entirely eBay based. Many Web businesses depend upon PayPal as their principal payment mechanism. Businesses advertise on Craigslist. A fair number use Twitter as a public relations outlet. Another point to note is that all these businesses have tens of millions of customers. Nearly all of them require very large data centers to cater to their millions of customers.

As we mention, because massively scaled data centers are designed to support a specific type of workload across millions of users, the cost efficiencies are so great that it is very hard to compete with them.

Looking at Web-based business services

You might be inclined to think that Web-based businesses are somehow different from the companies to which you outsource your energy generation or the companies that provide your communications, but they're very similar.

It's easy to be misled by the fact that many of these Web-based companies started out without a well-defined revenue stream and some of them have yet to demonstrate a viable business model for their activities.

This is currently the case, for example, with Twitter, Facebook, and YouTube, all of whom exist just because their investors (or Google in the case of YouTube) believe that they will eventually find a profitable way of operating.

Most of the businesses we mention are dominant in their field because these vendors have established very forbidding barriers to entry because of their scalable infrastructure and their ability to deliver services at a very low cost. There were quite a few Internet auction houses before eBay began to dominate the field, and there have been several attempts by would-be competitors to penetrate eBay's market, but none have made much of an impact.

With search, the situation is different. It is dominated by Google, but Yahoo! and Microsoft have significant market share, so the market is genuinely divided even though one company dominates. However, it's tough, even if you have the billions of dollars in funding available to Microsoft, to change the profile of the market.

Just like power generation and telecomms, such businesses have very high customer retention and the financial barriers to entry are very great. These Internet companies may have started out small, but they are now giants in their field. Just as no company is likely to think of building its own hydroelectric power station or telecommunications network, no company is going to build its own Internet search capability.

Delivering Business Processes from the Cloud

We're moving from one world (where companies built their own software or used packaged software for all their business processes) to another (where some of these business processes can be provided directly from the cloud).

Business process examples

Economic considerations indicate that the business processes that will be sold as a service will be those that can have a very large number of users and that can be defined relatively simply.

Consider three distinct examples:

- ✔ **A molecular modeling program:** Organic chemists carry out molecular modeling by using PC software. This capability could be delivered from the cloud. However, there just aren't enough organic chemists for a cloud business to be feasible right now. The economics wouldn't work.

- ✔ **An accounting capability:** Companies such as Intuit, NetSuite, Aplicor, and BizAutomation offer capable accounting software as a cloud service. They're excellent examples of SaaS, but they don't amount to outsourcing a business process because the business process of accounting, a required function at most businesses, varies according to the type of business and how the financial accounts are managed. While elements of the accounting process are common to lots of businesses — sending invoices or managing customer addresses — many elements are unique to each business. In other words, the accounting process requires someone to do the accounting.

  For this reason, while many vendors deliver accounting services in the cloud, the services aren't likely to grow to massively scaled applications in the same way as email applications have.

- ✔ **Email:** The business process of managing email can be standardized across millions of users. Few businesses need to run email systems from the data center. Running it from the cloud is far less expensive: Recent cost figures suggest between $\frac{1}{10}$ and $\frac{1}{20}$ of the price. What's more, both Google and Yahoo already provide email to many businesses.

Business processes destined for the cloud

Some applications that embody business processes are inevitably destined for the cloud because of the very high number of users and their ease of use in a cloud context.

These applications form two groups:

- ✔ Existing applications that are migrating to the cloud. The cloud makes the most sense for these established applications (such as email).
- ✔ New applications whose use in the cloud is taking off faster than its use through software installed in the data center, or where there isn't any data center choice available. Voice over IP (VoIP) is an example.

Hidden in the cloud

If you haven't had much contact with Web businesses, you may not know that nearly all their important business processes are run from the cloud, often at very low cost. For example, unless you run a very large Web site, the Web statistics software you use is most likely provided by Google. Your email system likely runs on your Web server, which itself is probably located in some Internet service provider (ISP) somewhere. If you carry ads on your Web site, you're probably using an ad server of some kind, which, again, doesn't run out of your offices. Selling ads to fill the available space on your site is probably outsourced to an advertising broker.

Your Web site itself is probably running on software built by someone else with various software modules provided by yet another company. The photographs displayed on your Web site may well be sourced from another Web site, and even some of the content may be sourced from content syndication operations.

It is easy to think up a list of the business processes and applications that will, as a general rule, be run from the cloud in the future. A few organizations will run such applications themselves, for reasons of security or possibly technology integration, but most will not because of cost.

Business processes already flying high

Here is a list of business processes that are already available from the cloud and are probably destined to reside in the cloud for the vast majority of companies:

✔ **Clerical activity:** Office software such as word processing, spread-sheets, and so on

✔ **Communications:** Unified communications, email, Instant Messaging (IM), voice, conferencing

✔ **Collaboration:** Desktop-to-desktop capabilities, from webinars through to collaborative work and file sharing

✔ **Data backup and disaster recovery**

✔ **Payment technology:** PayPal, credit cards, voucher schemes, and so on

✔ **Research:** Including marketing research, technical research, patent research, and almost all other areas of research

✔ **Web site work:** Design, content, advertising, and SEO.

We could add many other things to this list — for example, the businesses of insurance, banking, package delivery, travel booking, and hotel booking. We might not think of these businesses as cloud services, but by any reasonable definition, they are.

Predicting the future

The best way to understand what's likely to happen with cloud computing is to study what has happened with businesses that work mainly in the cloud. Web-based businesses are exactly like that. Even when Web-based businesses are large, many of their business processes are assembled by linking software together, often in a way that's no more sophisticated than simply linking to it from a Web page. Consider, for example, a small site belonging to a publisher that sells books over the Web, as well as selling them through Amazon.com.

Payment is likely to be by PayPal. A client may publish books through a printer, but most likely the books will be stored by the printer and fulfilled by the printer — with orders sent directly from the Web site by email. This will be the case for individual orders, but also for direct orders from Amazon. Much of the rest of the business involves attracting people to the Web site to market the books via search engine optimization. Proper search engine optimization increases the odds that a Web site will be returned in the results of a Web search, and is fostered by the analysis of Web site stats, the addition of appropriate content, and Web design. (For more on this topic, see *Search Engine Optimization For Dummies,* Wiley.)

Now try to envisage other businesses running in this way. It's not that hard to do, because the vast majority of small to medium businesses only do one or two unique things — and that means most of their business processes are common, mundane, and a good fit for cloud computing.

Mashups and other unintended consequences

One curious aspect of the move toward the cloud is the innovative behavior of some computer users. For example, when Twitter got started, some marketing people quickly realized that it could become a PR and marketing channel. They started to reinforce their marketing activity by posting messages on Twitter.

A similar phenomenon happened with Facebook. When it began to grow, some companies used it to replace their intranet, reducing their IT costs considerably. The use of Facebook in this way proved particularly effective in distributed organizations. Some companies are even using Facebook as part of their personnel systems.

The unpredictable use of such applications is encouraged by the fact that many of the vendors are very happy to publish their APIs (programmer interfaces). Not only is it possible to use (often free) applications in ways that were never intended, but you can link Web sites to create a service that neither site initially intended to deliver.

Aside from the fact that this has spurred some interesting uses of sites such as Google maps, it means that often you can integrate these Web services with software built in-house. There are no formal service contracts or agreed-upon service levels, but many companies seem not to care.

Chapter 14

Setting Some Standards

. . . .

In This Chapter

▶ Understanding the importance of standards

▶ Figuring out why standards are needed in the cloud

▶ Understanding what standards exist today

. . . .

*A*sk knowledgeable companies about their top worries about moving to the cloud. Two major reasons would no doubt be security and vendor lock-in. Read more about security in Chapter 15. This chapter tackles *vendor lock-in:* being stuck with one cloud provider because of interoperability or portability issues. Standards and best practices address these two concerns.

If standards are the directions, *best practices* are the blueprint for creating techniques or methods that result in predictable outcomes in the real world. For example, you might have a best practice designed to ensure security in cloud environments.

Understanding Best Practices and Standards

Best practices and standards provide a starting recipe, appropriate tools, required ingredients, and some tips and tricks.

The idea is fewer errors will occur if organizations follow best practices (because the processes, techniques, and methodologies they're using have been repeatedly tested). The same holds true for standards. Standards mean that you don't need to constantly reinvent the same thing. And, best practices and standards for managing critical aspects such as data security and privacy help ensure quality for crucial workloads in the cloud.

Best practicing makes perfect

Best practices are accumulated knowledge that can help individuals and organizations avoid mistakes others have made.

They provide

- ✔ A starting point for planning
- ✔ A common language
- ✔ A set of concepts that help you communicate and coordinate with large groups of people

Best practices range from recommendations for specific coding specifications to describing enterprise-wide management processes that have shown proven success.

Best practices can be found in many places:

- ✔ Industry organizations
- ✔ Independent books
- ✔ Training materials
- ✔ Vendor Web sites
- ✔ Consulting practices

Setting your sites on standards

Standards are a core set of common and repeatable best practices that have been agreed upon by a business or industry group. Typically, different vendors, industry user groups, and end users collaborate to develop standards based on the broad expertise of a large number of stakeholders. Organizations can leverage these standards as a common foundation and build on top of them.

Standards, or agreed-upon approaches, let you

- ✔ Move your infrastructure or applications from one cloud provider to another.
- ✔ More easily integrate applications between your on-premise data center and private and public cloud environments.

Standards are useless unless you implement them.

Standards are made two ways:

- ✔ **A big standards body develops it.** The International Organization for Standardization (ISO) is an example of a standards organization. This group is made up of representatives from countries all over the world. ISO has developed over 17,500 standards covering many subject areas, and more standards are developed every year. These standards are well documented so people can learn what they need to adopt a standard. ISO standards cover many areas of IT, including standards for IT service management and the governance of IT services.

- ✔ **A best practice becomes a de facto standard.** A *de facto standard* emerges because a product or approach is used enough that it becomes a standard. For example, the networking protocol called TCP/IP was adopted by so many vendors that over time it became the networking standard.

Clouding the Standards and Best Practices Issue

Cloud standards are in the early phases of being developed and implemented. Some are coming along, but, to many watching the development of these standards, it can seem like the Wild West.

Despite some potential hurdles, standards and best practices are important — especially in the cloud — because they help improve choice, reduce cost, and improve quality.

Standards are important for the cloud in a number of areas:

- ✔ Interoperability
- ✔ Portability
- ✔ Integration
- ✔ Security

Interoperability

Interoperability refers to cloud users being able to take their tools, applications, virtual images, and so on and use them in another cloud environment without having to do any rework. Say one application runs in one environment and you need that application to operate with a partner's application in another cloud environment. If the right interoperability standards are in place, you can do this without needing multiple versions of this application.

Simple Object Access Protocol (SOAP), Representational State Transfer (REST), and Atom Syndication Format and Atom PublishingProtocol (both standards referred to as Atom) are all examples of widely used interoperability standards and protocols.

Portability

Portability lets you take one application or instance running on one vendor's implementation and deploy it on another vendor's implementation. For example, you might want to move your database or application from one cloud environment to another.

Standards examples

One example of a standard that has gotten some traction in the cloud environment is the *Open Virtual Format (OVF)* developed by the Distributed Management Task Force (DMTF). It was developed jointly by the likes of Citrix, Dell, HP, IBM, Microsoft, and VMWare. The idea is to streamline the installation of a virtualized platform. This standard addresses interoperability issues for virtual machines. The multivendor format includes a set of *metadata* (virtual machine hard drives, information about resource requirements, a digital signature, and so on) that enables virtual machines to be used in multiple environments.

Another example of a standard that's getting some attention is ISO 27001 for information management. This existing standard was developed by the International Organization for Standardization (ISO) (www.iso.org). This specification for information security management system consists of policies and procedures that include legal, physical, and technical controls over an information infrastructure. The specification includes a six-part planning process that includes defining a security policy, conducting risk assessments, establishing control objectives, and preparing a statement of applicability.

Open Cloud Manifesto

The notion of an open cloud is so critical to the long-term success of the cloud that more than 200 vendors have already signed on to support a document called the Open Cloud Manifesto (www.opencloudmanifesto.org). The group realizes that although the cloud presents a great opportunity, a series of challenges must be overcome. These challenges include security, interoperability, portability, management and metering, and governance. The manifesto has a series of statements related to standards.

Integration

When you think *integration,* you generally think of combining various hardware and software components together to create something. The same idea applies in the cloud. One example of integration: easily integrating your data with a Software as a Service application. This is an example of taking some of your internal IT capability and integrating it into the cloud environment.

Portability and integration become major issues when cloud vendors have different platforms. This can lead to vendor lock-in, which means that moving to another cloud provider is so difficult that you don't even bother trying.

Security

Cloud security is such a big concern that we devote Chapter 15 to it. You need to make sure that the right controls, procedures, and technology are in place to protect your corporate assets. Your organization has invested a lot internally to protect your assets, and it's reasonable to assume that your cloud provider should do the same.

Cloud security standards are a set of processes, policies, and best practices that ensure that the proper controls are placed over an environment to prevent application, information, identity, and access issues (to name a few).

Two organizations that are very active in this area are the Cloud Security Alliance and a think tank called the Jericho Forum. These are profiled later in this chapter.

Standards Organizations and Groups

A number of organizations and informal groups are addressing standards issues in the cloud environment — we detail several in this section. Some of these organizations have been around for years; others are relatively new.

It is important to note that some of these standards bodies aren't necessarily looking to create new standards. One idea is to leverage existing best practices and standards such as those used in implementing the Web and service oriented architectures.

Several standards organizations have gotten together to create a cloud standards coordination *wiki* — a Web site that uses collaborative software (also called wiki) to allow many people to work together to post and edit content. All groups can post their work in one spot: `www.cloud-standards.org`.

Cloud Security Alliance

The Cloud Security Alliance (`www.cloudsecurityalliance.org`) formed in late 2008 when cloud security became important in user's minds. Its founding members include PGP, QualSys, Zscaler, and the Information Systems Audit and Control Association (ISACA).

The CSA's goal is to promote a series of best practices to provide security assurance in cloud computing. Its objectives include

- ✓ Promoting understanding between users and providers of cloud computing regarding security requirements
- ✓ Researching best practices for cloud security
- ✓ Launching awareness campaigns about cloud security solutions
- ✓ Creating consensus lists of issues and guidance for cloud security assurance

The Cloud Security Alliance recently published "Guidance for Critical Areas of Focus in Cloud Computing," which is available at `www.cloudsecurity alliance.org/guidance`.

Recently, the CSA announced that it will work together with Jericho Forum (`www.opengroup.org/jericho`), an independent security expert group, to promote best practices for secure collaboration in the cloud. The groups will provide guidance on how to operate securely in the cloud. Both groups recently published initial guidelines for cloud computing. The Jericho Forum published a Cloud Cube Model designed to be a tool to help businesses evaluate the risk and opportunity associated with moving in to the cloud. The paper is available at the Jericho Forum Web site at www.opengroup.org/jericho/cloud_cube_model_v1.0.pdf.

Distributed Management Task Force (DMTF)

The DMTF (www.dmtf.org) has been around for about 15 years, and may best be known for its common information model, which is a common view of IT equipment. In the cloud space, it focuses on IaaS (Infrastructure as a Service), and providing standards that enable IaaS to be a flexible, scalable, high-performance infrastructure. Part of this is to try to separate the infrastructure from the applications. Members include pretty much every major hardware, systems software, and networking vendor, as well as smaller companies and at least 50 universities.

The DMTF is the group that developed the OVF standard that is formally known as DSP0243 Open Virtualization Format (OVF) V1.0.0. It describes an open, secure, and portable format for packaging and distribution of software that will be run in virtual machines.

The DMTF has also launched the Open Cloud Standards Incubator, which will focus on standardizing interactions between cloud environments by developing cloud resource management protocols, packaging formats, and security mechanisms to facilitate interoperability. Of specific interest are specifications that can facilitate interoperability between public and private clouds.

National Institute of Standards and Technology (NIST)

NIST (www.nist.gov), which has been around since 1901, is a nonregulatory federal agency that is part of the U.S. Department of Commerce. Its goal is to promote innovation and U.S. competitiveness by advancing standards, measurement science, and technology. NIST has a hand in standards everywhere, from the fire-related standards that your mattress had to pass to the auto emissions your car must (not) pass on the road.

Recently, NIST has formed a cloud computing team to help federal agencies understand cloud computing and to determine the best way to secure those agencies implementing the technology. The team is creating a special publication that includes information for the government agencies around various cloud models, security issues including application security, cloud monitoring, and service level agreements, among others.

Open Cloud Consortium (OCC)

The OCC (www.opencloudconsortium.org) was formed in 2008. One of its goals is to support the development of standards for cloud computing and frameworks for interoperating between clouds. Members include Cisco and Yahoo as well as a number of universities including Northwestern.

The OCC has a number of working groups. Two in particular deal with cloud standards:

- ✔ **Working Group on Standards and Interoperability for Clouds That Provide On-Demand Computing Capacity:** The focus for this group is on developing standards for interoperating clouds that provide on-demand computing capacity. The group is developing standards for interoperability between storage clouds and compute clouds.

- ✔ **Working Group on Information Sharing, Security, and Clouds:** This group focuses on standards and standards-based architecture for sharing information between clouds. The emphasis is on clouds belonging to different organizations and subject to different policies. The group is also examining security in the cloud.

Open Grid Forum (OGF)

The OGF (www.ogf.org) is an open community that focuses on driving the adoption and evolution of distributed computing. This includes everything from distributed high-performance computing resources to horizontally scaled transactional systems supporting SOA as well as the cloud. The community shares best practices and drives these best practices into standards. It consists of more than 400 companies in 50 countries, including AT&T and eBay.

The Open Cloud Computing Interface Group (OCCI), formed in 2009, is a working group within the OGF that focuses on the creation of an API for interfacing infrastructure cloud facilities. The group is looking to deliver an API specification for remote management of cloud infrastructure that enables common tasks such as provisioning and managing virtual environments. It will also define these infrastructure cloud services.

The Object Management Group (OMG)

The OMG (www.omg.org) is an international group focused on developing enterprise integration standards for a wide range of industries including government, life sciences, and healthcare. The group provides modeling standards for software and other processes. These include embedded and specialized systems and architecture driven modernization and middleware. Its task forces have developed modeling standards including the *Unified Modeling Language (UML)* and *Model Driven Architecture (MDA)*.

OMG has recently begun efforts focusing on modeling deployment of applications and services on clouds to enable interoperability, portability, and reuse.

Storage Networking Industry Association (SNIA)

The SNIA (www.snia.org) has focused for more than ten years on developing storage solution specifications and technologies, global standards, and storage education. This organization's mission, according to the SNIA members, is "to promote acceptance, deployment, and confidence in storage-related architectures, systems, services, and technologies, across IT and business communities".

Very recently, the SNIA created the Cloud Storage Technical Work group to develop SNIA Architecture and best practices related to system implementation of cloud storage technology. It will act as a technical entity to help SNIA to identify and develop cloud standards for cloud storage. It also will produce a set of standards interface specifications and document system-level requirements under the guidance of the SNIA Technical Council and in cooperation with the SNIA Strategic Alliances Committee.

Cloud Computing Interoperability Forum (CCIF)

The Cloud Computing Interoperability Forum (CCIF at www.ccif.org) provides discussion forums to create a cloud computing ecosystem where organizations can work together for wider adoption of cloud computing technology and services. A major focus is on creating a framework that enables two or more cloud platforms to exchange information in a unified way.

Some experts state that the CCIF is not a standards body, per se. Rather, it's more of a discussion forum, focused on building community consensus, exploring emerging trends, and advocating best practices/reference architectures for the purposes of standardized cloud computing.

Vertical groups

In addition to these standards groups and discussion groups, *vertical industry groups* — groups comprised of members from a particular industry such as technology and retail — are also beginning to look at cloud standards.

Examples include

- ✔ **Telemanagement Forum (TM Forum):** This large group has more than 700 members in 75 countries including service providers, cable and network operators, software suppliers, equipment suppliers, and systems integrators. Its goal is to improve business effectiveness for service providers and their suppliers. The TM Forum serves the information, communications, and entertainment industries. It produces educational information such as industry research, road maps, best practices, training, and standards. Recently, it began working in the telecommunications initiative for cloud computing.

- ✔ **Association for Retail Technology Standards (ARTS):** This group is part of the National Retail Federation and its goal is to create an open environment where retailers and technology vendors can work together to create international retail technology standards. This includes the UnifiedPOS (a specification for point-of-sale, or POS, device interfaces). Recently, this group also started looking at researching this space and developing white papers to address cloud issues for this vertical.

Part IV

Managing the Cloud

The 5th Wave   By Rich Tennant

"We take network security here very seriously."

In this part . . .

*U*sing a cloud model doesn't mean giving away
responsibility for your corporate assets. Security,
governance, and standards, for example, are all critical
aspects. In this part, we explore what it takes to manage
the cloud.

Chapter 15

Managing and Securing Cloud Services

In This Chapter

▸ Recognizing security risks

▸ Carrying out required security tasks

▸ Managing user identity

▸ Using detection and forensics programs

▸ Encrypting data

▸ Creating a security plan

*A*ny IT manager thinking about the impact of cloud computing on the corporation worries about security first, second, and third. Whether you're looking at creating a private cloud or leveraging a public cloud, you need to have a security strategy. Without a secure environment, no organization would dare implement cloud computing.

Even if your IT organization already has a well-designed security strategy, different issues will surface with cloud computing. Therefore, your strategy has to take this different computing model into account. In fact, you want to make sure that your IT security strategy is lined up with your cloud security strategy.

Cloud service providers each have their own way of managing security. They might be compatible with the compliance and overall security plan of your business. On the other hand, the security approach may conflict with your company's rules. No governance body will accept the excuse that you simply didn't know how your provider protected your information. In this chapter, we show you how your company's information and technology security strategy needs to be integrated with your overall cloud computing strategy and plan.

Putting Security on the Spot with Questions

Starting with a list of issues and questions helps you to frame the way you understand the importance of security from a cloud computing perspective.

Here are the most critical security questions to ask the potential cloud provider:

✔ What is the cloud provider's security architecture and policy?

✔ Does the cloud provider use a third party to assess its own security risks?

✔ Does the cloud provider understand its responsibilities for governance issues (such as cross-border data transfers)?

✔ How comprehensive is the service level agreement between you and the cloud provider?

✔ Does the cloud provider understand your data preservation and protection needs?

✔ Where does your data physically live? Do you have the cloud provider's assurance that it will remain private?

✔ Does your cloud provider separate *(partition)* your data, applications, and/or management tools from other users of its cloud services?

✔ Are there clear penalties for a data or system breach?

✔ Is data portability part of the service provided by the cloud vendor?

✔ Does the cloud provider have a security baseline that it promises to adhere to?

✔ Are you allowed to inspect the cloud facility?

✔ Does your cloud provider have well implemented patch management policies and procedures?

✔ Does the cloud provider have application level firewalls and other tools that help keep your application or code safe?

✔ Can the cloud provider keep security information such as private keys private?

✔ Does the cloud provider provide encryption and key management?

✔ Does the cloud provider have a well-defined, well-executed identity and access management architecture?

✔ Has single sign-on been implemented for the customers of a cloud provider?

You're probably wondering if asking all these questions is necessary. It's your obligation to keep your company safe. While you might be directly responsible for your company's security strategy, you also need a good understanding of how a cloud provider might approach the topic.

But again, nothing is that straightforward. Many large enterprises are implementing private or hybrid clouds, essentially transforming their data centers to adopt the characteristics of a self-service, scalable resource.

However, even a private cloud can be a challenge for traditional security policies, which tend to assume a more static and controlled environment. Don't think that you're in more control of your security destiny if you have your own cloud.

An IT organization must ensure the right balance of protection, privacy, governance, and accessibility to key resources — whether in the traditional data center, the private cloud, or the public cloud. Security measures for monitoring access control, identity management, and the network need to be maintained in a consistent way across the internal data center and hybrid cloud environments. (See Chapter 9 for more information on private and hybrid clouds.)

IT security is a very complicated area of cloud computing for three reasons:

✔ You will be trusting your security to the cloud provider. If that provider hasn't done a good job securing its own environment, you could be in trouble.

✔ IT security is difficult to monitor and problems may not be apparent until something goes wrong.

✔ Measuring the quality of a provider's approach to security is difficult because many cloud providers don't expose their infrastructure to customers.

Understanding Security Risks

Cloud security has to be a part of your company's overall security strategy. Most companies place a high priority on the testing and monitoring of threats to their data center, buildings, people, and information.

Security risks, threats, and breaches can come in so many forms and from so many places that many companies take a comprehensive approach to security management across IT and the business. For example, many companies use technology that tracks someone's identity whether this person enters a company building or accesses corporate information, either from within the company's perimeters or from any external location.

A company planning to secure its IT environment will generally focus on the broad range of potential vulnerabilities to its data center as well as ways to safeguard sensitive corporate, customer, and partner information wherever it is located. A company's software applications may include lots of built-in application and data level protections (such as authentication, authorization, and encryption), but there are many situations where these protections aren't enough. The following section provides an overview of the types of security risks that companies should consider in any IT environment, including the cloud.

Even when cloud operators have good security (physical, network, OS, application infrastructure), it is *your* company's responsibility to protect and secure your applications and information.

Security services at both the application and the infrastructure level must be a top consideration for organizations.

Given the importance of security in the cloud environment, you might assume that a major cloud services provider would have a set of comprehensive service level agreements for its customers. In fact, many of the standard agreements are intended to protect the *service provider* — not the customer. Therefore, a company really must understand the contract.

The risks are lower if you're using storage on a temporary basis than if you're using a cloud service as a replacement for a critical service that touches your customers.

Currently, the IT industry faces a problem: Security approaches (including perimeter security) are becoming less effective. To understand why, you must know how security threats arise. About 70 percent of security breaches are caused by insiders (or by people getting help from insiders). Insiders rarely get caught. The cloud environment can have some of the same issues. After all, a cloud is managed by people who might be tempted to breach security. If your company is going to use a cloud service, you need to have a plan to deal with inside as well as outside threats.

The possibility that insiders will open a door for hackers or mount an inside attack makes it clear that perimeter security on its own will never be enough.

Secure history

PCs had no security at all initially, but a password-and-permissions system was added for networkwide security based on login. In IT security circles, this system is called *perimeter security* because it establishes a secure perimeter around the network, the applications it runs, and the data stored within. Many of the security products that organizations deploy, such as firewalls and *virtual private networks* (VPNs, which are encrypted communication lines), are also perimeter-security products. They improve the security of the perimeter, which is a bit like plugging holes in the castle walls. With the advent of networks, however, an operating system could be artificially extended to work across a network. With virtualization of everything from servers to networks, storage, and applications, the problem gets even more complicated.

Reducing Cloud Security Breaches

Make sure that the cloud provider has taken a structured approach to its own security model. In general, follow these steps to reduce the risk of suffering security breaches:

1. **Authenticate all people accessing the network.**

2. **Frame all access permissions so users have access only to the applications and data that they've been granted specific permission to access.**

3. **Authenticate all software running on any computer — and all changes to such software.**

   This includes software or services running in the cloud.

   Your cloud provider needs to automate and authenticate software patches and configuration changes, as well as manage security patches in a proactive way. Why is this so important to understand? Many cloud service provider outages typically come from configuration mistakes. If a cloud provider doesn't update security, your intellectual property could be at risk.

4. **Formalize the process of requesting permission to access data or applications.**

   This applies to your own internal systems and the services that require you to put your data into the cloud.

5. **Monitor all network activity and log all unusual activity.**

   In most cases, you should deploy intruder-detection technology. Although your cloud services provider may enable you to monitor activities on its environment, you should have an independent view. This is especially important for compliance.

6. **Log all user activity and program activity and analyze it for unexpected behavior.**

7. **Encrypt, up to the point of use, all valuable data that needs extra protection.**

8. **Regularly check the network for vulnerabilities in all software exposed to the Internet or any external users.**

If you think these steps are easy, you don't know how complex it is to implement all these rules across a large network. Very few networks come close to this level of protection. When you consider a cloud provider, this list will give insight into how sophisticated the provider is.

Point solutions usually cover specific vulnerabilities:

✔ Firewalls protect the internal network from the Internet.

✔ Antivirus software protects individual computers against known viruses.

✔ VPNs protect external connections coming into the network.

Such products reduce the risk of specific threats, but aren't an integrated approach to IT security. Right now, that approach doesn't exist outside the realm of government organizations such as the National Security Agency, and it may not exist inside such organizations, either. As the cloud services market matures, successful vendors will have to provide this type of comprehensive approach.

But some important products can make a significant contribution to building an integrated IT security platform. They come in three categories:

✔ Identity management

✔ Detection and forensics

✔ Data encryption

We discuss these products separately in the following sections.

Implementing Identity Management

Identity management is a very broad topic that applies to most areas of the data center. However, it's particularly important in protecting the cloud environment. Because the cloud is about sharing and virtualizing physical resources across many internal (and often external) users, you must know who has access to what services.

Identity management's primary goal is managing personal identity information so that access to computer resources, applications, data, and services is controlled properly. Identity management is the one area of IT security that offers genuine benefits beyond reducing the risk of security breaches.

Benefits of identity management

Identity management helps prevent security breaches and plays a significant role in helping your company meet IT security compliance regulations. The benefits of keeping your customer or company financial data safe from unauthorized access can be huge.

In addition, you reap many benefits from identity management that occurs every day, not just during a major threat.

- ✔ **Improved user productivity:** Productivity improvement comes from simplifying the sign-on interface (see "Single sign-on," later in this chapter) and the ability to quickly change access rights. Productivity is likely to improve further where you provide user self-service.

- ✔ **Improved customer and partner service:** Customers and partners also benefit from a more streamlined, secure process when accessing applications and data.

- ✔ **Reduced help desk costs:** IT help desks typically experience fewer calls about forgotten passwords when an identity management process is implemented.

- ✔ **Reduced IT costs:** Identity management enables automatic *provisioning* — providing or revoking users' access rights to systems and applications. Provisioning happens whether you automate it or not. When provisioning is manual, normally it's carried out by members of the IT operational staff or departmental staff. Considerable time and cost savings are possible when you automate the process (see "Provisioning," later in this chapter).

After you grasp the basics of identity management, you need to understand the special conditions needed for the cloud. Because the cloud is a highly distributed environment, identity management needs to be federated for you to benefit from the process. *Federated identity management* lets people keep the same identification across different applications, services, and networks of different companies.

This eliminates some of the boundaries to access for your employees, customers, and partners so they can use the applications and information from multiple environments (including the cloud).

Aspects of identity management

In this section, we cover the various aspects of an identity management program.

Corralling the data

Identity data generally is scattered around systems. Establish a common database or directory as a first step in gaining control of this information. This step involves inputting data to and gathering data from various user directories.

Integrating

An identity management system must integrate effectively with other applications. In particular, the system must have a direct interface to the following:

- ✔ Human resources system, where new joiners and leavers are first recorded

- ✔ Supply-chain systems, if partners and suppliers use corporate systems

- ✔ Customer databases (if customers require access to some systems), although customer identity management normally is handled by a separate component of an identity management system

Beefing up authentication

When you require authentication stronger than passwords, the identity management system must work with products that provide that authentication, such as biometric systems (fingerprints, handprints, iris verification, and the like) and identity token systems.

Provisioning

When you link all systems that use identity information, you can automate provisioning. If this process is automated, a single status change (of an employee or anyone else with access rights) can be defined in the identity management system and sent across all affected systems from that point.

When provisioning is automated, users rarely (or never) get more access than necessary. Providing broad levels of access happens frequently in manual provisioning because it's easier to specify broad access. Additionally, an automated process never fails to revoke former employees' access to the network.

Single sign-on

Single sign-on means providing all users an interface that validates identity as soon as a user signs on anywhere; this interface requires the user to enter a single password. Thereafter, all systems should know the user and her permissions.

Some single sign-on products don't provide the full gamut of identity management capabilities, but all identity management products deliver single sign-on capability.

Instead of being assigned to individuals, permissions are often assigned to roles (accounts clerk, sales assistant, programmer, and so on). Therefore, single sign-on also means capturing information about the administration hierarchy. Single sign-on naturally goes with portal technology, with the user having a Web-based initial interface that provides access to all applications that he's entitled to access. Thus, single sign-on may need to interface with a portal product.

Security administration

Identity management reduces security administration costs because security administrators don't have to manually authorize; the identity management system handles that workflow automatically.

The automatic ID management handling is particularly useful for organizations that have distributed security administration over several locations because it enables security administration to be centralized.

Analyzing data

After you centralize all user data, you can generate useful reports on resource and application use or carry out security audits. For example:

- ✔ If you're having problems with internal hacking you can check a log that lists every user's activity (see the following section).

- ✔ If you have logging software for databases and files, you can monitor who did what to any item of data and when, including who looked at specific items of data. This audit capability is important for implementing data privacy and data protection compliance.

Playing Detective: Detection and Forensics

In this section, we discuss three specific groups of IT security products:

- ✔ Activity logs
- ✔ Host-based intrusion protection systems and network-based intrusion protection systems
- ✔ Data audit

No one — intruder or legitimate user — should be able to use the preceding resources without leaving evidence. You want to detect any illegitimate activity as soon as it happens, but in many situations, you can't separate the legitimate from the illegitimate. If you don't detect an attack while it's happening, at least you have a record of what took place.

Activity logs

Many logging capabilities are included in operating systems, applications, databases, and devices such as hardware firewalls and network monitors. It costs to invoke logging capabilities: Turning on logging requires the system to write log records constantly, and it also involves managing and archiving such data until it's no longer needed.

Log files often provide some evidence of how fraud was perpetrated, however. Perpetrators of digital fraud often escape justice simply because the victim doesn't have sufficient evidence to prove what they did.

HIPS and NIPS

Companies that would like to see a cloud service provider take over their internal platform and infrastructure services need to take a careful look at infrastructure protection.

Host-based intrusion protection systems (HIPS) and *network-based intrusion protection systems (NIPS)* are the same thing: a collection of capabilities that make it tough to penetrate a network.

HIPS and NIPS can include the following elements:

- ✔ **System and log-file monitors:** This software looks for traces of hackers in log files. The monitors can watch login accounts, for example, and issue alerts when account permissions change — often an indication that something untoward is going on.

✔ **Network intrusion-detection systems (NIDS):** These security programs monitor data packets that travel through a network, looking for any telltale signs of hacker activity. The effectiveness of a NIDS depends on whether it can sort real dangers from harmless threats and from legitimate activity. An ineffective NIDS raises too many false alarms and, thus, wastes time.

✔ **Digital deception software:** This software deliberately misleads anyone who's attempting to attack the IT network. It can range from the simple spoofing of various service names to setting up traps known as *honeypots* or *honeynets*. (For more information, see the nearby sidebar "Fooling attackers by spoofing.")

Setting security traps is unusual and can be expensive. It's normally done by government sites or by companies that suspect digital industrial espionage.

✔ **White-listing software:** This software inventories valid executable programs running on a computer and prevents any other executables from running. White-listing severely hampers hackers, because even if they access a computer, they can't upload their own software to run on it. White-listing software reports on any attempt to run unauthenticated software. It also stops virus software stone dead.

✔ **Unified threat management:** This central function takes information from all the preceding components and identifies threats by analyzing the combined information.

Fooling attackers by spoofing

As a technical IT term, *spoofing* means pretending to be something else. In a so-called *phishing* attack, a false Web site pretends to be a genuine one. A phishing Web site might pretend to be a bank's Web site, for example, and try to tempt users to reveal their financial details. It's possible to spoof email addresses and, under some circumstances, Internet protocol (IP) addresses, but mounting an attack this way is difficult because a computer responds directly to the real address rather than to the spoofed address.

When you use spoofing as a defense, your aim is to confuse attacking software. Hackers use sniffing software to look for servers running specific versions of, say, Microsoft Windows. If you set the operating system to give out false information, which is easy enough to do, that false information confuses the attacking software into passing on by. Honeypots work by spoofing, too. They pretend to be vulnerable servers and thereby trick attackers into revealing details on where they're attacking from.

Data audit

Although databases do log the name of the individual who changed data, they normally don't log who *read* any piece of data. But read data is easily stolen. If you plan on storing data in a cloud environment, you must address this issue.

Enthusiasm for filling this gap increased considerably after the Sarbanes-Oxley legislation was enacted in 2002, specifically demanding that financial data be secured from unauthorized eyes. Consequently, a series of software products that log who looks at what quickly came into existence. These products generally are referred to as *data audit* products.

Encrypting Data

The IT world has a whole set of encryption techniques that can be regarded as completely safe. Thus, you can easily encrypt data and ensure that only the intended recipient can decrypt it.

You *could* encrypt everything. You could encrypt data when you write it to disc, when you send it down a wire, when you send it through the air by radio, and so on. Encrypting everything in a comprehensive way considerably reduces your exposure to data theft. Hackers aren't able to cover their tracks because they're not able to decrypt the log files.

Encryption poses a performance penalty, so be sure to focus encryption on specific data that needs protection.

Think about how you use encryption. A fairly recent case of data theft included data that was encrypted until it was delivered to the application that needed to use it. At that point, the data was decrypted for use — and that's exactly where the hacker struck. The loss could have been prevented if the receiving application itself had controlled the decryption on a record-by-record basis.

Because of the complexities it adds, encryption is used less frequently than perhaps it should be. The media have covered many cases of stolen laptops containing valuable data — including military secrets. Those thefts wouldn't have been problems if all the data on those laptops had been encrypted properly.

Data encryption becomes even more important when using cloud services. But keep in mind that your company is still responsible for the quality and integrity of your information.

Creating a Cloud Security Strategy

This book isn't *Cloud Security For Dummies,* so we won't go into creating a comprehensive security strategy. We do want to provide some pointers, though:

- ✔ In most circumstances, approach cloud security from a risk-management perspective. If your organization has risk-management specialists, involve them in cloud security planning.

- ✔ IT security monitoring has no simple key performance indicators, but be aware of what similar organizations spend on IT security. It also makes sense to keep track of time lost due to any kind of attack — a useful measurement of cost that you may be able to reduce over time.

- ✔ You need identity management for many reasons, and identity management offers many benefits. Give priority to improving identity management if your current capability is poor.

- ✔ Try to create general awareness of security risks by educating and warning staff members about specific dangers. It is easy to become complacent, especially if you're using a cloud service provider. However, threats come from within and from outside the organization.

- ✔ Regularly have external IT security consultants check your company's IT security policy and IT network and the policies and practices of all your cloud service providers.

- ✔ Determine specific IT security policies for change management and patch management, and make sure that policies are well understood by your service management staff and by your cloud service provider.

- ✔ Stay abreast of news about IT security breaches in other companies and the causes of those breaches.

- ✔ Review backup and disaster-recovery systems in light of IT security. Apart from anything else, IT security breaches can require complete application recovery.

When a security breach occurs on a specific computer, the applications running on that computer will likely have to be stopped. Consequently, security breaches can be the direct causes of service interruptions and can contribute to lower service levels. Also, data theft resulting from a security breach could result in a real or perceived breach of customers' trust in your organization.

Security is a very complex area for both internal IT organizations as well as the cloud service providers. Many organizations will have hybrid environments that include public as well as private clouds. Internal systems will be connected to cloud environments. New frontiers add complexity and risk.

Chapter 16

Governing the Cloud

. . . .

In This Chapter

▶ Defining governance inside the cloud

▶ Knowing what governance to expect for your provider

▶ Knowing the risks of monitoring inside the cloud

▶ Making cloud governance work

. . . .

*W*hen you move a workload to the cloud, there is a good chance, depending on the kind of workload, that you're no longer responsible for the care and feeding of that workload. You might move email or archived data to a storage cloud, for example. Wait! You turned over control of your assets to the cloud provider, but you're still ultimately responsible for its wellness. In other words, make sure that your assets are managed in a way that meets your business objectives.

This is where governance comes in.

At the end of the day, governance is about making good decisions regarding performance predictability and requiring accountability. This is the case whether you're governing your own data center or thinking about the cloud.

We know there must be a myriad of questions in your head about governing in the cloud: How do I make sure that the other guy is following my rules and policies? When does it matter if he doesn't follow my rules? What's the role of trust in this situation?

An overarching principle behind governance is trust. All parties involved in the cloud — you, the cloud provider, and other service providers — must be able to trust that each party will do what it's supposed to in accordance with established policies and procedures. Think about what would happen without these policies and procedures; the cloud environment might be chaos, which isn't appealing.

In this chapter, we cover the ins and outs of cloud governance, including understanding the risks.

Looking at IT Governance

At its most basic, *governance* is about applying policies relating to using services. It's about defining the organizing principles and rules that determine how an organization should behave.

Did you know that the word *governance* derives from the Latin word for "steering"? It is important to have a steering process because, well, it helps to make sure that you stay on the road!

Before diving in, take a step back and look at the IT governance process in general because many of the same principles are relevant to the cloud environment. IT manages a complex infrastructure of hardware, data, storage, and software environments. The data center is designed to use all assets efficiently while guaranteeing a certain service level to the customer. A data center has teams of people responsible for managing everything from the overall facility: workloads, hardware, data, software, and network infrastructure.

In addition to the data center itself, your organization may have remote facilities with technology that depends on the data center. IT management has long-established processes for managing and monitoring individual IT components, which is good.

IT governance does the following:

- Ensures that IT assets (systems, processes, and so on) are implemented and used according to agreed-upon policies and procedures.

- Ensures that these assets are properly controlled and maintained.

- Ensures that these assets are providing value to the organization (actually supporting your organization's strategy and business goals).

IT governance, therefore, has to include the techniques and policies that measure and control how systems are managed. However, IT doesn't stand alone in the governance process. In order for governance to be effective, it needs to be holistic. It is as much about organizational issues and how people work together to achieve business goals as it is about any technology. Therefore, the best kind of governance occurs when IT and the business are working together.

Governance defines who is responsible for what and who is allowed to take action to fix whatever needs fixing. Governance also sets down what policies people are responsible for and puts in place means to determine whether the responsible person or group has, in fact, acted responsibly and done the right thing.

A critical part of governance is establishing organizational relationships between business and IT, as well as defining how people will work together across organizational boundaries.

How does IT governance typically work? IT governance usually involves establishing a board made up of business and IT representatives. The board creates rules and processes that the organization must follow to ensure that policies are being met. This might include

✔ Understanding business issues such as regulatory requirements or funding for development

✔ Establishing best practices and monitoring these processes

✔ Responsibility for things like programming standards, proper design, reviewing, certifying, and monitoring applications from a technical perspective, and so on

A simple example of IT governance in action is making sure that IT is meeting its obligations in terms of computing uptime. This uptime obligation is negotiated between the business and IT, based on the criticality of the application to the business.

Deciding on a Governor

Cloud governance is a shared responsibility between the user of cloud services and the cloud provider. Understanding the boundaries of responsibilities and defining an appropriate governance strategy within your organization require careful balance. You must consider many factors, ranging from the performance levels of the IT environment's components to the *key performance indicators (KPIs)*, which measure the effectiveness of a business process — of your business. Your governance strategy needs to reflect the mix of IT services provided by your internal data center, as well as private and public clouds.

Cloud governance requires governing your *own* infrastructure as well as infrastructure that you don't totally control. For example, your organizations must monitor performance across all components in a way that reflects the overall impact of *all* IT performance on the business. You may not have as much insight into the cloud environment, which could create challenges when you need to satisfy governance requirements.

Here are two examples of how governance may become more complicated when you add cloud services into your IT environment.

Imagining a scenario

Say that you move some of your processing to the cloud and expect to get the same uptime that you had in your data center. You rely on your cloud provider for the availability of virtualized servers. Chances are, however, that you don't have a good view into that environment.

What do you need to be concerned about from a governance perspective?

- ✔ Can you enforce this same availability policy with your cloud provider?
- ✔ Will your cloud provider have tools that allow you to monitor whether service targets are being met?
- ✔ Your cloud provider may be meeting predefined service levels, but will the provider communicate this information to you?

Imagining another scenario

You're developing a new application on a cloud provider's platform. You expect a certain set of services to be available; in fact, you're planning your development around it.

What are some of the potential issues in this scenario?

- ✔ Does your cloud provider have a service registry or catalog that enables you to have good visibility into the management and availability of services?
- ✔ Will the services you want be available in the service catalog when you need them?
- ✔ Does your cloud provider have a policy for enforcing the service you want to be maintained and available in the service catalog?

Knowing the Risks of Running in the Cloud

IT governance is tightly woven with business goals and policies to ensure that services are optimized for customer expectations. Because IT and business goals are tightly woven in a governance strategy, we think it is important for you to also look at cloud governance from a holistic business perspective.

Your governance strategy needs to be supported in two key ways:

✔ **Understanding the compliance and risk measures the business must follow:** What does your business require to meet IT, corporate, industry, and government requirements? For example, can your business share data across country lines? These requirements would need to be supported through technical controls; automation and strict governance of processes, data, and workflows.

✔ **Understanding the performance goals of the business:** You may measure your business performance in terms of sales revenue, profitability, stock price, quality of product or service provided, and time to delivery. Your cloud provider must be able to support service delivery to optimize business performance.

Look at each of these in a bit more detail.

Understanding risk

Each industry has a set of governance principles based on its regulatory and competitive environment and its view of risk. There are different levels of risk. For example, in certain companies, information cannot be shared across international boundaries. In financial services, certain data practices need to be followed. In software development, there are risks associated with getting the product out in the market on time. The healthcare industry has patient privacy concerns.

For example, suppose you have a corporate policy that states that no data from a credit card system can be used by the company's marketing analysis systems. If the CIO later discovers, for example, that this information has been used by the system, the business is put at risk and IT governance has failed. Others besides the CIO needed to know that this information was not to be used by marketing because of privacy concerns.

Deducing IT risk

In the heterogeneous IT environment, IT needs to juggle various tasks: meeting customer expectations, optimizing business goals, recognizing resource constraints, and adhering to rules and requirements. The cloud can further complicate this juggling act because it is yet another resource that IT is responsible for. This means that the governing body is responsible for overseeing the provider relationship.

Of course, the level of involvement and risk around governance might vary with how your organization is using the cloud. For example, the cloud can be used in the following ways, each of which you must evaluate — separately — to determine the level of governance that your company feels comfortable with:

- ✔ For temporary computing power
- ✔ As a SaaS model
- ✔ As a platform to build a service

Risk list

Consider these risks as you move into the cloud:

- ✔ **Audit and compliance risks** including issues around data jurisdiction, data access control, and maintaining an audit trail.
- ✔ **Security risks** including data integrity, data confidentiality, and privacy.
- ✔ **Information risks** (outside of security), including protection of intellectual property.
- ✔ **Performance and availability risks,** including availability and performance levels that your business requires to successfully operate. This includes alerts, notifications, and provider business continuity plans. Along with this, does the provider have forensic information in case something does go wrong?
- ✔ **Interoperability risks,** which are associated with developing a service that might be composed of multiple services. Will the infrastructure continue supporting your service? What if one of the services that you're using changes? What policies are in place to ensure that you'll be notified of a change?
- ✔ **Contract risks** associated with not reading between the lines of your contract. For example, who owns your data in the cloud? If the service goes down, how will you be compensated? What happens if the provider goes out of business?
- ✔ **Billing risks** associated with ensuring that you're billed correctly and only for the resources you consume.

Remember when we said that governance was all about trust? Well, the reality is that, if you move into the cloud, you need to trust the cloud provider and every other provider that the cloud provider is working with. Currently, there are no professional standards or laws related to cloud computing.

Managing risk can't be emphasized enough; unlike internal IT governance where all parties work for the same legal entity, the cloud relationship is with an external provider and governance agreements need to be contractually stated.

Measuring and monitoring performance

Measuring performance as a means to help improve performance is a concept that is well understood by competitive athletes. Imagine the countless hours spent during training measuring, recording, and monitoring changes in time and distance. But what if the runner were taking steroids? Was she in compliance? Clearly, even if all other measurements were positive, breaking the rules changes everything.

How does this example apply to cloud governance?

Although measuring and monitoring may help you improve performance, that performance is irrelevant if you don't follow the company's governance rules.

Measurement methods

You can measure business performance by comparing production, sales, revenue, stock price, and customer satisfaction with your goals. You can measure IT performance by comparing server, application, and network uptime; service resolution time; budgets; and project completion dates with your goals. Businesses use all these measures to rate their performance compared with that of competitors and the expectations of customers, partners, and shareholders.

In cloud computing, you need to measure the impact of IT performance on the business that, by definition, now includes the performance of the cloud provider.

Of course, your own internal governance committee needs to answer the following questions to get started:

- ✔ How can IT performance measures support the business?
- ✔ What should management measure and monitor to ensure successful IT governance?
- ✔ Can customers get responses to requests in the expected amount of time?
- ✔ Is customer transaction data safe from unauthorized access?
- ✔ Can management get the right information at the right time?
- ✔ Can IT demonstrate to business management that your organization can recover from anticipated outages without damaging customer loyalty?

✔ Can your company monitor systems proactively so you can make repairs before faulty services affect rules and regulations?

✔ Can you justify your IT investments to business management?

Making Governance Work

We believe that effective cloud management is accomplished partly through people and processes, and partly through technology. It's really a three-part solution:

✔ Your organization needs a governance body to deal with cloud issues (this can be your existing governance board, if you like) and processes to work with the business around these issues. This board should have oversight and collaborate with the business (it should include business members as well) around cloud issues that directly impact your organization. It can also develop best practices for managing cloud environments.

✔ The cloud needs governance bodies that deal with standardization of services and other shared infrastructure issues. Your organization needs some sort of interface to this group. Your level of involvement depends on your level of involvement in the cloud.

✔ Your organization needs technology that helps you automatically monitor what happens in the cloud.

Establishing your governance body

You need your own group of people who understand your business to deal with the business of the cloud. This governance board might consist of representatives of corporate, departmental, and IT management to help encourage communication — the kind necessary to link IT management and the business. This board may also create other groups responsible for different aspects of governance. For example, it might create a group that needs to understand cloud standards, or it may leverage an IT security group.

Of course, an important part of this governance structure will be a group of individuals who actually *deal* with the cloud providers to negotiate terms and conditions and to be the point group(s) for managing the cloud provider(s).

This governing body should be ongoing, with authority across the enterprise and with a mechanism for communicating business objectives and changes to IT management. Ideally, it will have executive-level endorsement to make its job easier.

Monitoring and measuring IT service performance

In addition to interacting with your cloud provider(s), you must also monitor what these cloud providers are doing. Depending on the situation, this may mean investing in technology that sees into cloud operations.

Many companies use a *dashboard,* which is an interface that holds the different services and shows how your performance measures up to your goals. This dashboard also needs to include information from the cloud. Quite a few emerging vendors provide tools that enable companies to monitor their cloud providers.

Monitoring can help answer questions like these:

- ✔ What are we aiming for?
- ✔ What are our KPIs?
- ✔ How are we performing according to our established KPIs?
- ✔ How does our performance compare with last week's or last year's?
- ✔ Are rules and processes implemented correctly?
- ✔ Does each service meet technical standards?

Cataloging control and compliance data

Many organizations use a *service catalog* as a record of IT services. This should be extended to the cloud. The catalog can include information such as

- ✔ Whom to contact about a service
- ✔ Who has authority to change the service
- ✔ Which critical applications are related to the service
- ✔ Outages or other incidents related to the service
- ✔ Information about the relationships among services
- ✔ Documentation of all agreements between IT and the customer/service user

Chapter 17

Virtualization and the Cloud

In This Chapter

▶ Discovering virtualization

▶ Dealing with management issues

▶ Moving virtualization to the cloud

Any discussion of cloud computing typically begins with virtualization. *Virtualization* is using computer resources to imitate other computer resources or whole computers.

We think of cloud computing as the transformation of computing that brings together service orientation with distributed manageability combined with the economies of scale from virtualization. In a world where almost everything is a service, virtualization is a fundamental mechanism for delivering services. Indeed, virtualization provides a platform for optimizing complex IT resources in a *scalable* manner (efficiently growing), which is ideal for delivering services.

When you think about cloud management, it's important to separate resources from their physical implementations. Without virtualization, the cloud becomes very difficult to manage. Virtualization is so important for cloud computing because it is possible to simplify many aspects of computing.

In this chapter, we present an overview of virtualization and how this process makes cloud computing work.

Visualizing Virtualization

Virtualization separates resources and services from the underlying physical delivery environment.

Characteristics

Virtualization has three characteristics that make it ideal for cloud computing:

- **Partitioning:** In virtualization, many applications and operating systems (OSes) are supported in a single physical system by *partitioning* (separating) the available resources.

- **Isolation:** Each virtual machine is isolated from its host physical system and other virtualized machines. Because of this isolation, if one virtual-instance crashes, it doesn't affect the other virtual machines. In addition, data isn't shared between one virtual container and another.

- **Encapsulation:** A virtual machine can be represented (and even stored) as a single file, so you can identify it easily based on the service it provides. In essence, the encapsulated process could be a business service. This encapsulated virtual machine can be presented to an application as a complete entity. Therefore, encapsulation can protect each application so that it doesn't interfere with another application.

Applications

Virtualization can be applied very broadly to just about everything that you could imagine:

- Memory
- Networks
- Storage
- Hardware
- Operating systems
- Applications

What makes virtualization so important for the cloud is that it decouples the software from the hardware. *Decoupling* means that software is put in a separate container so that it's isolated from operating systems. See Chapter 19 for more on this issue.

Forms

To understand how virtualization helps with cloud computing, you must understand its many forms. In essence, in all cases, a resource actually emulates or imitates another resource. Here are some examples:

- **Virtual memory:** Disks have a lot more space than computer memory. Therefore, with virtual memory, the computer frees valuable memory space by placing information it doesn't use often into disk space. PCs have *virtual memory,* which is a disk area that's used like memory. Although disks are very slow in comparison with memory, the user may never notice the difference, especially if the system does a good job of managing virtual memory. The substitution works surprisingly well.

✔ **Software:** Companies have built software that can emulate a whole computer. That way, 1 computer can perform as though it were actually 20 computers. The application consolidation results can be quite significant. For example, you might be able to move from a data center with thousands of servers to one that supports as few as a couple of hundred. This reduction results in less money spent not only on computers, but also on power, air conditioning, maintenance, and floor space.

Using a hypervisor in virtualization

A *hypervisor* is an operating system, which means that it knows how to act as a traffic cop to make things happen in an orderly manner. The hypervisor sits at the lowest levels of the hardware environment.

Because in cloud computing you need to support many different operating environments, the hypervisor becomes an ideal delivery mechanism. The hypervisor lets you show the same application on lots of systems without having to physically copy that application onto each system. One twist: Because of the hypervisor architecture, it can load any (or many) different operating system as though it were just another application. Therefore, the hypervisor is a very practical way of getting things virtualized quickly and efficiently.

Scheduling access

You should understand the nature of the hypervisor. It's designed like a mainframe OS rather than like the Windows operating system. The hypervisor therefore schedules the *amount* of access that guest OSes have to everything from the CPU; to memory; to disk I/O; and to any other I/O mechanisms. With virtualization technology, you can set up the hypervisor to split the physical computer's resources. Resources can be split 50–50 or 80–20 between two guest OSes, for example. Without the hypervisor, you simply can't do that with Windows.

The beauty of this arrangement is that the hypervisor does all the heavy lifting. The guest operating system doesn't care (or have any idea) that it's running in a virtual partition; it thinks that it has a computer all to itself.

A short history of virtualization

IBM introduced virtualization in the early 1960s to enable users to run more than one operating system on a mainframe. Mainframe virtualization became less relevant in the 1980s and 1990s. Indeed, in the 1990s, companies stopped worrying about the efficiency of the computer platform because computers were getting so powerful.

For more than a decade, IT organizations expanded the capabilities of their data centers by adding servers. Servers had become so cheap that each time a new application was added, it was easier to buy a new server than to share resources with other applications. Eventually, organizations realized that maintaining, upgrading, and managing a large (and growing) number of servers was getting out of hand. The number of support-staff employees required to operate the data center was climbing swiftly, so the manpower cost of maintaining the data center (as a percentage of the total cost) was rising. At the same time, other costs were growing in an unpredicted manner, particularly the costs of electricity (to power the computers), air conditioning (to cool them), and floor space (to house them).

One of the main problems was that the servers were horribly inefficient. In the days of the mainframe, great efforts were made to use 100 percent of the computer's CPU and memory resources. Even under normal circumstances, it was possible to achieve better than 95 percent utilization. On the cheap servers that IT departments had been deploying, however, CPU efficiency was often 6 percent or less —

sometimes as low as 2 percent. Memory and disk input/output (I/O) usage were similarly low.

This situation seems almost insane until you realize that applications simply don't require a great deal of resources, and with the servers that were being delivered by the year 2000, you didn't put more than one application on a server. Why? Because the operating systems that almost everyone had — Windows and Linux, typically — can't effectively schedule resource use between competing applications. In a competitive hardware market, vendors began increasing the power of servers at an affordable price. Most of these servers had more power than typical applications needed. The same inefficiencies of Windows and Linux didn't address the efficiency problem, however. If an organization decided to stay with older but lower-powered hardware, it couldn't find people to maintain those aging platforms.

If you had an application that only ever needed 5 percent of a current CPU, what were you going to do other than provide it with its own server? Some companies actually used old PCs for some applications of this kind, maintaining the PCs themselves; but there's a limit to the amount of old equipment that you can reuse.

The solution to this squandering of resources was to add scheduling capability to computers, which is precisely what one IT vendor, VMware, introduced. Adding scheduling changed the dynamics of computer optimization and set the stage for the modern virtualization revolution. The mainframe is dead; long live the mainframe!

Defining types

Different hypervisors support different aspects of the cloud. Hypervisors come in several types:

- ✓ **Native hypervisors,** which sit directly on the hardware platform are most likely used to gain better performance for individual users.

- ✓ **Embedded hypervisors** are integrated into a processor on a separate chip. Using this type of hypervisor is how a service provider gains performance improvements.

- ✓ **Hosted hypervisors** run as a distinct software layer above both the hardware and the OS. This type of hypervisor is useful both in private and public clouds to gain performance improvements.

Abstracting hardware assets

One of the benefits of virtualization is the way that it *abstracts* hardware assets, in essence allowing a single piece of hardware to be used for multiple tasks.

The following list summarizes hardware abstraction and its management:

- ✓ **File system virtualization:** Virtual machines can access different file systems and storage resources via a common interface.

- ✓ **Virtual symmetric multiprocessing:** A single virtual machine can use multiple physical processors simultaneously and thus pretend to be a server cluster. It also can emulate a fairly large grid of physical servers.

- ✓ **Virtual high-availability support:** If a virtual machine fails, that virtual machine needs to automatically restart on another server.

- ✓ **Distributed resource scheduler:** You could think of the scheduler as being the super-hypervisor that manages all the other hypervisors. This mechanism assigns and balances computing capability dynamically across a collection of hardware resources that support the virtual machines. Therefore, a process can be moved to a different resource when it becomes available.

- ✓ **Virtual infrastructure client console:** This console provides an interface that allows administrators to connect remotely to virtual center management servers or to an individual hypervisor so that the server and the hypervisor can be managed manually.

Managing Virtualization

For cloud computing to operate consistently, the service provider has to track all the virtualized resources.

You must keep track of

- ✔ Where everything is
- ✔ What everything has to accomplish
- ✔ For what purpose

When managing virtualization, the service provider (whether in your own organization or in a private cloud) must be able to do the following:

- ✔ Know and understand the relationships among all elements of the network.
- ✔ Be able to change things dynamically when elements within this universe change.
- ✔ Keep the placement of virtual resources in step with all the other information held in the *configuration management database (CMDB)*. Given that few organizations have anything approaching a comprehensive CMDB, that's asking for a lot. In fact, the CMDB needs to know how all service management capabilities are integrated.

Foundational issues

Managing a virtual environment involves some foundational issues that determine how well the components function as a system. These issues include

- ✔ How licenses are managed
- ✔ How workloads are controlled
- ✔ How the network itself is managed

In cloud environments, customers request additional add CPU cycles or storage as their needs grow. They're protected from the details, but this protection doesn't happen by magic. The provider has to do a lot of work behind the scenes to manage this highly dynamic environment.

The foundations have to be in synch between the two worlds. And when your company reviews different cloud options, management must understand how the cloud provider deals with foundational issues:

✔ **License management:** Many license agreements tie license fees to physical servers rather than to virtual servers. Resolve these licenses before using the associated software in a virtual environment. The constraints of such licenses may become an obstacle to efficiency.

✔ **Service levels:** Measuring, managing, and maintaining service levels can become more complicated simply because the environment itself is more complex. When cloud computing is added in to the mix, the cloud consumer is responsible for establishing service levels for both internally virtualized environments as well as those living in the cloud.

✔ **Network management:** The real target of network management becomes the virtual network, which may be harder to manage than the physical network.

✔ **Workload administration:** Set policies to determine how new resources can be provisioned, and under what circumstances. Before a new resource can be introduced, it needs to be approved by management. Also, the administrator has to be sure that the right security policies are included.

✔ **Capacity planning:** Although it's convenient to think that all servers deliver roughly the same capacity, they don't. With virtualization, you have more control of hardware purchases and can plan network resources accordingly.

Abstraction layer

Managing virtualization requires an *abstraction layer* that hides and manages things between the physical storage subsystems. The virtualization software needs to present the whole storage resource to the virtualized environment as a unified, sharable resource. That process can be more difficult than it sounds.

All the administrative functions that you'd need in a physical data center have to be deployed in a virtualized environment, for example. Following are some of the most important considerations:

✔ **A business can use virtualized storage for backup, recovery, and disaster recovery.** Virtualized storage can reinforce or replacing existing backup and recovery capabilities. It can also create *mirrored systems* (duplicates of all system components) and, thus, might participate in disaster-recovery plans. This issue must be resolved both for internally virtualized environments as well as those leveraging external clouds.

✔ **A service provider or a business investing in its own private cloud can perform backups of whole virtual machines or collections of virtual machines in any given state as disk files.** This technique is particularly useful in a virtualized environment after you change applications or complete configurations. You must test — and, therefore, simulate — this configuration before putting it in a production environment.

✔ **Whether you're a business leveraging virtualization in your own cloud or a service provider, you must manage the service levels of the applications running in a virtualized environment.** The actual information delay from disk varies for data held locally, data held on a *storage area network (SAN)*, and data held on *network access storage (NAS)*, and the delay differences may matter. Test different storage options against service levels.

For more information on SANs, see *Storage Area Networks For Dummies,* Second Edition, by Christopher Poelker and Alex Nikitin (Wiley).

✔ **In the long run, establish capacity planning to support the likely growth of the resource requirement for any application (or virtual machine).**

Provisioning software

Provisioning software lets you manually adjust the virtualized environment. Using provisioning software, you can create new virtual machines and modify existing ones to add or reduce resources. This type of provisioning is essential to managing workloads and to moving applications and services from one physical environment to another.

If you're using a cloud service provider, make sure that the company offers provisioning software in a consistent manner and can work with your internal resources.

Provisioning software enables management to prioritize actions based on a company's key performance indicators. It enables the following:

✔ Migration of running virtual machines from one physical server to another

✔ Automatic restart of a failed virtual machine on a separate physical server

✔ *Clustering,* or grouping, of virtual machines across different physical servers

Managing data center resources is hard under any circumstance — and even harder when those resources are running in virtual partitions. These managed resources need to provide the right level of performance, accountability, and predictability to users, suppliers, and customers. Virtualization must be managed carefully.

Virtualizing storage

Increasingly, organizations also need to virtualize storage. This trend currently works in favor of NASes rather than SANs, because a NAS is less expensive and more flexible than a SAN.

Because the virtualized environment has at least the same requirements as the traditional data center in terms of the actual amount of data stored, managing virtualized storage becomes very important.

In addition to application data, virtual machine images need to be stored. When virtual machines aren't in use, they're stored as disk files that can be instantiated at a moment's notice. Consequently, you need a way to centrally store virtual machine images.

Hardware provisioning

Before virtualization, hardware provisioning was simply a matter of commissioning new hardware and configuring it to run new applications (or possibly repurposing hardware to run some new application).

Virtualization makes this process a little simpler in one way: You don't have to link the setup of new hardware to the instantiation of a new application. Now you can add a server to the pool and enable it to run virtual machines. Thereafter, those virtual machines are ready when they're needed. When you add a new application, your cloud data center administrator or your service provider (via a self-service interface) will enable you to configure it to run on a virtual machine.

One of the key benefits that companies have found with cloud computing is the ability to quickly and effectively provision additional hardware resources from Infrastructure as a Service providers.

Provisioning is now the act of allocating a virtual machine to a specific server from a central console. Be aware of a catch, however: You can run into trouble if you go too far. You may decide to virtualize entire sets of applications and virtualize the servers that those applications are running on, for example.

Although you may get some optimization, you also create too many silos that are too hard to manage. (For more information on silos, see the nearby sidebar, "Static versus dynamic virtualization.") You may have optimized your environment so much that you have no room to accommodate peak loads.

The hypervisor (refer to "Using a hypervisor in virtualization," earlier in this chapter) lets a physical server run many virtual machines at the same time. In a sense, one server does the work of maybe ten. That arrangement is a neat one, but you may not be able to shift those kinds of workloads without consequences. A server running 20 virtual machines, for example, may still have the same network connection with the same traffic limitation, which could act as a bottleneck. Alternatively, if all those applications use local disks, many of them may need to use a SAN or NAS — and that requirement may have performance implications.

Security issues

Using virtual machines complicates IT security in a big way for both companies running private clouds and service providers. Virtualization changes the definition of what a server is, so security is no longer trying to protect a physical server or collection of servers that an application runs on. Instead, it's protecting virtual machines (or collections of them).

Because most data centers support only static virtualization, it isn't yet well understood what will happen during dynamic virtualization. Definite issues have been identified, however, and we address several of them in the following sections.

Network monitoring

Current network defenses are based on physical networks. In the virtualized environment, the network is no longer physical; its configuration can actually change dynamically, which makes network monitoring difficult. To fix this problem, you must have software products (available from companies such as VMWare, IBM, Hewlett-Packard, and CA) that can monitor virtual networks and, ultimately, dynamic virtual networks.

Hypervisors

Just as an OS attack is possible, a hacker can take control of a hypervisor. If the hacker gains control of the hypervisor, he gains control of everything that it controls; therefore, he could do a lot of damage. (For more details, see "Using a hypervisor in virtualization," earlier in this chapter.)

Static versus dynamic virtualization

There are two types of virtualization: static and dynamic. Static virtualization is difficult, but the dynamic type is even more so.

In *static virtualization,* application silos become virtualized application silos. (A *silo* is an isolated piece of software and hardware that can't interact with other components; it's a world unto itself.) You use virtualization to reduce the number of servers, but the virtualization is done via a fixed pattern that ensures that applications always have sufficient resources to manage peak workloads. This arrangement makes life relatively simple because that virtual machine will stay on the same server. Static virtualization is significantly more efficient than no virtualization, but it doesn't make optimal use of server resources.

If you want to optimize your environment, you need to be able to allocate server resources dynamically, based on changing needs within the business. *Dynamic virtualization* is complex, however. It's so complex that the market currently doesn't offer products that can implement it effectively. But those products will be available in time, because the virtualization cat is out of the bag.

Why is dynamic virtualization inevitable? The workloads in the data center are dynamic, especially considering that Internet applications change their transaction rates wildly over time. As the key performance requirements of the environment change, the virtual environment must change to meet those needs. In the long run, envision a world in which the whole network is treated as though it were a single resource space that can be shared dynamically based on changing workloads.

Configuration and change management

The simple act of changing configurations or patching the software on virtual machines becomes much more complex if the software is locked away in virtual images; in the virtual world, you no longer have a fixed static address to update the configuration.

Perimeter security

Providing perimeter security, such as firewalls, in a virtual environment is a little more complicated than in a normal network because some virtual servers are outside a firewall. This will be the responsibility of the service provider.

This perimeter security problem may not be too hard to solve because you can isolate the virtual resource spaces. This approach places a constraint on how provisioning is carried out, however.

Veiling virtualization from the end user

A cloud service provider (or a business with a private cloud) has a lot of details to manage. All the virtualization technology that supports these requirements is hidden from the end user. Although the business customer may expect to run a wide variety of software services on the cloud, with virtualization the business has little, if any, input into the how those underlying services are managed.

Taking Virtualization into the Cloud

As we indicate earlier in this chapter, virtualization is rapidly becoming a requirement for managing a data center from a service-delivery perspective. Despite its economies , however, companies are seeking even better economies when they're available.

If you like, you can think of cloud computing as being the next stage of development for virtualization. The problem for the data center is that workloads are very mixed; the data center needs to execute internal transactional systems, Web transactional systems, messaging systems such as email and chat, business intelligence systems, document management systems, workflow systems, and so on. With cloud computing, you can pick your spot and focus on getting efficiency from a predictable workload.

From this somewhat manual approach, you can move to industrial virtualization by making it a repeatable platform. This move requires forethought, however. What would such a platform need?

For this use of resources to be effective, you must implement a full-service management platform so that resources are safe from all forms of risk. As in traditional systems, the virtualized environment must be protected:

- ✔ The virtualized services offered must be secure.
- ✔ The virtualized services must be backed up and recovered as though they're physical systems.
- ✔ These resources need to have workload management, workflow, provisioning, and load balancing at the foundation to support the required type of customer experience.

Without this level of oversight, virtualization won't deliver the cost savings that it promises.

Chapter 18

Managing Desktops and Devices in the Cloud

In This Chapter

▶ Checking out the virtualized desktop

▶ Moving desktops to the cloud

▶ Managing desktops in the cloud

▶ Checking reality

*I*n some ways, what goes around comes around. Over the past few years, the notion of a virtual desktop has been getting a lot of attention. With a *virtual desktop,* the PC doesn't run its own applications — they run on a server in a data center. Sound sort of familiar? And, as virtualized servers move into the cloud, the idea of using a virtual desktop is gaining steam. In this chapter, we examine what a virtual desktop is all about, what it means to move it into the cloud, and how to manage this environment.

Virtualizing the Desktop

In a virtualized desktop, the applications, data, files, and anything graphic are separated from the actual desktop and stored on a server in a data center (not on the individual machine).

Why is it attractive? Think about a PC's *total cost of ownership (TCO):* acquisition, maintenance, support, help desk, hardware, software, and power. In a typical enterprise situation, the annual support cost per PC is anywhere between three and five times the cost of the PC itself. Because PCs are outdated after about four years, the TCO can be anywhere from 9 to 20 times the cost of the PC itself.

Virtualizing the desktop can bring down the TCO because it helps manage and centralize support. Standardizing infrastructure that needs to be managed via virtualization makes it easier to optimize IT resources.

Across industries

Virtualization is popular in a number of industries. For example, in healthcare, clinicians are using a virtualized desktop to gain access to information in any patient room or office. In science labs, where space is at a premium and contaminant-free work areas are a priority, virtualized desktops eliminate the server and other hardware from the room.

Other examples include using virtualized desktops for temporary workers or remote workers who need access to applications, or even traders who need to move around the trading floor, but need to gain access to the information they need, when they need it. Moving the desktop into the data center covers every possible means of replacing physical PCs with graphics terminals (also known as *thin clients*).

The name *thin clients* comes from the fact that such devices — although they're computers with CPUs, memory resources, keyboards, and mice — aren't PCs in the sense that they don't have disks or DVD drives. These devices also run an operating system, but the OS is used only to emulate the user interface of a PC. The reality is that thin clients are not always *that* thin — they usually have some local memory.

The client desktop

Virtualizing the *client* desktop can happen four ways, each of which is described in the following sections:

- ✔ Session-based computing
- ✔ Operating-system streaming
- ✔ Virtual Desktop Infrastructure (VDI)
- ✔ PC blade

You could loosely describe every one of these techniques as *client virtualization,* because in each technique the PC is controlled from the data center (not from the desktop). In practice, however, only one of these techniques, VDI, is based on *true* virtualization, which is the use of software to emulate a computing environment within another computer.

Client virtualization involves emulating a whole PC in software on a data center server and displaying the user interface on a graphics terminal.

Computers have become powerful enough to do this, and users are unlikely to detect the difference between client virtualization and a desktop.

Session-based computing

In session-based computing, the user is really running a session on a server. The server is running a single instance of the Windows operating system with multiple sessions. Only the screen image is actually transmitted to the user, who may have a thin client or possibly an old PC.

Products that provide this capability include Citrix MetaFrame and Microsoft Terminal Services.

Operating-system streaming

In this approach, the Windows OS software is passed to the client device — but only as much of the software that's needed at any point in time. Technically, this process is called *streaming.*

Some of the processing occurs on the disk and some in local memory. Thus, the Windows OS and its applications are split between the client and the server. Streaming applications run at about the same speed as reading the application from the disk.

You can use this approach by using PCs on the desktop (diskless PCs and laptops are options) or by using thin clients. Both Citrix and Hewlett-Packard provide this capability.

Virtual Desktop Infrastructure

Here, *virtual PCs* (complete emulations of a PC) are created on the server. The user has what *appears* on the server to be a complete PC. The graphics are being sent to a desktop. Today, most people refer to this kind of client virtualization as *Virtual Desktop Infrastructure (VDI).*

VDI is the ability to have shared client sessions on the server rather than on the client. The software you need to use sits on the server and an image can be viewed on your device. It is a type of virtualization hosted on the server. It's widely used and appropriate in many client environments.

In the VDI model, virtual machines are defined on a back-end infrastructure. Users connect into their virtual desktop from various clients (thin, PC, mobile, and so on) through something called a *connection broker.* The users are really accessing the image of the desktop. The IT administrator simply makes a copy of the *golden image* (server image used as a template) of a desktop and provisions that to a user.

VMware and Citrix both provide software that delivers this capability.

The PC blade

A *server blade* is a server computer contained entirely on a single computer board that can be slotted into a *blade cabinet* — a purpose-built computer cabinet with a built-in power supply. The server blade can contain a number of PC blades.

Each user is typically associated with one PC blade — although some environments let multiple users share one PC blade — and a whole PC sits on a server blade in the data center. Normally, the desktop is a thin client.

You can share a PC blade by putting a *hypervisor* (a program that enables multiple operating systems to run in conjunction with another operating system) on the blade. Whether or not you want to do this depends on how much CPU power you have and what type of applications you are running. For example, if you have two users who want to share a blade and both are running the same CPU-intensive application like Photoshop, they may not get the performance they were hoping for.

Putting Desktops in the Cloud

You get two big advantages to moving desktops to the cloud:

✔ **You can create desktops at your own speed.** You might first virtualize your desktops wherever they are, and replace them with thin clients. The PC blades or VDI servers (or whatever the provider uses to house your virtual desktops) are located at the provider's data center. You pay the provider a fee for this.

The average deployment time for a server in a data center is about five days. This includes all the setup and provisioning of the server. You might get five–ten virtual servers from this. If your resources are in the cloud, and the provider already has the infrastructure and management software ready for you to set up these desktops, your *provisioning* (adding capacity at will) time might be five seconds. This means, for example, that you decide when you want to provision the HR department — you can do it all at once, or over the course of a month — it is at your own speed.

✔ **You can get as many resources as you need for these desktops.** And, if the HR department needs more resources, the cloud provider has them ready, as well. Say you have offices in New York and Hong Kong: When the New York office is dark and everyone is asleep, you can use the same resources for Hong Kong because of the virtualization on the back end.

Moving an image of every desktop into a cloud environment doesn't make sense: The hardware and support costs would be astronomical.

How does this work in the real world? The principle here is economies of scale. The idea is to move common implementations into a virtualized environment. The golden image — a server image that's used as a template — of the OS and common applications and data are housed in the virtualized servers.

For example, it may make sense to move call center applications to this model. You provide a golden image of the OS and the call center support applications (and the data) that are used by numerous call center agents. The agents access this information via their thin clients. The applications don't run on their desktops; they run in the cloud. This is a desktop virtualization in the cloud model rather than a SaaS model because of the specific interface (the thin client), not the mode of accessing the application.

Further pros

The business advantages of desktops in the cloud are the same as in other forms of PC virtualization, reducing desktop ownership costs and support efforts in a big way. This approach also has some other advantages:

- ✔ The upfront investment is very low and transforms most client computing costs from fixed to variable (from capital to operating expense).
- ✔ It's quick to deploy and easy to scale incrementally.
- ✔ It's particularly attractive to companies that are running out of data center space.

Desktop as a Service (DaaS)

How can you deploy and manage these desktops? What is your window into this process? Recently a new class of services are being referred to *Desktop as a Service* or *DaaS* (not to be confused with Data as a Service, which may use the same acronym). DaaS removes a layer of complexity associated with deploying and managing VDI.

The provider takes all the virtualization technology infrastructure and unifies it with a management front end that enables your IT to provision these desktops and monitor resource usage. Of course, this idea works as well in a public cloud as it does in a private cloud.

Two players in this space are Desktone and Virtual Bridges.

Desktone

Desktone (www.desktone.com) offers what it calls the Desktone Virtual-D Platform, which is a unified desktop virtualization platform. It actually integrates discrete virtualization technology (application, network, and so on) and allows the whole thing to be managed from a single console.

The platform is two tiered:

- ✔ **Enterprise:** The enterprise manages the operating system, applications, and licensing.
- ✔ **Service provider:** The physical data center infrastructure is run by service providers (or enterprises acting as service providers), using a VDI model.

Desktone's offering is based on a private cloud that will be owned and run by service providers (IBM and Verizon are two examples). The approach is intended to treat the virtual desktop as PCs connected to a service provider that provides the "virtual container" for the desktops. In essence, the end customer is responsible for their own operating system and PC application licenses.

Desktone provides a virtual desktop grid — what it calls an *access fabric*. This fabric is a software service that manages desktop virtualization.

Virtual Bridges

Virtual Bridges (www.vbridges.com) was established in 2000 to create VDI on Linux servers. It offers Virtual Enterprise Remote Desktop Environment (VERDE), which is a desktop virtualization solution for Linux and Windows that use VDI.

It recently partnered with IBM and others to offer SMART, a business cloud computing strategy. This solution runs open standards-based email, word processing, spreadsheets, unified communication, social networking, and other software to any laptop, browser, or mobile device from a virtual desktop login on a Linux-based server configuration. The solutions combines VERDE with the Ubuntu desktop Linux OS from Canonical (www.canonical.com) and IBM's collaboration and productivity software.

What's the difference between desktop virtualization that runs in your data center and desktop virtualization that runs in a cloud? The technology is basically the same. However, the data center usually supports lots of *workloads* (lots of different applications with lots of different operating systems and middleware) with different requirements and much less automation. A cloud, on the other hand, is optimized for more specialized and fewer workloads and therefore is easier to automate. Chances are you won't run an application that only services 50 people in a cloud environment. Leave that for the data center.

Managing Desktops in the Cloud

From a management perspective, you should understand that cloud desktop virtualization doesn't remove the need for management at the desktop. Additionally, you may still need to manage laptops and PCs that can't be virtualized, and that task may still place a heavy demand on support.

In terms of managing desktops in the cloud, you need to monitor at least two *key performance indicators (KPIs)* regardless of the model you choose:

- ✔ **Annual support costs per device:** This metric is preferable to the total cost of ownership, which includes variable uncontrollable costs such as software licenses and device purchases.

- ✔ **Availability:** This metric, which measures uptime, should be close to 100 percent with virtualized cloud desktops.

You may monitor additional KPIs, depending on your level of maturity in terms of your current PC management strategy. Of course, companies are at different levels of maturity when it comes to managing desktops. At one end of the spectrum, client management is fragmented and reactive; organizations at the other end have automated client environment management to the point where PC applications are provisioned and patched automatically, and the PC environment is centrally controlled.

The reality for most organizations is that the client environment is managed quite separately from the data center, with a separate support staff. For efficiency reasons — and because the technology to enable it is improving fast — the management of the two domains will become more integrated in coming years — especially given this cloud model.

Watching four areas

Even if your desktops move to the cloud, you're still responsible for keeping track of your assets, as well as monitoring how your services are running.

Your provider may be allocating disk space and dividing up bandwidth. Because they're managing a large resource pool, they'll also no doubt be monitoring availability.

In fact, we believe you need to track at least five areas whatever your cloud model:

- ✔ **Asset management:** No matter what the client environment is (cellphone, BlackBerry, thin client, and so on), activities within that container need to be registered, monitored, and tracked; based on both the hardware itself, the software that runs on the platform, and how various groups use it.

- ✔ **Service monitoring:** Activities in this process area monitor what's happening at each client, as well as the tasks required to maintain the right level of service. The service desk (see Chapter 17) provides coordination for monitoring.

- ✔ **Change management:** Activities in this process area involve managing and implementing all changes in applications and hardware. Although you may often be working off a golden image, this is still important.

  A *golden image* means that every user will have the identical environment. If something goes wrong, an administrator simply gives that user a new copy of the same image so there is less management needed for each individual desktop user.

- ✔ **Security:** Activities in this process area involve securing the whole client domain against external threats and authenticating which users can get into which facilities.

- ✔ **Governance:** Cloud services need to be considered in connection with your governance strategy and your ability to comply with industry and government regulations (like Sarbanes-Oxley, Health Insurance Portability and Accountability Act, and Payment Card Industry Security Standards). For example, desktops in the cloud allow for all types of data to pass through and be stored. You need a plan to ensure continued compliance with regulations.

In the next few sections, we examine each of these in detail.

Managing assets

Desktop and device asset management help you select, buy, use, and maintain desktop hardware and software. What must you do to manage desktops and mobile devices thoroughly? Here's a list of necessary activities:

- ✔ **Establish a detailed hardware asset register.** A *register* is a database that itemizes hardware assets and records all the details. It lets you analyze hardware assets (including peripherals) and provides a foundation for many user services, including provisioning and security. It also may be fed with information by asset discovery software.

✔ **Establish a software register.** A software register tracks all the software elements of devices. It complements the hardware register and offers a foundation for better automated provisioning of software.

✔ **Control software licenses.** Even if you move your desktops to the cloud and have common implementations, you must manage the software licenses. Watching software licenses reduces costs and efforts; it also eliminates the risk that the company will be running more versions of software than it has paid for.

✔ **Manage device costs.** Often, companies have devices that are no longer used but that still require time and effort to maintain. By tracking device use, you can reduce redundancies and maintain hardware more efficiently.

Monitoring services

The support service is driven by the data center's trouble-ticketing system, which tracks a problem to its resolution and quickly identifies situations in which the data center applications are the cause of the problem. We talk a lot more about monitoring in Chapter 22.

Even if your desktops are running in the cloud, make sure that you can monitor the following:

✔ **Application monitoring:** Users are quick to blame IT when the performance of their applications is poor. Poor performance can have a multitude of causes, one of which is simply that the client device doesn't have enough power. Consequently, IT must be able to monitor client device performance based on actual application use.

✔ **Service-level maintenance:** Service levels should be applied both to hardware and applications running on client devices. If service levels aren't defined accurately, they can't be monitored effectively. Service-level maintenance becomes even more important as organizations virtualize the client environments.

✔ **Automated client backup:** An automated backup system reduces the risk of data loss and speeds recovery times when failures occur.

✔ **Remote management and maintenance:** Users may be spread around the country or the globe. Depending what your situation is and what your service provider is actually providing, find out who's managing both client related hardware and software and if this can be done remotely.

✔ **Client recovery:** Normally, this task involves restoring data from automated backups, but it also can involve reconfiguration or a software upgrade, depending on the diagnosis. Determine how this will be done.

✔ **Root-cause analysis:** If your desktops go down, you may want to call your service provider to see if something happened on their end. There may be some finger-pointing. On the other hand, many monitoring products place a software agent on the client device to capture the behavior of the hardware and software in real time. Simply knowing whether a failure is caused by hardware or software leads to faster recovery. The more information you can gather about CPU, memory, and application resource use, the easier it is to diagnose a problem.

Change management

Managing change means that you have to provide standardized processes for handling IT changes. Although cloud desktop virtualization may minimize the amount of change that occurs, change remains a fact of life across your organization.

You should meet these key requirements for handling change management:

✔ **Hardware provisioning:** Rapid deployment of devices minimizes the time needed to support staff changes. New staff members have to be provisioned just as quickly as those leaving the organization.

✔ **Software distribution and upgrade:** Being able to distribute changed software to devices across the organization is mandatory in tight financial times. Many companies create a standard desktop client environment that facilitates distributing and changing software.

✔ **Patch management:** *Patches* are software changes that fix bugs rather than upgrade functionality. When well automated, patch management minimizes the impact of patch implementation while reducing the risk associated with the bugs being fixed. Many such fixes address IT security problems.

✔ **Configuration management:** This process lets your company automate the configuration settings in a desktop software environment, making it easier to manage the client environment. Specifically, it manages which applications are loaded and may include IT security settings that provide or deny administrative capabilities. (See the following section.)

Security

Ensuring the security of every user access device in a company can be tough. We devote all of Chapter 15 to security in the cloud.

Here are some security approaches to safeguard your access devices:

✔ **Secure access control:** This approach may involve simple password protection, or it may involve more sophisticated (token-based or biometric) authentication. Secure access control reduces security breaches.

✔ **Identity management:** Identity management defines the user in a global context for the whole corporate network. It makes it possible to link users directly to applications or even application functions. This approach delivers networkwide security, associating permissions with roles or with individual users.

✔ **Integrated threat management:** Normally, you have to counter a variety of security threats through several security products, both on the client and in the data center:

• Virtual private networks secure remote communications lines for using virtualized desktops from home or from remote offices.

• Intruder-detection systems monitor network traffic to identify intruders.

• White-listing products limit which programs are allowed to run.

✔ **Automated security policy:** Ultimately, with the right processes and technology, you can manage some aspects of IT security to some degree via policy. Some products manage logging activity so that all network users' activities are logged, for example. Also, you can define policies within identity management software to designate who has the right to authorize access to particular services or applications.

Getting a Reality Check

We would be remiss if we didn't point out that not all PCs can be virtualized, much less moved to the cloud. The reality is that probably no more than 80 percent can be virtualized. Think about your organization.

You may find that about 50 percent of your organization uses the same sets of applications. These are the low-hanging fruit that could easily be virtualized in a cloud environment.

Maybe another 30 percent of your people use specialized programs: You might need to determine whether these programs could work in a cloud environment: Are there enough people using the applications? Can the application be shared on a server? Even if you discover that all these specialized apps can ultimately be virtualized, that still leaves about 20 percent of applications that don't fit the virtualization model at all.

Chapter 19

Service Oriented Architecture and the Cloud

In This Chapter

▶ Understanding service oriented architecture (SOA)

▶ Defining loose coupling

▶ Finding SOA components

▶ Pairing SOA and cloud services

▶ Benefiting from SOA and the cloud

A cloud has some key characteristics: elasticity, self-service provisioning, standards based interfaces, and pay as you go. This type of functionality has to be engineered into the software. To accomplish this type of engineering requires that the foundation for the cloud be well designed and well architected.

What about cloud architecture makes this approach possible? The fact is that the services and structure behind the cloud should be based on a modular architectural approach. A modular, component-based architecture enables flexibility and reuse. A *service oriented architecture (SOA)* is what lies beneath this flexibility. In this chapter, we provide an overview of what SOA is and how it enables the characteristics of the cloud.

Defining Service Oriented Architecture

SOA is much more than a technological approach and methodology for creating IT systems. It's also a *business* approach and methodology. Companies have used the principles of SOA to deepen the understanding between the business and IT and to help business adapt to change.

One of the key benefits of a service oriented approach is that software is designed to reflect best practices and business processes instead of making the business operate according to the rigid structure of a technical environment.

Combining the cloud and SOA

Cloud services benefit the business by taking the best practices and business process focus of SOA to the next level. These benefits apply to both cloud service providers and cloud service users. Cloud service providers need to architect solutions by using a service-oriented approach to deliver services with the expected levels of elasticity and scalability. Companies that architect and govern business processes with reusable service-oriented components can more easily identify which components can be successfully moved to public and private clouds.

A *service oriented architecture (SOA)* is a software architecture for building business applications that implement business processes or services through a set of loosely coupled, black-box components orchestrated to deliver a well-defined level of service.

This approach lets companies leverage existing assets and create new business services that are consistent, controlled, more easily changed, and more easily managed. SOA is a business approach to designing efficient IT systems that support reuse and give the businesses the flexibility to react quickly to opportunities and threats.

Characterizing SOA

The principal characteristics of SOA are described in more detail here:

- ✔ **SOA is a black-box component architecture.** The *black box* lets you reuse existing business applications; it simply adds a fairly simple adapter to them. You don't need to know every detail of what's inside each component; SOA hides the complexity whenever possible.

- ✔ **SOA components are loosely coupled.** Software components are *loosely coupled* if they're designed to interact in a standardized way that minimizes dependencies. One loosely coupled component passes data to another component and makes a request; the second component carries out the request and, if necessary, passes data back to the first. Each component offers a small range of simple services to other components.

A set of loosely coupled components does the same work that software components in tightly structured applications used to do, but with loose coupling you can combine and recombine the components in a bunch of ways. This makes a world of difference in the ability to make changes easily, accurately, and quickly. (See the next section for more information on loose coupling.)

✔ **SOA components are orchestrated to link through business processes to deliver a well-defined level of service.** SOA creates a simple arrangement of components that, together, deliver a very complex business service. Simultaneously, SOA must provide acceptable service levels. To that end, the components ensure a dependable service level. Service level is tied directly to the best practices of conducting business, commonly referred to as *business process management (BPM)* — BPM focuses on effective design of business process and SOA allows IT to align with business processes.

Loosening Up on Coupling

In traditional software architecture, various software components are often highly dependent on each other. These software component dependencies make the process of application change management time consuming and complex. A change made to one software component may impact lots of other dependent software components, and if you don't make all the right changes, your application (or related applications) may fail. One small change to an application can make its way through the whole application, wreaking havoc and leading to massive software code revision.

Loose coupling makes it simpler to put software components together and pull them apart. Because they aren't codependent, you can mix and match components with other component services as needed. This mix-and-match capability allows you to quickly create new and different applications from existing software services.

For example, if a credit card–checking service is loosely coupled from an ecommerce application and you need to change it, you simply replace the old one with the new one without touching any of the other applications that use the service.

An important aspect of loose coupling is that the component services and the *plumbing* (basic interaction instructions for the pieces) are separated so that the service itself has no code related to managing the computing environment. Because of this separation, components can come together and act as if they were a single, tightly coupled application.

If the notion of loose coupling sounds familiar to you, it should. It isn't unlike interchangeable parts that sparked the industrial revolution. For example, many of the early factories used the concept of interchangeable parts to keep their machines running. When a part failed, they simply replaced it with another one. Automobile manufacturers have also used this concept. For example, the same steering column is used in many different car models. Some models may modify it, but the basic steering column doesn't change. Because the steering column was designed to be used in different models, the power steering columns can be substituted for manual columns without alteration to the rest of the car. Most car manufacturers don't view the basic steering mechanism as a significant differentiator or source of innovation. Likewise, a data service or an email service are not necessarily differentiators, but they may be used to build services that can help companies do lots of different things.

Making SOA Happen

In this section we highlight some of the key components of a service oriented architecture.

You can find lots more information on SOA, including the basics, technical details, and real-life company experiences and best practices in another book written by our team, *Service Oriented Architecture For Dummies,* Second Edition (Wiley).

Figure 19-1 shows the main SOA components:

- ✔ The **Enterprise Service Bus (ESB)** makes sure that messages get passed back and forth between the components of an SOA implementation.

- ✔ The **SOA Registry and Repository** have important reference information about where the SOA business services are located.

- ✔ The **Business Process Orchestration Manager** provides the technology to connect people to people, people to processes, and processes to processes.

- ✔ The **Service Broker** connects services to services, which in the end enables business processes to flow.

- ✔ The **SOA Service Manager** makes sure that the technology underneath the SOA environment works in a consistent, predictable way.

Each component has a role to play, both independently and with each other. The goal is to create an environment where all these components work together to improve the business process flow.

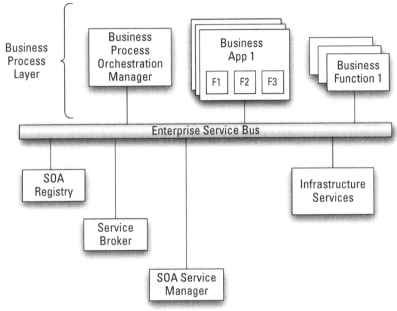

Figure 19-1:
Funda-
mentals of
SOA
components.

When all these component parts work together and sing the same tune, the result is dependable service levels. A finely tuned SOA helps guarantee service levels.

Catching the Enterprise Service Bus

In service oriented architectures, all the different pieces of software talk to each other by sending messages — a lot of messages. The messages are critical to delivering *end-to-end services* — delivery from the service provider to the service consumer. They must be delivered quickly, and their arrival must be guaranteed. If that doesn't happen, "end-to-end service" quickly becomes "lack of service."

To transport the messages between software components, SOAs typically use an ESB. The ESB is so important to SOA that some people think that you can't have a SOA without one. Other folks think that if you have an ESB, you have an SOA. Neither statement is accurate. You don't need an ESB to have an SOA, but you *do* need a way for the services to communicate with each other. The ESB is a reasonable, effective way to accomplish this goal.

The ESB is a collection of software components that manage messaging from one software component to another. A software component connects to the ESB and passes it a message by using a specified format along with the address of the software component that needs to receive the message. The ESB completes the job, getting the message from the sending component to the receiving component.

Telling your registry from your repository

The self-contained and reusable software components that you create to carry out your important business processes are called *business services*. Business services are often made up of a group of component services, some of which may also have additional component services. Each service provides a function.

Simply, here's the difference between the repository and the registry:

- **Repository:** Central reference point for all the components within the software development environment from which services are built

- **Registry:** Central reference point for definitions, rules, and descriptions associated with every service within an SOA environment

Registry

Information describing the function of each reusable component is recorded in the *SOA registry* — a type of electronic catalog. The SOA registry has two roles:

- **One rooted in the operational environment:** In the day-to-day working business computing environment, the SOA registry provides reference information about software components that are running or available for use. This information is of particular importance to the service broker — the software in a SOA framework that brings components together by using the rules associated with each component.

- **One rooted in the world of programmers and business analysts:** For programmers and business analysts, on the other hand, the SOA registry acts as a reference that helps them select components and then connect them to create composite applications that represent business processes. It also stores information about how each component connects to other components. In other words, the SOA registry documents the rules and descriptions associated with every given component.

The SOA registry is extremely important because it acts as the central reference point within a service oriented architecture. The SOA registry contains information *(metadata)* about all the components that the SOA supports. For that reason, it defines the domain of the architecture.

The SOA registry is where you store definitions and other information about your software components so developers, business analysts, and even your customers and business partners can find the services they need. Business services are *published* in a registry to make them easier to find and use.

The idea of *publishing* Web services is critical to SOA. You can only reuse services that are available for reuse, which means they have to be published first.

Repository

Comparatively, the repository is like a central reference point within the software development environment. It stores the source code and the linking information used to build all the programs that run in the operational environment. The SOA repository feeds the service oriented architecture with changes and new components, working within the operational environment. It is the counterpart of the registry within the development environment.

Cataloging services

It isn't enough to assemble all the key components and create a central reference point for your business services. You need to plan for managing those services; otherwise, your SOA implementation won't meet your expectations. Service catalogs provide a foundation for good service management.

If you want to create, use, change, or manage a service, then you need access to documentation about that service. These services may include business services that represent a company's important business processes and they may include a range of IT services such as software services, networking services, communications services, or data services.

Many organizations are creating catalogs of business and IT services. These catalogs help companies standardize the approach to delivering and managing services across all units. Some organizations have merged catalogs of different types of services to improve their ability to manage and govern *all* the services delivered to the business.

A service catalog should be dynamic to keep pace with the changing needs of the business. A sample of the information included in the service catalog follows:

- Whom to contact about a service
- Who has authority to change the service
- Which critical applications are related to the service
- Outages or other incidents related to the service

✔ Information about the relationships among services

✔ Documentation of all agreements between IT and the customer or user of the service

A banking institution's service catalog, for example, may have information about its online banking service, the key performance indicators — measurement indicating the effectiveness of a process — for that service, and the service level agreements between IT and the online banking business. If an outage occurs, the bank's IT service management team can read the service catalog to locate the root cause of problems with the service.

Understanding Services in the Cloud

When you have some of the background on what it means to take a service-oriented approach to architecting technology systems, you can begin to see the relationship between SOA and cloud computing. Services are important for cloud computing from both an infrastructure and an application perspective.

Service orientation permeates the cloud itself and the cloud serves as an environment that can host other services (either at technical or business levels). What does this mean?

✔ On the one hand, cloud providers have built the cloud infrastructure on well-designed services with clearly defined black-box interfaces. These black-box services (think capacity, for example) allow the cloud to scale. The cloud infrastructure itself is service oriented.

✔ On the other hand, companies building applications designed for the cloud tend to build them out as services; this makes it easier for customers and partners to use them. For example, Software as a Service providers need an ecosystem of partners that provides either complementary components or full applications that are important to sustaining and growing their businesses. A service oriented architecture is the only way partners can economically build on these platforms.

In Part III of this book, we introduce you to the various elements of the cloud and describe the different cloud models — *Infrastructure as a Service (IaaS)*, *Platform as a Service (PaaS)*, and *Software as a Service (SaaS)*. We illustrate how each of these models exhibits some important characteristics, like elasticity and self-service provisioning.

Look at each of these models again so that you can understand why smart cloud providers are using a services approach.

Infrastructure as a Service (IaaS)

The Infrastructure as a Service layer offers storage and compute resources that developers and IT organizations can use to deliver custom business solutions. A cloud provider wants the provisioning capability associated with the IaaS to be designed as a modular service with published interfaces so it can be used for many different situations.

Say you have a group of applications that you want to run in a public cloud because you want capacity on demand. You sign up with an IaaS provider. Via your Web browser, you can buy this capacity and start running your applications on the service. The service is provisioning the capacity. While you're running the application, the service provisions hardware to run it and then de-provisions the virtualized servers when you're done.

As a user of this capacity provisioning service, you don't need to know how the provider is making the service happen; it is a black box to you. If the cloud weren't service oriented, you'd have to figure out how to provision your application to the environment. With the cloud, you can use a single provisioning service.

Platform as a Service (PaaS)

The Platform as a Service layer offers development environments that IT organizations can use to create cloud-ready business applications. This is offered as a set of black-box services that lets developers build applications on top of the compute infrastructure. This might include developer tools that are offered as a service to build services, or even data access and database services, or even billing services.

In these situations, the principles of SOA (such as loose coupling and reusability) have been applied to IT infrastructure components that are delivered as cloud services to PaaS users. Developers in your organization may locate the platform services they need by referencing a service catalog.

Software as a Service (SaaS)

With Software as a Service, the provider hosts the software for you so you don't need to install it, manage it, or buy hardware for it. All you have to do is connect to it and use it.

For example, you might make use of CRM as a service or accounting as a service. Many of these providers have created their services in a modular way to enable scalability (because you're using these services along with perhaps thousands of other clients). A services-oriented approach allows the provider, for example, to swap out functionality easily.

Don't confuse SOA with SaaS. SOA is software designed as a service; SaaS is software managed and distributed as a service.

In all these models, companies will use a set of well-defined services that they can access through interfaces. Companies can leverage these services in many different ways depending on what problems they are trying to solve.

Are all cloud providers totally committed to a SOA? Probably not. But any smart cloud provider wants to make sure that it can change and modify its offering to solve your problems. Service orientation is the most pragmatic way to achieve that goal.

Serving the Business with SOA and Cloud Computing

Bringing IT and the business together to find ways to use technology to serve the needs of the business is a core concept for both service oriented architecture and cloud computing. SOA is a business and technical approach used to architect your company's business process as reusable, inter-changeable, black-box software components. Cloud computing is about delivering IT infrastructure (not just software, but hardware, storage, and IT services too) as efficient and reusable services according to the needs of the business.

Concepts like reusability and loose coupling that are central to SOA are also integral to the scalability of cloud services. The use of reusable and loosely coupled components makes scalability and elasticity a reality for cloud service providers. And, consider what might happen in the not-too-distant future. Say you have built a private cloud that deals with some of your company's applications and data, but you're using a public cloud for some other applications.

You don't want these applications to be stove piped. They need to act together. If there are well-defined interfaces that enable you to share data, for example, between these applications (no matter where they are) you will be well served. If you are working with vendors where the platform has lots of dependencies that will lock you in, you will not be able to gain the business advantages you expect.

Companies benefit from SOA and the cloud because both of these approaches place a priority on understanding what the business needs, when it needs it, and how efficiently and cost effectively the business can be served.

Chapter 20

Managing the Cloud Environment

. . . .

In This Chapter

▶ Grasping the complexities of managing services in the cloud

▶ Helping customers fix problems

▶ Determining the root cause

▶ Tracking service levels

. . . .

*W*hen you deploy applications on your own premises, you can control your resources and you (hopefully) know who's responsible for maintaining the integrity of the overall environment. When you move some of your computing to a cloud environment, the way you think about managing changes dramatically.

You need to find the right balance between the oversight you must provide to internal customers and the way you monitor your cloud provider. We expect that many companies will have a combination of on-premise data centers combined with some cloud-based services. Therefore, you have to juggle a variety of management approaches.

Whatever path you choose, one thing is clear: You do not relinquish authority at the door. You need a consistent view across both on-premise and cloud-based environments. You need to make sure that you understand how the provider is going to support what you're doing in the cloud, whether it's computing capability, building your own applications, or using another provider's applications.

When you begin to leverage cloud services, you must have a clear understanding of how that resource will be managed by that provider. The company you have partnered with has to manage the underlying infrastructure that you're using (along with its multitude of other customers). This includes the physical servers, networks, and storage, as well as any virtual servers. Someone also has to manage the databases and applications that are running on top of this infrastructure. That's a lot of managing — and for the most part, you're not in control.

The cloud is a complex environment and many parties may be part of the cloud service delivery model. These parties may include the cloud infrastructure provider, a SaaS provider, and your own set of developers and delivery team.

Managing this hybrid environment, in some ways, is in its infancy. Therefore, it's important to have a good understanding of the issues and questions you should present to your cloud partners before starting your migration.

Managing the Cloud

Chapter 2 introduces a simple model of cloud computing that has three models:

- ✓ Infrastructure as a Service
- ✓ Platform as a Service
- ✓ Software as a Service

All are surrounded by a management layer, as you can see in Figure 20-1.

We mention that the management layer is where life in the cloud can get very complicated. It's simple enough to describe how to use some kind of cloud computing service, but you also have to integrate cloud oversight and management into the company's IT operations; that isn't necessarily a simple thing to do.

The point is that when you look at managing the cloud environment, you need to consider this from the point of view of the service provider(s) and the end customer.

There are many dimensions involved in managing a cloud. If you're a service provider, for example, you have to think about the different types of customers that will be using the cloud. One might be using the cloud as a commercial platform while another might be a single business user. Obviously, the customer using the cloud for commercial uses needs to understand the provider's management approach; the business user also has to understand the provider's approach.

The following sections look at what this means.

The service provider

Many types of cloud service providers are required to provide management services. The cloud provider has to make sure that it has a well-designed management infrastructure so that all of its services operate efficiently and safely. Unlike a traditional data center, the cloud service provider has to manage both virtual as well as physical components. The provider has to make sure that each customer's data is well protected and supported. When the provider has done a good job, you may be unaware of it. This is something the customer rarely ever sees.

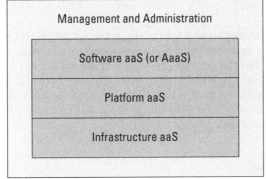

Figure 20-1:
Various
cloud
services
layers.

Managing based on services

Management service types depend on the type of cloud service the vendor provides. For example:

- ✔ A vendor providing cheap storage may not necessarily have a sophisticated set of management services.

- ✔ Another provider might have different levels of customer support and may act more like an outsourced service provider.

Managing several cloud providers

You may end up working with several different cloud providers — one for a Software as a Service (SaaS) application and another for Infrastructure as a Service (IaaS), for instance. Although each vendor will have its own management services, your organization is responsible for oversight.

Here's a simple scenario that drives home this point: Assume you have contracted with a SaaS service to manage your sales leads. This company doesn't have its own cloud center, so they contract an IaaS provider. When something goes wrong, it may be tough to figure out the source. If you're the customer using the SaaS application, you'll call your provider. How sophisticated is their service management system? Can they quickly trace the cause of the problem?

It may be harder than it seems. For example, the problem might occur because the platform provider just upgraded to a new version of an operating system and forgot to upgrade a script or a component. The problem may be a power outage.

Many companies today are using emerging cloud providers that offer very inexpensive, or even free, services. While this can dramatically improve your bottom line, it may also cause problems. What happens when your free service quits working? Some free (or nearly so) services provide online service status updates, but many do not.

Many of these issues related to service levels and oversight in the cloud are a function of the relative immaturity of the cloud market itself. It may be hard to assess how sophisticated the service management environment of a specific cloud provider is. In fact, you'll likely sign up with a SaaS provider without knowing anything about the way it manages its own environment. However, this may be one of the most important questions to ask — especially if you're dependent on the application.

Customers

If you're a business manager using a cloud provider, you need visibility into both the computing infrastructure and the applications you're using in the cloud. You need to understand some key factors so you can manage both your cloud-based services as well as your own data center. (Read more about this topic in the "Gaining Visibility" section later in this chapter.)

From an overall management perspective, you need to at least be able to do what's described in the following sections.

Provision resources in the cloud

If you're using a public or private cloud, you need a mechanism that enables you to provision new resources when you need them. Can this be automated, or does someone have to manually do it? This administrative function includes setting up your cloud environment as well as building and deploying applications in the cloud. This administrative process will be needed regardless of whether you're using a public or a private cloud.

It is also true, in a slightly different way, in the SaaS environment. The service provider manages the performance levels of the overall environment that might require the addition of servers, increasing processing power, and so on in a compute environment. It may include provisioning a database or mapping your data to your new cloud application.

Deal with incidents and problems

When your organization begins adopting some cloud computing capabilities, you must have a plan to handle problems such as unexpected outages. Although the cloud computing vendor will have its own infrastructure and tools for this, you have to be proactive too. Know how your provider handles changes to its environment.

Depending on how critical the cloud service is to your business, you have different levels of support. For example, if you're a large corporation using a cloud service for all your company's email services, you probably want to establish a plan with your provider for direct support to handle problems.

Work with your cloud provider if you're dependent on these services to run your business. You need to have a process for handling incidents and problems. You also need to explain to your management what happens if and when a service fails.

Monitor and measure

Of course, you want to make sure that you can see the performance level of the services in the cloud. This monitoring should be incorporated into your overall capacity plan for your company.

You really need these things overall:

- ✔ A dashboard that provides you with insights across the applications and services that are running in your data center and those that are running in a cloud.
- ✔ A service level agreement across your own services and those provided by cloud providers to get a true picture of the service you are providing to your company.

Bill and other services

All cloud providers will bill your company based on one of the following:

- ✔ How many users are supported
- ✔ How much capacity you use
- ✔ How many services you leverage

As with any service you purchase, it is important that you have oversight. You should be able to "see into" your billing, especially if you're automatically provisioning capacity. Most service providers will provide customers with an application that will include information about what resources they are being charged for. If the service provider can't provide this accounting information, something is wrong.

Hybrid environments

Your company will probably have a *hybrid* environment: a traditional data center, a private cloud, and some cloud services. That hybrid is part of what makes cloud management so complex. They may use virtualized servers as well as dedicated physical servers.

Chapter 17 defines *virtualization* as using computer resources to imitate other computer resources or even whole computers. The term is very broad and can include virtualizing everything from memory to software, but we keep it simple for right now.

This hybrid environment requires management of both the virtual servers and the physical infrastructure beneath. And, because there is a good chance that most enterprises won't move *all* of their computing resources to the cloud, they have to be concerned with how this hybrid environment gets managed. Two important capabilities need to be in place to manage this hybrid world: the service catalog and the Configuration Management Database (CMBD).

The service catalog

One of the important factors in managing a cloud is to ensure a way to manage IT assets and activities. Enter the service catalog (defined as part of the *Information Technology Infrastructure Library [ITIL]* Service Design best practice). The catalog is a component list that makes up internal and external services that are available to an organization.

A typical service catalog includes such items as the definition of the service, its service level, who is entitled to use that service, and what components are required to execute that service. Clearly, a service catalog is required for organizations to manage services in a hybrid world — across data centers, private and public clouds, as well as hosted environments. The service catalog is an essential tool for both cloud providers and customers that need a view into the assets they are using. Many cloud providers package a service catalog to help their customers work between their cloud and external resources.

The Configuration Management Database (CMDB)

To understand what services are being managed across your various computing environments, you should keep track of changes. That is the role of the *Configuration Management Database (CMDB)*. For example, many cloud environments use extensive virtualization to add efficiency. Virtualization enables the abstraction of hardware assets so that these assets can be used for multiple purposes. These varied uses increase the difficulty of tracking changes to these resources. However, it's important for the cloud provider (even if that's you in your private cloud) to track these assets and understand what's been changed and what state that service is in.

The CMDB will evolve into an important capability because it ensures that cloud services don't fail because of an inadvertent configuration change.

Often, when vendors talk about managing the cloud, they're only talking about how you manage resources over a virtualized infrastructure — about a self-service portal that lets you provision resources and some sort of automated resource allocation. They're not talking about fixing problems, providing service level agreements, or managing security.

Building Up Support Desks

One of the fundamental truths of managing services is that when you do it well, the service management team is like the wizard behind the curtain in the Land of Oz. If your email never goes down and your technical equipment never fails, you don't go looking behind the curtain to understand what went wrong.

The reality is that services *do* fail and errors *do* occur — and when they do, customers (or service users) need questions answered and problems resolved. Whatever a problem is, it must be reported, diagnosed, evaluated, and fixed quickly. One critical component of this equation is the service desk. If your cloud provider doesn't have one, you need to ask, "Why not?"

For many businesses, the service desk is the first port of call when there is an incident or a problem. Imagine the lost productivity and revenue (and the all-around chaos) that would occur in the cloud if your provider couldn't manage service delivery and deal with problems effectively. The service desk does this.

Service desk goals

A service desk provides a single point of contact for IT users and customers to report any issues they may have with the service. It generally has three goals:

✓ **Problem resolution:** First and foremost, the desk is there to help resolve issues as quickly as possible. This task involves

 • Recognizing and resolving relatively simple issues

 • Prioritizing problems that may have a greater impact

An outage in the cloud that provides corporate email services, for example, may take higher priority than a free service to consumers.

✔ **Service restoration:** The desk works to restore service as quickly as possible to maintain service level agreements (which require a lot of negotiation). Therefore, a key service desk role is ensuring that the agreements are enforced to the best of the company's ability, which means tracking and monitoring service levels.

✔ **System support:** The service desk provides system support, which includes dealing with any server incidents (and may also mean dealing with issues such as change and configuration management).

Varying support levels

Your own data center will obviously provide a service desk, but does your cloud provider offer service support? It should.

However, providers offer different levels of support:

✔ Basic support might mean a two-day response time via a Web-based portal where you ask your question.

✔ It might also simply mean access to a Web-based community.

✔ A premium package may get you a two-hour response time, but no guarantees about service levels.

✔ Some providers state that they will provide a one-hour response time for "urgent" issues, but don't specify what *urgent* actually means.

Keep this in mind: If you can't find any support information on a cloud provider's Web site, there is a good chance that you won't get any.

Examining support services

Although cloud management is still evolving, some cloud providers have a service desk in place to support customers. Many service desks deal with issues beyond incident and problem reporting, such as change management, customization, and so on. A service desk can provide many services. What about your cloud provider?

Depending on the level of service required for a cloud service, you might need to ask about some of these services.

Communication via multiple channels

Does your provider support a wide variety of communication styles, including phone, email, online forms, and even mobile communications?

This communication is a two-way street: People can use the channels to report issues, and the provider can use the channels to notify customers about the status and resolution of issues. This means that you might receive proactive communications from your provider if there is a problem. Or, you could receive notification when problems will be fixed.

Incident and problem management

The service desk should support the assessment, prioritization, resolution, notification, and reporting of small incidents or major problems. An *incident* becomes a *problem* when it happens more than a few times.

Management includes recording, routing, and resolving an issue; notifying interested parties of the status of the issue; and reporting on the issue. Although some of these might seem like remote possibilities, these types of problems do happen and often cause the most serious outages. Ask your cloud provider how they deal with the following issues:

- ✔ **Configuration management:** Someone made an error while changing a configuration.
- ✔ **Network:** The network gets overloaded.
- ✔ **Database:** A database table needs to be optimized.
- ✔ **System management:** A server's processors failed and the failover didn't work.
- ✔ **IT security:** A denial-of-service attack is in progress.
- ✔ **Application:** A program has a bug.

When you decide to go with a cloud provider, make sure that the proper level of support is there for you.

Change management

Suppose you want to customize your application or need some other type of support. The service desk should support the management of change requests, including information about how system parts interact. Often, the provider will include some support for customization in the contract. This might consist of one-on-one interactions with someone on the cloud staff. You need to find out.

Knowledge base

If service desk personnel don't have the right information to do their jobs, their jobs won't get done well. Knowledge management ensures that people get the information they need to do their jobs correctly. Service management systems often link to a database for past incidents and how they were resolved; this database speeds incident resolution.

Google this

Google provides an application status dashboard called the Google Apps Status Dashboard (google.com/appsstatus#). Customers can use this Status Dashboard to check on current Google services such as email, calendar, chat functions, word processing, spreadsheets and presentation software, and video. The dashboard shows the status of each of these applications, by day. If a problem occurs, information about that problem is on the dashboard. Overall service metrics (such as the downtime or disruption for each application type by month) aren't presented. However, in this case, you get what you pay for (which is nothing, in the case of many of these free services).

Configuration management

The desk should support mapping resources to the business processes that they support. Configuration management often entails a Configuration Management Database (CMDB) or some other kind of data store for holding all the cloud data center assets.

Gaining Visibility

At a minimum, you need to be able to see into these arenas in the cloud:

- ✔ Security
- ✔ Performance
- ✔ Service availability

Your dashboard should give visibility into those services that you are using on a regular basis. Ideally, you want a dashboard that gives you uniform visibility across your own resources and those of your cloud and hosting providers.

You should track security, performance levels, and service availability, all of which are discussed.

Monitoring securitySecurity is important whether you're consuming IaaS (Infrastructure as a Service), PaaS (Platform as a Service), or SaaS (Software as a Service), cloud services. To monitor security, you need to

- ✔ Scan networks
- ✔ Scan operating systems

✔ Scan applications

✔ Perform some sort of testing

For example, at the IaaS level, you need to validate appropriate levels of network, operating system, and middleware security to prevent intrusion and denial-of-service attacks. Please refer to Chapter 15 for more information on managing security in the cloud.

Ensuring adequate performance levels

Make sure that the cloud's performance doesn't go below the agreed-upon service level. To see into this aspect, you might use a tool that tests for

✔ Bandwidth

✔ Connectivity

✔ Scalability

✔ Quality of end-user experience across your cloud services

Monitoring service availability

You need a tool that can help you determine the availability of your services. You can use this tool to monitor whether your cloud network is up or down and if your provider is meeting its service level agreements. (See the next section for more on SLAs.)

Tracking Service Level Agreements

A *service level agreement (SLA)* is a contractual obligation between you and your cloud provider. Negotiating SLAs is often a dance between IT and the provider.

Some service levels are nonnegotiable, such as a mission-critical application. By nonnegotiable we mean that if that application needs to be available except for one hour per month, you can't agree to a compromise. If that's the case and the provider can't meet the service level, you should reconsider the cloud option. Other SLAs have more wiggle room.

IT and the service provider must work together to establish these SLAs. Typical SLAs include the following:

- ✔ Response times (possibly varying by transaction)
- ✔ Availability on any given day
- ✔ Overall uptime target
- ✔ Agreed-on response times and procedures in the event a service goes down

The agreement theoretically gives you some assurance that the provider will meet certain service levels.

But, buyer beware! You need to determine the following:

- ✔ **Downtime:** Depending on how critical your applications running in a cloud are, you will need a certain level of availability. Is 99.9 percent enough for you? Or, do you require five nines? How does the provider plan to ensure that it will meet its SLA? What failover and disaster recovery mechanisms does the provider have in place? Are you comfortable with them?

  You need to read the fine print. Does the SLA include planned maintenance, or is that separate? If so, how does planned maintenance affect you?

- ✔ **How the lines of responsibility are drawn:** You don't want to be in a situation where the SaaS provider is pointing a finger at the infrastructure provider, saying it wasn't their fault.

- ✔ **Cost of downtime:** What does it mean to your operations if the cloud is down? Service providers might compensate simply based on the number of hours systems are down. What about the cost to your business?

- ✔ **Past incidents:** Has your provider struggled with excessive downtime in the past? Check the record. Also look at service desk metrics, including

    - **Time to identify problem:** Did a problem exist for a long time before it was reported? Is performance varying widely without warning? If this is true, it means that the monitoring system isn't performing well and should be reviewed.

    - **Time to diagnose:** Time between an event report and the identification of the cause of the problem.

    - **Time to fix:** Time between diagnosis and system repair or resumption of service.

Ideally, you can see the operations of your service provider.

The SLA information you should capture from your provider is part of the overall *key performance indicators (KPIs)* for your company.

Part V
Planning for the Cloud

The 5th Wave   By Rich Tennant

Now maybe these folks got a decent disaster recovery plan and maybe they don't...

DANGER
WILD RHINOCEROS

In this part . . .

There's more to cloud computing than technology. Planning is a critical part of any cloud computing endeavor. In this part, we look at economics and suggest some ways of starting your cloud journey.

Chapter 21

Banking on Cloud Economics

- -

In This Chapter

▶ Exploring the allure of the cloud

▶ Discovering the economics of the data center

▶ Checking out some interesting ratios

- -

*W*hen company management begins thinking about implementing a cloud, the first thing they think about is the economic impact. In other words, if somehow I can get rid of my data center and move to a cloud, all my financial problems are over! Like everything else in life, it isn't that simple.

Many issues come into perspective when you're evaluating the economics of the cloud:

✔ The data center itself isn't static; it changes constantly.

✔ Not every workload is more economical in the cloud.

✔ Emerging technologies make some decisions more complicated.

In this chapter, we discuss the cloud from an economic perspective.

$eeing the Cloud's Allure

Cloud computing capabilities aren't easily replicated in the traditional data center. Cloud computing can easily handle the following types of situations:

✔ Your organization is ramping up for a new but short-term initiative and you temporarily need some extra CPU capacity and extra storage.

✔ You're a startup and want to create an online presence without spending money on hardware or software, so you use a cloud-based platform to get started.

✔ You decide that running sales automation is much simpler with a Software as a Service solution. (See Chapter 12 for more about Software as a Service.)

✔ You're changing your email system and decide that selecting a massively scaled application service in the cloud makes sense.

In the next few sections, we take a look at each of these scenarios from an economic perspective. We examine the economic justification for each of these in the context of the data center.

Filling the need for capacity

Some pragmatic workloads fit perfectly into the Infrastructure as a Service (IaaS) model. Include basic computing services to support unexpected workloads or test and development requirements. Economically, organizations can access what they need right away, without having to buy new hardware or go through the long process of manual provisioning.

What does this mean in practical terms?

✔ **Software evaluation:** Testing new software is both a cumbersome and long-lived process. Typically developers need to acquire servers and specialized development software. While this is a necessary process, it doesn't add to the bottom line of revenue. It is overhead. Therefore, offloading is likely to be inexpensive because it's fairly infrequent.

✔ **System testing:** Similar to software evaluation, resources are required for a relatively short time. Despite that, testers typically want to own their own resources, which isn't cost effective. In addition, if someone is testing a fast-growing workload, they have to spend massive amounts of money to achieve the same thing that they can via a service for a fraction of the cost.

✔ **Seasonal or peak loading:** Some companies are already using IaaS for the unexpected or planned high-load periods. The flexibility of using IaaS means that the company doesn't have to overinvest in hardware. These companies must be able to adapt to higher loads to protect their companies.

Getting the work done without capital investment

Only a few opportunities to take advantage of PaaS are tactical. Some PaaS operations are doing little more than providing an open-source Internet software stack and development environment; therefore, migrating to such an environment might be possible without much disruption.

If the developers have enough experience, they can use this free resource to develop applications with a PaaS approach. This saves a lot of money for experienced teams.

Organizations may decide to use a platform to create software for a special project between collaborators that will go away when the project is finished. Some organizations simply want to get started without additional capital expenses. However, in large organizations, there are usually multiple development environments, and moving strategic parts of the development environment into the cloud is likely to be a complex decision rather than a tactical one.

In this situation, organizations have to make a decision by looking at both initial costs and long-term support. A pure open-source PaaS provides great economic value, but in the long run other costs appear (in terms of development and support).

Selecting a SaaS for common applications

The ease with which SaaS offerings can be adopted varies. If the application is fairly independent of the overall applications and information environment of the company, SaaS is a tactical and pragmatic approach. And because many of the SaaS vendors publish their interfaces, some applications can be used in conjunction with SaaS offerings. Also, SaaS has enormous benefit for organizations that don't want to support their own hardware and support environment.

Selecting the massively scaled application

Some of the earliest cloud adopters are large companies that want to take a massively scaled application (such as email) and put it into a cloud. Companies are finding that a more cost-effective approach. In essence, this is the type of application of the cloud where the economics can't be matched by the data center. When applications support this type of massively scaled infrastructure, the cloud will often win out. For more about massive scaling, see Chapter 13.

When it's not black and white

Not all situations are clear cut. Accurately forecasting the economics of the cloud versus the data center is complicated. The problem for many organizations will be that they do not have an accurate model of data center costs that allows them to consider cloud propositions on an apples-to-apples basis.

Creating an Economic Model of the Data Center

It's hard for most organizations to accurately predict the actual costs of running any given application in the data center. A particular server may be used to support several different applications. How do you accurately judge how much of your personnel resources are dedicated to a single application? While there may be a particular month when your staff is updating one application, in another month, those same staff members may be troubleshooting another application. In some organizations, there may have been attempts to tie computing costs to specific departments, but if so, the model is likely to have been very rough.

Consider, as a simple example, the use of email. Some departments are very heavy users, whereas others barely touch it at all. Pockets *within* a single department may be heavy users. Although technically you can monitor individual use, doing so would require more overhead than it's worth.

If you want to have a rational economic approach to cloud adoption, unfortunately you'll have to analyze IT costs down to that kind of level.

The simple fact is that the cloud won't necessarily be less expensive and it won't necessarily provide the same level of service as your data center. Your own data center may have a service level agreement with a 99.999 percent uptime record. Will your cloud provider offer that same level of service? Probably not. You have to weigh how critical that level of predictable uptime is to your internal customers.

Listing application costs

In creating an economic model of an application, determine all the costs in a way that allows you to do a fair comparison. Here is a fairly comprehensive list of the possible costs, with notes:

- ✓ **Server costs (A):** With this and all other hardware components, you're specifically interested in the total annual cost of ownership, which normally consists of the cost of hardware support plus some amortization cost for the purchase of the hardware.

- ✓ **Storage costs (B):** In situations where a *storage area network (SAN)* or *network attached store (NAS)* is used for an application, a proportional cost over the whole SAN or NAS needs to be determined, including management and support cost for the hardware.

- ✓ **Network costs (C):** This needs to be carefully considered because the fact that an application moves into the cloud does not necessarily mean that all the network traffic it generates disappears. For example, data may need to be pulled from the application's database to be added to a data warehouse. Alternatively, when Web applications are moved into the cloud, corporate Internet bandwidth requirements may be reduced. Clearly, the ability to access external applications requires substantial bandwidth.

✔ **Backup and archive costs (D):** The actual savings on backup costs depends on what the backup strategy will be when the application moves into the cloud. The same is true of archiving. Will all backup be done in the cloud? Will your organization still be required to back up a percentage of critical data?

✔ **Disaster recovery costs (E):** In theory, the cloud service will have its own disaster recovery capabilities, so there may be a consequential savings on disaster recovery. However, you need to clearly understand what your cloud provider's disaster recovery capability is. Not all cloud providers have the same definition of disaster recovery. IT management must determine the level of support the cloud provider will offer.

✔ **Data center infrastructure costs (F):** A whole series of costs including electricity, floor space, cooling, building maintenance, and so on can't easily be attributed to individual applications, but can usually be assigned on the basis of the floor space that the hardware running the application occupies. For that reason, try to calculate a floor space factor for every application.

For example, if your data center is only 40 percent full, the economics of putting lots of additional capacity into the cloud is not financially viable. However, if your data center is 90 percent full and has been expanding at 10 percent a year, you'll run out of data center next year. At that point, you may have to build a data center that could cost as much as $5 million. The cloud will be a much more economical choice.

✔ **Platform costs (G):** Some applications only run in specific operating environments — Windows, Linux, HP-UX, IBM zOS, and so on. The annual maintenance costs for the application operating environment need to be known and calculated as part of the overall costs.

✔ **Software maintenance costs (package software) (H):** Normally this cost element is simple because it comes down to the software's annual maintenance cost. However, it may be complicated if the software license is tied to processor pricing. The situation could be further complicated if the specific software license is part of a bundled deal.

✔ **Software maintenance costs (in-house software) (I):** Such costs exist for all in-house software, but may not be broken out at an application level. For example, database licenses used across many different applications may be calculated at a corporate level. It may be necessary to allocate these database cost at a per-application level. There may also be these kinds of costs for packaged software if in-house components have been added or if integration components have been built to connect this application to other applications.

✔ **Help desk support costs (J):** It's necessary to analyze all help desk calls at an application level to determine the contribution of an application (if any) to help desk activity. The support costs for some applications may be anomalous and may disappear with the movement into the cloud. Some applications require more support than others. Understanding the different support requirements is key to making the right decision on the cloud.

✔ **Operational support personnel costs (K):** There is a whole set of day-to-day operational costs associated with running any application. Some are general costs that apply to every application, including staff support for everything from storage and archiving, to patch management and networks and security. Some support tasks, however, may be particular to a given application, such as database tuning and performance management.

✔ **Infrastructure software costs (L):** A whole set of infrastructure management software is in use in any installation, and it has an associated cost. For example, management software is typically used for many different applications and can't easily be divided across specific applications.

We now present a simple formula that states the annual data center cost of application ownership:

$$A + B + C + D + E + F + G + H + I + J + K + L$$

We refer to this cost as the *Total Cost of Application Ownership (TCAO)*.

To be thorough, you should calculate this figure for every application and make sure that the overall total for all applications reconciles with the actual data center costs as recorded in the company accounts. If there is any discrepancy, the model needs to be adjusted accordingly.

Recovering costs

It would be pleasant if you could simply compare the Total Cost of Application Ownership to the cost of running the application in the cloud and, if the cloud costs were less, schedule its move to the cloud. Unfortunately, you must also be concerned whether the application costs are actually recoverable, or how much of the costs are actually recoverable. Most of the factors we mention in the preceding section need to be considered in this regard. The following are worth noting:

✔ **Server costs:** If an application is relatively small, running in a virtual server, or perhaps only running occasionally, it's unlikely that moving it to the cloud will result in any server hardware savings.

✔ **Storage costs:** Similarly, if very little storage is consumed by the application, there may be no reduction in SAN or SAN costs.

✔ **Network costs:** Unless the amount of network capacity or Internet bandwidth saved is large, it will probably be negligible.

✔ **Data center infrastructure costs:** The floor space in the data center will not be reduced by the removal of a few servers and it may make little difference to cooling costs. There usually needs to be quite a significant change in order to bring down these costs.

✔ **Platform costs:** There may be a global license for platforms, especially where open source is used. Thus, the removal of an individual application may result in no cost reduction. Is some situations you need to maintain the licenses for technologies such as middleware when you move to the cloud (because most companies end up having a hybrid).

✔ **Software maintenance costs (package software):** This cost may be difficult to calculate if the software license is tied to processor pricing and the situation could be further complicated if the specific software license is part of a bundled deal or a global usage deal.

✔ **Operational support personnel costs:** Savings only occur here if there's a possibility of saving a whole person or delaying the recruitment of another person.

✔ **Infrastructure software costs:** Infrastructure management software costs may not come down with the movement of a few workloads into the cloud.

On a per-application basis, you need to adjust costs to allow for factors like these.

Adjusting the Economic Model even Further

A number of other considerations may alter the economics of cloud migration. All of them are strategic in nature. Amend the economic model to accommodate them.

Private cloud and allocation costs

In most cases, picking up an application and moving it to the cloud isn't simple. Most likely there will be some configuration work and some testing done first. In addition, that application may not be well designed for the highly distributed nature of the cloud environment in its current form and it may need to be rewritten. This is another cost that needs to be taken into consideration when deciding whether to move an application into the cloud.

While you might assume that all applications can move to the cloud, it isn't true. Don't look at the TCAO as a black-and-white situation. For those applications and those workloads that *are* appropriate for the cloud, this TCAO is ideal. However, in the real world you have to split the economic analysis that takes into account those workloads that must remain in the data center.

We discuss the private cloud in Chapter 9 and note that one of its primary functions is to allow the IT department to transform a data center into a more elastic and self-service environment.

The same cost factors apply where there's a private cloud, but how the IT department assesses the costs of the private cloud is a matter of policy. The private cloud may be built as a staging area for moving applications to the cloud, or as a way to move workloads to a more efficient, automated environment. Many companies will leverage their existing hardware, software, and networking assets as the foundation for a private cloud.

From a policy perspective, companies shouldn't simply take an action because it seems cheaper. They need base policy on what must stay in the traditional data center and why (for example, privacy and complexity and singularity of the workload). They then must have a policy that states that automation and self-provisioning will support the business and enable them to react to opportunities much faster. There also needs to be policy that specifies when a workload can safely be moved to a public cloud: Is the data safe enough in the private cloud? Is there an additional level of safety because of a *virtual private network (VPN)*. All these questions are part of the larger economic decision-making process.

Based on the questions we pose, most companies will clearly use some combination of public and private cloud resources (called a *hybrid*). These private cloud environments may live in your company's internal data center or they may be hosted by a private cloud vendor. Each company will have its own way of dealing with the allocation of capital expenditures versus operating expenditures with private cloud environments. For more details on private and hybrid clouds, see Chapter 9.

Service levels and compliance costs

It's unlikely that a cloud service will provide exactly the same service level that the data center has provided for an application. There will either be a hidden cost or benefit. In order to put a value on this, you need to estimate the cost to the business of the application being unavailable. This can then added (or subtracted) as a further cost factor involved in moving the application to the cloud.

Compliance (external or internal) can also be thought about as a service level cost. It may be necessary to get the cloud service audited to see that it meets the appropriate compliance requirements, which may relate to IT security or recovery procedures or any other such IT activity that must obey compliance standards.

Strategic considerations and costs

The IT context of your organization and its strategic direction need to be taken into account when deciding how any cloud costing model is applied. There are two important points worth paying attention to here:

- ✔ **Data center capacity:** Many organizations are running out of data center space. If they do run out of space, there's likely to be a massive cost in getting extra space. Thus, for some organizations, freeing up space in the data center creates capacity that's more valuable than it might otherwise appear (because it will delay or even eliminate the need for additional data center space).

- ✔ **Application grouping:** Because of the advent and widespread adoption of service oriented architecture (see Chapter 19), the interdependence of application services has increased. For technical integration and performance reasons, it may be impractical to think of applications on an individual basis, and instead to group them together when considering cloud migration.

Summarizing an Economic Cost Model

The economic costing model we outline involves the following steps:

1. Identify costs for all applications (or logical groups of applications) in terms of the Total Cost of Application Ownership (TCAO).

2. Adjust costs to reflect actual cost savings that might be achieved.

3. Factor in the cost of the private cloud (if there is one).

4. Factor in service level and compliance.

5. Take into account strategic factors (data center capacity and application groupings).

This creates an apples-to-apples comparison that can help you make cloud migration decisions.

IT is a dynamic environment and is likely to remain so. The cloud computing market is only just being established and prices may change considerably over time. Similarly, data center costs will not remain static, and neither will technology. You therefore have to review the economic model on a regular basis.

Chapter 22

Starting Your Journey to the Cloud

· ·

In This Chapter

▶ Anticipating cultural issues with the cloud

▶ Assessing risks

▶ Identifying low-hanging fruit

▶ Planning for leveraging the cloud

· ·

*T*he cloud model has lots of benefits, but there are also many issues — as there are with any new technology. In Chapter 4, we address how to develop a cloud strategy. Assuming you have decided to go with the cloud model, how do you get started? What factors do you need to consider as you begin?

In this chapter, we try to boil it down for you. We start off by examining how to deal with the inevitable cultural issues that arise when you ask people to do things differently. And, although we discuss the risks associated with the cloud throughout the book, we highlight some of the more important ones again because risk assessment needs to be part of getting started. Finally, we talk about some other issues that you may or may not have considered, such as planning your long-term cloud strategy.

Putting the Kibosh on Cloud Cultural Issues

Anytime something new comes along, it may take people time to accept it. This was probably the case when zippers were introduced, and it will certainly be the case with the cloud. The reality is that change usually causes people to react. Sometimes they react positively to change, and sometimes this isn't the case.

Anticipating (but not with relish)

Because you don't know what might happen, it is important to anticipate issues and plan accordingly.

Generally, issues associated with introducing new technology to an organization fall into one of the following categories:

- ✔ **People just don't get it.** Remember the Rutherford B. Hayes famous quote about the telephone: "An amazing invention — but who would ever want to use one?" Why did he say this? At the time, people used telegraphs and it wasn't obvious to some why they'd want to actually hear another person's voice when communicating long distance. Similarly, in the cloud, people need to be educated about how the model works and what the benefits are.

- ✔ **People have legitimate concerns.** There are, of course, legitimate reasons for not wanting to adopt a certain technology. These reasons are usually about risk. In the cloud, people worry about security, manageability, and availability. These are risks that consumers should be aware of, and we talk more about them in the next section.

- ✔ **People feel threatened by new technology because they think it may affect their livelihood.** This does happen — for example, the telephone switch replaced the telephone operators who used to connect your telephone call. Your staff may be concerned about the impact that the cloud will have on their jobs. Even though they might not lose their jobs, they still want to understand what the impact will be to their current situation.

- ✔ **People agree in principle with a technology, but it still might take some getting used to.** Remember when the ATM was introduced? People liked the convenience of being able to get money whenever they wanted, but were used to writing checks and cashing them at the bank. It took time to trust this new way of doing things.

Any or all of these reactions should be expected as you deploy cloud technology in your enterprise. Whether it's the technician who's concerned about putting virtual desktops in the cloud (and how the change will impact people staffing the IT help desk), or the database administrator who's concerned about the security around a cloud database, or the scientist who's thrilled at the prospect of being able to perform calculations in the cloud on demand — many people will be affected by the change, and you have to help smooth the transition.

Smoothing the transition

What can you do about it? Here are some ideas that will help smooth the transition to the cloud model.

Get executive support

The move to the cloud will be smoother if you have executive support. If one of these executives can be designated the champion, so much the better. This person will send the message from the top and people will be more likely to listen.

Understand the culture

If your culture is one that embraces innovation and change, that's great. However, if your company has been doing something one way for the last ten years, you need to understand that there will no doubt be some resistance. You need to plan your rollout accordingly.

Communicate the message

When you have executive support and understand the culture you're dealing with, communicate the cloud message to those who will be impacted. There are many ways to do this, depending on your culture:

- ✔ Department meetings
- ✔ Memos
- ✔ Podcasts
- ✔ Internal social networks

It's also a good idea to have a formal statement about the business case for cloud, in case you have to really convince your staff. Additionally, for those whose jobs will be significantly impacted, it is important to communicate the message directly. Never underestimate the human side of the equation.

Educate the troops

Everyone in the organization who's involved with cloud computing needs to understand three things:

- ✔ Why the company is moving some operations to the cloud model
- ✔ What the benefits of the move will be for the organization
- ✔ How individual people will be impacted by the move to cloud computing

This is the case for the remote worker who may now have a thin client on his desk; this is the case for the data center operator who now must monitor off-site computers.

Get people involved

If people feel that they're part of the change, they aren't as likely to resist it. So, get people involved! Form transition committees and appoint people to lead the charge.

Train your staff

Even if you're just moving all your clinicians to a thin client virtualized cloud desktop, you may still need to do some training. Of course, the type of training will depend on the job function.

- ✔ If you're moving a lot of your workload to the cloud and your cloud provider has monitoring tools that you aren't used to, obviously your staff will have to be trained on this.

- ✔ If there are processes that change as a result of moving to the cloud model, there would be training involved in that, as well.

- ✔ If you move to a SaaS model for some of your applications and they are new, people will have to be trained on that, as well.

Measuring Twice: Assessing Risks

Throughout this book we cover some of the risks you may face when moving to the cloud. Some of the people and business culture issues discussed earlier in this chapter are considered as risk elements in the chapter on cloud strategy; see Chapter 4. The chapters on cloud delivery models (see Chapters 10 through 12) consider the business process risks of adopting each of these models. In Chapter 16 we discuss risks from a technology and compliance perspective, including risks associated with data protection, security, customer expectations, performance levels, and interoperability.

Playing risk with categories

You need to manage several categories of risk as you move to the cloud:

- ✔ People
- ✔ Process
- ✔ Technology resource

Ask yourself these questions:

- ✔ **What are the people and process risks associated with any new technology?** How does this move mesh with people's skills? For example, if you move your desktops to virtualized desktops in the cloud, your IT help desk might need some new skills. Or, if you move to a private cloud model, you may want to make sure that your team can manage the data center. Can the team be trained?

- ✔ **How might my processes change in the cloud?** How will that impact your organization? Chances are that you can effectively address any people or process issues, but you shouldn't forget about them.

- ✔ **What about the technology resources?** Every company (large and small) has its own tolerance level when it comes to risk. It may vary by application type. The more critical the application, the lower the tolerance. As you begin your journey into the cloud, consider each type of asset that is cloud bound and assess the risk associated with the move.

Assess the risk associated with a move to the cloud model. And know that this assessment isn't a one-time thing. Monitor what your cloud provider is up to; make sure that your risk remains at an acceptable level.

Top company concerns

This chapter is about getting started with the cloud. We have pulled together some of the top questions companies consider when moving to the cloud:

- ✔ **What are my security and privacy concerns?** These are two of the top concerns that companies cite about a move to the cloud. In Chapter 15, we talk a lot about security. We note that in most circumstances, cloud security needs to be approached from a risk-management perspective. If your organization has risk-management specialists, involve them in cloud security planning.

- ✔ **How available and reliable will my resources be?** When you ran the data center, availability and reliability were under your own company control. Your IT organization probably has negotiated certain service level agreements with the departments in your company based on the criticality of your applications. With a move to the cloud, you need to ask yourself what levels of availability you need and what risk you're willing to take if your service provider doesn't meet agreed-upon levels. There may be some applications where you're willing to take the risk and some where you are not. But you need to assess the risk. Remember too that you may not be compensated the way you think you should be if your provider's service goes down.

✔ **What about my data?** If you're thinking about moving applications and data to the cloud, you need to address a number of questions. These include, but aren't limited to, the following:

- Can my data be stored anywhere or does my company not allow data to cross country boundaries?

- What happens if the data is lost?

- Can I recover?

- Who owns my data?

In other words, you need to weigh the risks associated with putting certain applications that rely on certain types of data into the cloud. It may well be that you're comfortable with the risk, but you still need to look at it. Look back at Chapter 8 for more information about managing data in the cloud.

✔ **Is my vendor viable?** What happens if your service provider goes out of business? Will you be able to recover your assets? Who owns the intellectual property?

✔ **Will I be locked into one vendor?** Although there are some movements afoot to move to an open cloud model (see Chapter 14), the cloud isn't there yet. This means there are proprietary data formats and APIs out there. Assess what they are and whether it will be easy to move your assets from one provider to another.

✔ **Are there other compliance or regulatory issues I need to be aware of?** Make sure that your provider can adhere to any regulatory or compliance issues your company has in place. You also need to make sure that they're willing to change if something changes in your own industry. Assess the risk and the cost that might be associated with this.

Much of this boils down to trust and doing your homework. Do you trust your vendor and have you put the right contracts in place to protect yourself? Have you done your homework? If you haven't, you need to do it. If you don't trust the vendor, you shouldn't be working with them.

Picking the Right Targets for Success

As we mention in Chapter 4, there's no one right path to leveraging cloud services within your business. It depends on the following:

✔ The state of your data center

✔ Your applications

✔ Your service portfolio

✔ Your changing business requirements

We also think that it goes without saying (but we'll say it anyway) that you probably don't want to move all your applications and resources to the cloud too quickly. And, as we point out through this book, certain areas may *never* be right for the cloud. If you move too quickly, you might end up living your own worst nightmare.

Instead, start by reviewing your IT portfolio to identify your first target. Select a specific area that demonstrates the value that you will get from a cloud model.

Picking the low-hanging fruit

Some areas are definitely ripe for cloud computing, which we refer to as *low-hanging fruit* (no pun intended). Here are a few examples:

✔ You might want to get your feet wet with something like moving application testing to a cloud environment. This has been a popular model for many companies. Instead of provisioning test servers on the company's premises, testing is done, on demand, in the cloud. The benefits include as much capacity as needed and no provisioning time for the servers in the test environment. Some companies are also moving development to the cloud for similar reasons.

✔ Another relatively low risk example is simply provisioning overflow capacity for something like a marketing campaign.

✔ Beta testing an application. Here is an interesting one. Some business analytics companies find that companies like to try applications out in the cloud first, before buying them. Go figure!

Approaching other areas

If you're planning to move some of your applications to the cloud, identify those applications that will give you the biggest bang for the buck. For example, 70 percent of your company might use the same email and scheduling package in the same manner. Right now, you're servicing these applications on the desktop, but it might make sense to move it to the cloud. On the other hand, there may be an analytical application that five of your scientists use. It probably wouldn't make sense to move this application to a cloud model because you wouldn't gain any economies of scale.

Do your homework for other types of applications and resources. Can you gain economies of scale by moving these to the cloud and at the same time manage your risk tolerance? For example, what if there is an application that a large percent of your staff use, but they tend to customize it for their own purposes? You have to evaluate whether it makes sense to move it to a cloud environment. You need to consider a range of costs and whether people will be able to do their jobs effectively under a new model.

Planning for Leveraging the Cloud

Say that you've moved to the cloud and started transitioning some of your applications to the cloud model. We think that while leveraging the cloud can be a good idea for many companies, you have to make sure that you manage the move properly. What do we mean?

Clearly, some of the move to the cloud will require that you think about managing your IT assets in a slightly different way. These changes fall into two categories: planning and doing.

These examples illustrate the need for proper planning so that your transition to the cloud makes sense. We hope that these scenarios don't happen in your company. However, these two somewhat simplistic examples show how important it is to plan for the cloud in a holistic manner. Otherwise, your company might be doomed to repeat some of the sins of the past.

Example 1

Say you're an electronics distributor that was using a CRM application that no one was particularly happy with. Fred over in the camera department decides to move all that group's sales information to a SaaS provider. However, Jane in the printer department decides to move that same sales function for her department to another SaaS provider.

When the CEO wants to know how sales are going across the two divisions, Fred and Jane scramble to get their data integrated. This problem sounds like the problem companies have had for ages with *siloed* information — data from different systems isolated into different environments, making it hard to integrate and manage. The same sort of thing can happen in the cloud if your cloud provider uses a proprietary format for storing data.

Example 2

Two divisions in a company with separate IT departments decide that they want to store some of their data in the cloud. Unknown to each other, they pick the same cloud provider and negotiate separate contracts with that provider. Now the company has two contracts to manage where it could have had one (probably more favorable). This can potentially cost the company more in the long run.

Part VI
The Part of Tens

The 5th Wave   By Rich Tennant

"Great goulash, Stan. That reminds me, are you still in charge of our system architecture?"

In this part . . .

In this part, we offer some cloud resources and caveats. We also include a glossary of terms frequently used when people discuss the cloud. While we strive to define terms as we introduce them in this book, we think you'll find the glossary a useful resource.

Chapter 23

Ten (Plus One) Swell Cloud Computing Resources

In This Chapter

▶ Seeking standards from the government

▶ Camping in the clouds

▶ Keeping the cloud open

▶ Finding free resources from your favorite vendorst

We have one cardinal rule for all would-be cloud computing enthusiasts — don't go it alone!

*I*n this chapter, we compile a list of resources we hope you find useful.

Hurwitz & Associates

The authors of this book are partners at Hurwitz & Associates. We're happy to help you with your questions about cloud computing. We can give a talk, provide service oriented architecture (SOA) training, and help you find the right technology partners. We invite you to subscribe to our blogs and visit our site at www.hurwitz.com.

National Institute of Standards and Technology

The National Institute of Standards and Technology (NIST) is a U.S. government agency that focuses on emerging standards efforts. This organization has done a considerable amount of work defining and providing good information on cloud computing. Check out their Web site at `http://csrc.nist.gov/groups/SNS/cloud-computing/index.html`.

CloudCamp

Everyone fondly remembers fun times at summer camp. CloudCamps aren't exactly the same, but they *are* great gatherings all over the world that bring together thinkers and doers. Check for a CloudCamp near you at `www.cloudcamp.com`.

Through a series of local CloudCamp (started by Dave Nielson) events, attendees exchange ideas, knowledge, and information in a creative and supporting environment, advancing the current state of cloud computing and related technologies. As an informal, nonprofit, member-supported gathering, they rely entirely on volunteers to help with meeting content, speakers, locations, equipment, and recruitment. They also have corporate sponsors that provide financial assistance with venues, software, books, discounts, and other valuable donations. To become a member, simply register online. Anyone may attend a meeting — there are no fees or dues.

SaaS Showplace

The SaaS Showplace was started by Jeff Kaplan, president of THINKStrategies, a SaaS consulting firm. The firm provides a constantly updated list of up-and-coming SaaS vendors. See a listing at `www.saas-showplace.com/home.html`.

TechTarget

TechTarget.com (`www.techtarget.com`) is a comprehensive online resource for all sorts of IT-related information, providing links to IT communities that focus on different areas of interest. SearchCloud.com, for example, is a TechTarget site with lots of information about products, services, and software vendors targeted at the needs of chief information officers and senior IT executives. Two other sites that might be useful are SearchSOA.com and SearchCompliance.com.

The Cloud Standards Wiki

This single place gives you access to lots of groups working on cloud standards. Check out their site at `http://cloud-standards.org/wiki`. The wiki contains information about all the organizations working in the area.

Finding OASIS

Creating standards takes a lot of work — often volunteer, financially uncompensated work by dedicated people determined to get things right. People who sit on standards committees deserve the undying gratitude of the rest of us. We thank you, standards committee members.

OASIS, the Organization for the Advancement of Structured Information Standards (`www.oasis-open.org`), is a global consortium focused on the creation and adoption of standards for electronic business. The consortium is a nonprofit organization that relies on contributions from its member organizations. OASIS creates topic-specific committees that are beginning to focus on cloud computing.

The Eclipse Foundation

The Eclipse Foundation is an open-source community focused on providing a vendor-neutral open development platform and application frameworks for building software. It's nonprofit and has widespread participation from developers and corporations around the globe. The Eclipse platform is written in Java and runs on most popular operating systems, including Linux, HP-UX, AIX, Solaris, QNX, Mac OS X, and Windows. Check out the Eclipse Foundation at `www.eclipse.org`.

The Cloud Security Alliance

The Cloud Security Alliance was established to promote the use of best practices for providing security assurance within cloud computing, and to educate people about the uses of cloud computing to help secure all other forms of computing. Check out their Web site at `www.cloudsecurityalliance.org`.

Open Cloud Manifesto

Open Cloud Manifesto is a community of more than 250 vendors intended to establish a core set of principles for cloud standards. The group has published several white papers that are worth reading. You can find them by clicking the Blogs, Wikis, and More link at www.opencloudmanifesto.org.

Vendor Sites

All the major cloud computing vendors provide great resources online. We recommend checking out vendors such as Google, VMware, EMC, Amazon, IBM, HP, Cisco, and Oracle. This is only a partial list. Hundreds of vendors are in the space, so don't stop with this list; check sites of all the vendors we mention throughout the book. You can find great resources on systems integrators sites. Take advantage.

Chapter 24

Ten Cloud Dos and Don'ts

In This Chapter
▶ Choosing the right starting point
▶ Standing on the shoulders of SOA giants
▶ Watching your back
▶ Being part of a SOA team

*W*e spend most of this book describing the cloud in great detail. In this chapter, we focus on a few simple dos and don'ts.

Don't Be Reactive

Many businesspeople who want to save money fast are tempted to throw out the data center and put all computing into a public cloud. Although this might sound good for a few hours, it isn't a thoughtful approach. In the end, you *might* decide which capabilities that you should put into the cloud, but you need to do your homework first. For example, do you have compliance issues to consider? What is the difference in cost between a public, private, hybrid, or even a traditional data center? You need to make sure that all the possible impacts have been considered before you spring into action.

Do Consider the Cloud a Financial Issue

You might start looking at some approaches to the cloud that sound really good. But before you jump in, do the math. How large is your company? What's the nature of your computing environment? How many applications do you support? How much does your current environment cost? How much spare capacity do you have in your data center? Are there applications that can cost effectively be moved to a Software as a Service model? Before you do anything, follow the money.

Don't Go It Alone

Although some companies have the sophistication to build their own clouds, they're the exception. Most companies need help, so don't go into this alone. An entire industry is just waiting out there to help you. Don't ignore it. Beg, borrow, steal, but get help. Talk to your peers who have done some early cloud projects. Consult with systems integrators, technology companies, and other consultants who have solid experience with best practices. Some cloud Web sites and organizations have great ideas and collaboration opportunities.

Do Think about Your Architecture

Just because you're thinking about moving into the cloud doesn't mean architecture is no longer important. In fact, it's more important than ever. You'll probably have business services that are designed for reuse that should be stored in a private or public cloud that need to be designed for reuse. You will likely have a hybrid environment that needs to be well planned to conform to your company's service level agreement and performance requirements.

Don't Neglect Governance

If you don't pay attention to compliance and governance, you're putting your company at risk. For example, some industries require that you store data in a very specific way. Some countries require that your customer data never is stored outside of its territory. You still have to comply with government regulations. These issues don't disappear into a cloud.

Don't Forget about Business Process

Start with the business process that you want to automate with your cloud initiatives. No matter which form of cloud you're considering, process is the building block. If you haven't figured out how business processes will be managed in this new distributed world, your business could be at risk.

Do Make Security the Centerpiece of Your Strategy

It's easy to get caught up in the mix-and-match euphoria and forget about the nitty-gritty issues. Pay close attention to the security implications of moving to the cloud. You still need a well-planned security strategy.

Don't Apply the Cloud to Everything

Don't get carried away. Not everything belongs in a cloud. For example, your data center might have a large, complex, and customized application used by a dozen people. It's critical to your business. You have no economic or business reason to move that application to the cloud.

Do your homework so you have guidelines to help you determine if an application or a function belongs in the data center, a public cloud, or a private cloud.

Don't Forget about Service Management

It's easy to make the assumption that if something is in the cloud, you don't have to worry about managing it. This isn't true. Although many cloud providers allow you to have a portal view of their own service levels, it's your responsibility to keep track of any service you have put into either a public or a private cloud. Because many companies inevitably have a hybrid environment, you need to manage your overall service level.

Do Start with a Pilot Project

Cloud computing will be around for a long time, so get experience now. Start with a pilot project. For example, you might want to start with a Software as a Service platform. You might use a public cloud for testing a new application before it goes into production. This gives you a feeling for what it means to give up this level of control.

You are still responsible for the integrity and security of your information. Finding out how to manage your cloud vendors is an important starting point.

Glossary

access control: Determining who or what can have access to what, and when and how they can access it.

ACID: atomicity, consistency, isolation, and durability. These are the main requirements for proper transaction processing.

API: application programming interface. A collection of subroutine calls that allow computer programs to use a software system.

application hosting: It comes in several models. One model requires the vendor to run an entire application for a customer. Software as a Service (SaaS) is another form of application hosting.

architecture: In information processing, the design approach taken in developing a program or system.

archiving: The process by which a database or file data that is seldom used or is outdated, but is required for historical or audit reasons, is copied to a cheaper form of storage. The storage medium may be online, tape, or optical disc.

ASP.NET: This is a Web application framework, from Microsoft, that programmers use to build Web applications and Web services. It's versatile because it allows programmers to write ASP.NET code using any supported .NET language.

asset management: Software that allows organizations to record all information about their hardware and software. Most such applications capture cost information, license information, and so on. Such information belongs in the configuration management database. *See also* CMDB.

audit: A check on the effectiveness of a task or set of tasks and how the tasks are managed and documented.

audit trail: A trace of a sequence of events in a clerical or computer system. This audit usually identifies the creation or modification of any element in the system, who did it, and (possibly) why it was done.

authentication: The process by which the identity of a person or computer process is verified.

AWS: Amazon Web Services. The set of Web services that Amazon offers to help Web developers build Web applications and use Amazon's cloud computing environment.

Azure: Windows Azure is an operating system for cloud computing from Microsoft. The hosting and management environment are maintained at Microsoft data centers, so there's no need to use internal data center resources when developing applications in Azure.

backup: A utility that copies databases, files, or subsets of databases and files to a storage medium. This copy can be used to restore the data in case of serious failure.

bandwidth: Technically, the range of frequencies over which a device can send or receive signals. The term is also used to denote the maximum data transfer rate, measured in bits per second (bps), that a communications channel can handle.

Basel II: Known more formally as the International Convergence of Capital Measurement and Capital Standards — A Revised Framework. Basel II is an internationally recognized set of rules for evaluating a bank's finances in light of various risks. It's also one of the big compliance regulations making organizations do things that they wouldn't otherwise feel compelled to do. (Basel, by the way, is named after a very lovely city in Switzerland.)

batch: A noninteractive process that runs in a queue, usually when the system load is lowest; generally used for processing batches of information in a serial and usually efficient manner. Early computers were capable of only batch processing.

best practice: An effective way of doing something. It can relate to anything from writing program code to IT governance.

binding: Making the necessary connections among software components so that they can interact.

biometrics: Using a person's unique physical characteristics to prove his identity to a computer — by a fingerprint scanner or voice analyzer, for example.

black box: A component or device with an input and an output whose inner workings need not be understood by or accessible to the user.

BPaaS: Business Process as a Service. A whole business process is provided as a service involving little more than a software interface, such as a parcel delivery service.

BPEL: Business Process Execution Language. A computer language based on WSDL (Web Services Description Language, an XML format for describing Web services) and designed for programming the orchestration of business services. *See also* XML.

BPM: business process management. A technology and methodology for controlling the activities — both automated and manual — needed to make a business function.

broker: In computer programming, a program that accepts requests from one software layer or component and translates them into a form that can be understood by another layer or component.

browser: A program that lets you access information on the Internet. Browsers are on computers, cellphones, and personal digital assistants, and soon will appear on refrigerators.

bus: A technology that connects multiple components so they can talk to one another. In essence, a bus is a connection capability. A bus can be software (such as an enterprise service bus) or hardware (such as a memory bus). *See also* ESB.

business process: The systematic arrangement of rules and practices that constitute a business.

business process modeling: A technique for transforming how business operates into a systematic arrangement of source in code so that it can be translated into software.

business rules: Constraints or actions that refer to the actual commercial world but may need to be encapsulated in service management or business applications.

business service: An individual function or activity that is directly useful to the business.

center of excellence: A group of key people from all areas of the business and operations that focuses on best practices. A center of excellence provides a way for groups within the company to collaborate. This group also becomes a force for change, as it can leverage its growing knowledge to help business units benefit from experience.

change management: The management of change in operational processes and applications.

client/server: A model of computing in which the various processes are classified as either consumers of services (clients) or providers of services (servers). This classification was once used as the basis for dividing processes among the available processors.

cloud computing: A computing model that makes IT resources such as servers, middleware, and applications available over the Internet as services to business organizations in a self-service manner.

CMDB: configuration management database. In general, a repository of service management data. *See also* repository.

CMMI: Capability Maturity Model Integration. A process-improvement best practice used to improve processes in a project or overall. The Software Engineering Institute of Carnegie Mellon University, along with representatives of industry and government, developed CMMI.**COBIT:** Control Objectives for Information and Related Technology. An IT framework with a focus on governance and managing technical and business risks.

component: A piece of computer software that can be used as a building block in larger systems. Components can be parts of business applications that have been made accessible through Web service-related standards and technologies. *See also* Web service.

compute unit: Within its EC2 service, Amazon uses computer units to measure the infrastructure used by virtual server instances. Currently, one EC2 Compute Unit provides the equivalent CPU capacity of a 1.0–1.2 GHz 2007 Opteron or 2007 Xeon processor. Other IaaS providers also have units for measuring resource usage.

configuration: The complete description of the way in which the constituent elements of a software product or system interrelate, both in functional and physical terms.

configuration management: The management of configurations, normally involving holding configuration data in a database so that the data can be managed and changed where necessary.

container: In computer programming, a data structure or object used to manage collections of other objects in an organized way.

CRM: customer relationship management. Software intended to help you run your sales force and customer support operations.

data cleansing: Software used to identify potential data-quality problems. If a customer is listed multiple times in a customer database due to variations of the spelling of her name, the data-cleansing software makes corrections to help standardize the data.

data fabric: The part of the computer network devoted to transmissions.

data federation: Data access to a variety of data stores, using consistent rules and definitions that enable all the data stores to be treated as a single resource.

data profiling: A technique or process that helps you understand the content, structure, and relationships of your data. This process also helps you validate your data against technical and business rules.

data quality: Characteristics of data such as consistency, accuracy, reliability, completeness, timeliness, reasonableness, and validity. Data-quality software ensures that data elements are represented in a consistent way across different data stores or systems, making the data more trustworthy across the enterprise.

data transformation: A process by which the format of data is changed so it can be used by different applications.

data warehouse: A large data store containing the organization's historical data, which is used primarily for data analysis and data mining.

database: A computer system intended to reliably store lots of information in an organized way. Most databases provide users convenient access to the data, along with helpful search capabilities.

dedicated hosting: Dedicated hosting is where the customer is given full control over the server that is hosted in the cloud. This contrasts with managed hosting, where management is the responsibility of the hosting company.

dedicated server: A dedicated server is one the customer does not share with any other users of the hosting cloud service.

directory: The word is used in both computing and telephony to indicate an organized map of devices, files, or people.

distributed processing: Spreading the work of an information processing application among several computers.

early binding: Making necessary connections among software components when the software system is built.

EC2: Elastic Compute Cloud from Amazon. This is Amazon's commercial Infrastructure as a Service (IaaS) Web service that has pioneered cloud computing.

elasticity: The ability to expand or shrink a computing resource in real time, based on need.

ERP: Enterprise Resource Planning. A packaged set of business applications that combines business rules, process, and data management into a single integrated environment to support a business.

ESB: enterprise service bus. A distributed middleware software system that allows computer applications to communicate in a standardized way.

eSCM: eSourcing Capability Model. A framework developed at Carnegie Mellon University to provide a best-practices model for improving relationships between customers and suppliers in outsourcing agreements.

ETL: Extract — Transform — Load. Tools for locating and accessing data from a data store (data extraction), changing the structure or format of the data so it can be used by the business application (data transformation), and sending the data to the business application (data load).

eTOM: enhanced Telecom Operations Map. A framework that provides a business process model for the telecommunications industry.

fault tolerance: The ability of a system to provide uninterrupted service despite the failure of one or more of the system's components.

federation: The combination of disparate things so that they can act as one — as in federated states, data, or identity management — and making sure that all the right rules apply.

framework: A support structure for developing software products.

GPL: GNU General Public License. An open-source copyright license created by Richard Stallman that, in its strictest form, requires programs built on code licensed under GPL to adopt the same license.

granularity: An important software design concept, especially in relation to components, referring to the amount of detail or functionality — from fine to coarse — provided in a service component. One software component can do something quite simple, such as calculate a square root; another has a great deal of detail and functionality to represent a complex business rule or workflow. The first component is fine grained, and the second is coarse grained. Developers often aggregate fine-grained services into coarse-grained services to create a business service.

grid computing: A step beyond distributed processing, involving large numbers of networked computers (often geographically dispersed and possibly of different types and capabilities) that are harnessed to solve a common problem. Clouds are usually organized as a computer grid.

HIPAA: Health Insurance Portability and Accountability Act of 1996. A set of extensive regulations that healthcare organizations and providers in the United States must follow. One of the goals is to control the healthcare system to protect patients' right to privacy regarding information about their health. The policies and regulations place significant demands on technology systems that have anything to do with healthcare.

HTML: Hypertext Markup Language. A data-encoding scheme invented by Tim Berners-Lee in 1991 and the basic way that information is encoded over the World Wide Web.

HTTP: Hypertext Transport Protocol. The basic way that information is linked and transmitted over the World Wide Web. HTTPS is a version of HTTP with encryption for security.

IaaS: Infrastructure as a Service. Infrastructure, including a management interface and associated software, provided to companies from the cloud as a service.

identity management: Keeping track of a single user's (or asset's) identity throughout an engagement with a system or set of systems.

information integration: A process using software to link data sources in various departments or regions of the organization with an overall goal of creating more reliable, consistent, and trusted information.

infrastructure: The fundamental systems necessary for the ordinary operation of an IT department. In IT, infrastructure includes basic computer hardware, networks, operating systems, storage, and other software that applications run on top of.

infrastructure services: Services provided by the infrastructure. In IT, these services include all the software needed to make devices talk to one another, for starters.

Internet: A huge computer network linking almost all the computers in the world and enabling them to communicate via standard protocols (TCP/IP) and data formats. *See also* SMTP, TCP/IP, and XML.

interoperability: The ability of a product to interface with many other products; usually used in the context of software.

IP: Internet Protocol. A systematic technique for communicating data across a packet-switched network. IP can also mean intellectual property such as patents, trademarks, copyrights, and trade secrets. *See also* TCP/IP.

ISO: International Organization for Standardization. An organization that has developed more than 17,000 international standards, including standards for IT service management and corporate governance of information technology.

ITIL: Information Technology Infrastructure Library. A framework and set of standards for IT governance based on best practices.

JCA: J2EE Connector Architecture. A technology that enables Java programs to talk to other software, such as databases and legacy applications.

key performance indicator: KPI. An indicator used to measure the effectiveness of a process.

LAMP: An increasingly popular open-source approach to building Web applications. LAMP comprises the Linux operating system, the Apache Web server, a MySQL database, and a scripting language (such as PHP, Perl, or Python).

late binding: Deferring the necessary connections among applications to when the connection is first needed. Late binding allows more flexibility for changes than early binding does, but it imposes some cost in processing time.

legacy application: Any application more than a few years old. When applications can't be disposed of and replaced easily, they become legacy applications. The good news is that they're still doing something useful when selected pieces of code can be turned into business services with new standardized interfaces.

Linux: Linux is an open-source operating system based upon and similar to Unix. In cloud computing it is the dominant operating system, primarily because there are no license fees for Linux.

Linux Web hosting: The vast majority of Web sites run on the Linux operating system managed by a Linux Web hosting service using the LAMP (Linux, Apache, MySQL, PHP) software stack.

loose coupling: An approach to distributed software applications in which components interact by passing data and requests to other components in a standardized way that minimizes dependencies among components. The emphasis is on simplicity and autonomy. Each component offers a small range of simple services to other components.

malware: The general term for computer software that intentionally does ill, such as viruses, Trojans, worms, and spyware.

managed hosting: This is where the customer gives control of his leased server to the managed hosting service, which then provides a guaranteed quality of service. *See also* dedicated hosting.

markup language: A way of encoding information that uses plain text containing special tags often delimited by angle brackets (< and >). Specific markup languages are often created, based on XML, to standardize the interchange of information between different computer systems and services. *See also* XML.

mashup: A program (possibly installed on a Web page) that combines content from more than one source, such as Google Maps and a real-estate listing service.

master-slave: An arrangement in which one system or process is designated as a controller and other participating systems or processes respond to this controller. Should a master fail, the slaves are unable to continue.

metadata: The definitions, mappings, and other characteristics used to describe how to find, access, and use the company's data and software components.

metadata repository: A container of consistent definitions of business data and rules for mapping data to their actual physical locations in the system.

middleware: Multipurpose software that lives at a layer between the operating system and application in distributed computing environments.

mission critical: Something, such as an application, that a business cannot afford to be without at any time.

MOM: message-oriented middleware. A precursor to the enterprise service bus. *See* ESB.

multi-tenancy: This refers to the situation where a single instance of an application runs on a SaaS vendor's servers, but serves multiple client organizations (tenants), keeping all their data separate. In a multi-tenant architecture, a software application partitions its data and configuration so that each customer has a customized virtual application instance.

MySQL: An open-source option for relational databases.

.NET: Pronounced *dot-net;* the latest Microsoft programming framework, with heavy emphasis on Web services. *See also* Web service.

.NET Framework: In the cloud, the .NET Framework has become a key foundational component of Microsoft's Azure platform for cloud computing.

network: The connection of computer systems (nodes) by communications channels and appropriate software.

OASIS: Organization for the Advancement of Structured Information Standards. A consortium promoting e-business and Web services standards.

open source: A movement in the software industry that makes programs and the source code used to create them freely available so that others can inspect and modify how they work.

P2P: peer to peer. A networking system in which nodes in a network exchange data directly instead of going through a central server.

PaaS: Platform as a Service. This is a cloud service that not only includes infrastructure (that is, hardware and operating software) but also a development environment and possibly other software development lifecycle tools.

Perl: Practical Extraction and Report Language. A powerful scripting language in widespread use in system administration, Web development, and other activities.

PHP: PHP Hypertext Processor. An open-source scripting language (originally designed in Perl) used especially for producing dynamic Web pages.

portal: In computing, a window that contains a means of access, often a menu, to all the applications throughout the whole network that the user is able to run. Often, the window is segmented into smaller windows, or *portlets,* that provide direct access to applications such as stock-market price feeds or email.

private cloud: As opposed to a public cloud, which is generally available, a private cloud is a set of computing resources within the corporation that serves only the corporation, but which is set up to operate in a cloudlike manner as regards its management.

programming in the large: An approach to developing business software that focuses on the various tasks or business processes needed to make the business function — processing an order, for example, or checking product availability — as opposed to low-level technical tasks such as opening a file.

protocol: A set of rules that computers use to establish and maintain communication among themselves.

provisioning: Making resources available to users and software. A provisioning system makes applications available to users and makes server resources available to applications.

real time: A form of processing in which a computer system accepts and updates data at the same time, feeding back immediate results that influence the data source.

real-time event processing: A class of applications that demand timely response to actions that take place out in the world. Typical examples include automated stock trading and radio frequency identification (RFID). *See also* RFID.

registry: A single source for all the metadata needed to gain access to a Web service or software component.

repository: A database for software and components, with an emphasis on revision control and configuration management (where they keep the good stuff, in other words).

response time: The time from the moment at which a transaction is submitted by a user or an application to the moment at which the final result of that transaction is made known to the user or application.

RFID: radio frequency identification. A technology that uses small, inexpensive chips attached to products (or even animals) that then transmit a unique identification number over a short distance to a special radio transmitter/receiver.

RPC: remote procedure call. A way for a program running on one computer to run a subprogram on another computer.

Ruby on Rails: Ruby is a programming language, and Rails is a Ruby framework built specifically for Web applications. It is regarded as an efficient language for programming Web applications.

SaaS: Software as a Service. This self-service application is based on a cloud infrastructure.

SAML: A standard framework for exchanging authentication and authorization information (that is, credentials) in an XML format called *assertions*.

Sarbanes-Oxley: The Public Company Accounting Reform and Investor Protection Act of 2002, a U.S. law enhancing standards for all U.S. public companies' boards of directors, resulting in substantial new requirements for corporate IT.

scalability: Regarding hardware, the ability to go from small to large amounts of processing power with the same architecture. Regarding software products such as databases, it refers to the consistency of performance per unit of power as hardware resources increase.

scripting language: A computer programming language that is interpreted and has access to all or most operating-system facilities. Common examples include Perl, Python, Ruby, and JavaScript. It is often easier to program in a scripting language, but the resulting programs generally run slower than those created in compiled languages such as C and C++.

secure Web hosting: This Web hosting environment is made secure by the use of Secure Socket Layer (SSL) certificates and HTTPS.

semantics: In computer programming, what the data means as opposed to formatting rules (syntax).

server array: This is a collection of single server types that is normally used for horizontal scaling. Typically, most private and public clouds are built as server arrays and managed with virtualization software.

server farm: A facility filled with computer servers, often needed to run large Internet sites.

service: A purposeful activity carried out for the benefit of a known target. Services are often made up of a group of component services, some of which may also have component services. Services always transform something, and they complete by delivering an output.

service catalog: A directory of IT services provided across the enterprise, including information such as service description, access rights, and ownership.

service desk: A single point of contact for IT users and customers to report any issues they may have with the IT service (or, in some cases, with IT's customer service).

service level agreement: SLA. A document that captures the understanding between a service user and a service provider as to quality and timeliness.

service management: Monitoring and optimizing a service to ensure that it meets the critical outcomes that the customer values and the stakeholders want to provide.

servlet: A program that runs on a Web server in response to an action taken by the user via a browser.

silo: In IT, an application with a single narrow focus, such as human resources management or inventory control, with no intention or preparation for use by others.

silver bullet: A proposed solution that seems too good to be true and usually is.

Simple Storage Service: S3. This distributed storage service, from Amazon, constitutes part of AWS. Amazon provides the capability to read, write, and delete objects (of data) that are up to 5 gigabytes in size. This isn't a database capability — just a place to store and access files.

Six Sigma: A statistical term meaning six standard deviations from the norm. Also the name of a quality-improvement program that aims at reducing errors to one in a million.

SMTP: Simple Mail Transfer Protocol. The basic method used to transmit e-mail over the Internet.

SOA: service-oriented architecture. An approach to building applications that implements business processes or services by using a set of loosely coupled black-box components orchestrated to deliver a well-defined level of service.

SQL: Structured Query Language. The most popular computer language for accessing and manipulating databases.

SSL: Secure Sockets Layer. A popular method for making secure connections over the Internet, first introduced by Netscape.

standards: A core set of common, repeatable best practices and protocols that have been agreed on by a business or industry group. Typically, vendors, industry user groups, and end users collaborate to develop standards based on the broad expertise of a large number of stakeholders. Organizations can leverage these standards as a common foundation and innovate on top of them.

subroutine: A piece of computer code that can easily be used (called) by many other programs, as long as they are on the same computer and (usually) are written in the same programming language.

TCP/IP: Transmission Control Protocol/Internet Protocol. The complex stack of communications protocols that underlies the Internet. All data is broken into small packets that are sent independently over the network and reassembled at the final destination.

thin client: Client hardware in the client/server environment that is dependent on the server for loading applications. Most hardware designed for this purpose is similar to a cut-down PC, with no floppy disk drive or hard drive.

throughput: The rate at which transactions are completed in a system.

TLS: Transport Layer Security. A newer name for SSL. *See also* SSL.

TQM: Total Quality Management. A popular quality-improvement program.

transaction: A computer action that represents a business event, such as debiting an account. When a transaction starts, it must either complete or not happen at all.

UDDI: Universal Description, Discovery, and Integration. A platform-independent, XML-based services registry sponsored by OASIS. *See also* OASIS and XML.

virtualization: Technically, virtualization is emulation. Virtual memory is the use of a disk to store active areas of memory to make the available memory appear larger. In a virtual environment, one computer runs software that allows it to emulate another computer. This kind of emulation is commonly known as virtualization.

VMware: VMware provides the technology, which currently dominates the virtualization of servers. In the cloud, however, the Xen hypervisor is also widely used as it is open source.

VPS: virtual private server. This is a virtual server that is dedicated to a single customer, whereas the server it resides on is actually shared among several customers, who are completely unaware of each other. Each VPS runs its own operating system, bandwidth, and disk space, and can be individually booted.

W3C: World Wide Web Consortium. An organization that coordinates standards for the World Wide Web.

Web service: A software component created with an interface consisting of a WSDL definition, an XML schema definition, and a WS-Policy definition. Collectively, components could be called a service contract — or, alternatively, an API. *See also* API, WSDL, WS-Policy, and XML.

workflow: This sequence of steps carries out a business process. Workflow technology automates the passage of information between the steps.

World Wide Web: A system built on top of the Internet that displays hyper-linked pages of information that can contain a wide variety of data formats, including multimedia.

WSCI: Web Services Choreography Interface. An XML-based interface description language that describes the flow of messages exchanged by a Web Service when it participates in choreographed interactions with other services.

WSDL: Web Services Definition Language. An XML format for describing Web services.

WS-Policy: The Web Services Policy Framework, which provides a means of expressing the capabilities, requirements, and characteristics of software components in a Web services system.

WSRP: Web Services for Remote Portlets. A protocol that allows portlets to communicate by using standard Web services interfaces.

XML: eXtensible Markup Language. A way of presenting data as plain-text files that has become the lingua franca of SOA. In XML, as in HTML, data is in tags that are enclosed in angle brackets (< and >), although the tags in XML can have many more meanings. *See also* SOA.

XML schema: A language for defining and describing the structure of XML documents.

XSD: XML schema definition. The description of what can be in an XML document.

XSLT: eXtensible Stylesheet Language Transformations. A computer language, based on XML, that specifies how to change one XML document into another. *See also* XML.

Index

• A •

abstraction, 68
abstraction layer, 203–204
Accenture company, 99
access control
  comprehensive security importance, 34
  data management, 79
  defined, 275
  scheduling access, 199
  security, 219
account and billing management
  automation, 32
  billing service, 235
  potential problem with, 32
accounting, 157
ACID (automicity, consistency, isolation,
    and durability), 275
activity log, 183
ad-hoc workload, 112
administration, security, 181
allocation cost, 251–252
Amazon
  EBS (Elastic Block Store), 103, 111
  EC2 (Elastic Compute Cloud), 109–113
  SimpleDB database, 83
  S3 (Simple Storage Service), 103, 111
  Virtual Private Cloud, 91
  Web site, 13
Amazon Work Space (AWS), 91, 276
amortization, 51
anchored lifecycle platform, 122
Apache Hadoop open-source distributed
    platform, 82
Apex programming language, 129
API (application programming interface)
  data transformation issue, 33
  defined, 275
  managing multiple, 33
  overview, 11
  REST, 132
  standardized, 33
  well-planned workload service, 68–69

AppJect company, 21
application
  business process, 158
  data architecture and, 33
  incident and problem management, 239
  monitoring, 217
  virtualization, 198
application hosting, 275
application programming interface. See API
Application Service Provider (ASP), 21
AppLogic 3Tera company
  as IaaS company, 115
  private cloud offering, 102–103
architecture do's and don'ts, 272
archive
  cost, 249
  data management, 84
  defined, 275
ARTS (Association for Retail Technology
    Standard), 170
ASP (Application Service Provider), 21
ASP.NET, 275
assertion, 285
asset management
  asset register, 216
  capacity planning, 73
  defined, 275
  desktop management, 216
  license, 217
  remote management, 217
  service management, 37
  workload, 73
asset performance, 30
Association for Retail Technology Standard
    (ARTS), 170
Atom Publishing Protocol, 164
Atom Syndication Format, 164
atomicity, consistency, isolation, and
    durability (ACID), 275
attack. See security
audit
  data audit product, 184
  defined, 275
  risk, 192

audit trail, 275
authentication
  comprehensive security importance, 34
  defined, 276
  identity management, 180
authorization, 34
automation
  application, 22
  backup, 217
  Runbook, 73
  security, 219
availability risk, 192, 259
AWS (Amazon Work Space), 91, 276
Azure (Microsoft), 125–126, 276

• *B* •

backup
  automated, 217
  as business process, 159
  cloud data center, 62
  cost, 64, 249
  data management, 79
  defined, 276
  traditional data center, 62
bandwidth
  defined, 276
  ensuring performance level, 241
  performance management, 36
Basel II, 276
batch, 276
best practice. *See also* standard
  about this book, 1
  avoiding mistake through, 162
  basic description of, 161
  consulting practice, 162
  defined, 276
  independent book, 162
  industry organization, 162
  training material, 162
Bigtable database (Google), 83
billing and account management
  automation, 32
  billing service, 235
  potential problem with, 32
billing and metering of service, 11
billing risk, 192

binding, 276
biometric, 276
black-box, 222, 276
blade cabinet, 212
Bloor, Robin (*Service Oriented Architecture For Dummies*), 32
BPEL (Business Process Execution Language), 277
BPM (business process management), 223, 277
breach, security, 177–178
broker, service, 224, 277
browser, 277
building cost, 58
bus, 277
business agility support, 15
business leader, 8
business management, 9
business process
  accounting capability, 157
  application, 158
  backup and disaster recovery, 159
  clerical activity, 159
  collaboration, 159
  communication, 159
  computer-dependent, 29
  defined, 277
  do's and don'ts, 272
  email, 157
  future of, 159
  molecular modeling program, 157
  monitoring, 29
  payment technology, 159
  research, 159
  as service, 28, 155
  Web site work, 159
  Web-based, 159
Business Process Execution Language (BPEL), 277
business process management (BPM), 223, 277
business process modeling, 277
business rule, 277
business service, 226–227
Business Week Magazine (Computing Heads for the Clouds), 50

• C •

CA company
  eHealth Performance Manager
    product, 101
  private cloud offering, 100–101
  Spectrum Automation Manager
    product, 101
  Spectrum Infrastructure Manager
    product, 101
Canonical Web site, 214
Capability Maturity Model Integration
    (CMMI), 278
capacity planning
  asset management, 73
  service management, 37
  virtualization, 203
capital expenditure
  private cloud, 92–93
  reduction, 15
capital investment, 30, 246–247
CCIF (Cloud Computing Interoperability
    Forum), 169–170
center of excellence, 277
change management
  configuration management, 218
  data management, 79
  defined, 278
  desktop management, 216
  hardware provisioning, 218
  patch management, 218
  software distribution and upgrade, 218
  support desk, 239
Cisco Webex Collaboration company, 148
Citrix GotoMeeting company, 148
clerical activity, 159
client
  caching, 65
  thin, 210, 288
  virtualization, 210–212
client desktop, 210–212
client/server, 278
cloud
  defining the, 9
  leveraging the, 262–263
  open, 165
  participant, 9
  trusted, 116–117

cloud computing evolution, 8–9
Cloud Computing Interoperability Forum
    (CCIF), 169–170
cloud data center
  backup, 62
  cost to operate, 51–52
  hardware cost, 60–61
  traditional data center cost comparison,
    55–58
cloud database, 83
cloud ecosystem, 33
cloud resource management. See resource
    management
Cloud Security Alliance (CSA), 166–167, 269
cloud service. See also service
  administering, 30–32
  advantages of, 14–15
  APIs, 11
  billing and metering of service, 11
  business agility support, 15
  business drivers for consuming, 14–15
  capital expenditure reduction, 15
  characteristic, 10
  defined, 9
  delivery model, 17–18
  elasticity characteristic, 10
  free, 11
  as important value to company, 9
  multi-tenancy, 9
  performance monitoring and
    measurement, 12
  scalability characteristic, 10
  self-service provisioning characteristic,
    10–11
  social network, 9
cloud service provider
  as cloud participant, 9
  customer, 234–235
  evaluation of, 31
  having more than one, 31
  investigating reliability and viability of,
    30–31
  IT service provider comparison, 12–14
  management service type, 233
  managing multiple, 233–234
  responsibilities of, 232–233
  roles of, 13
Cloud Standards Wiki, 269

cloud washing, 94
CloudCamp Web site, 268
cluster, 82
clustering, 204
CMDB (Configuration Management
    Database)
  defined, 278
  hybrid environment, 236
  optimization, 65
  virtualization, 202
CMMI (Capability Maturity Model
    Integration), 278
CODA software company, 145
collaboration
  as business process, 159
  defining the cloud, 9
collaboration as a service, 146, 148–149
communication
  as business process, 159
  unified, 148
communications cost, 64
compatibility testing, 149
compliance
  cost, 252–253
  data management, 43, 85
  risk, 192
  as a service, 151
component, 278
composite application, 120
comprehensive strategy, 28
compute cycle, 15
compute unit, 110, 278
Computer Sciences Corporation (CSC),
    98–99
computer-dependent business process, 29
computing cost, 52
Computing Heads for the Clouds (*Business
    Week Magazine*), 50
Concur company, 147
configuration management
  change management, 218
  defined, 278
  incident and problem management, 239
  service management, 37
  workload, 74
Configuration Management
    Database (CMDB)
  defined, 278
  hybrid environment, 236

optimization, 65
  virtualization, 202
connectivity, 241
Constant Contact company, 147
consultant, security, 185
consulting practice, 162
container, 278
container workload, 71
continuity plan, data management, 85
contract. *See also* SLA
  data management, 85
  risk, 192
  termination, 85
cooling cost, 61
cost
  allocation, 251–252
  archive and backup, 249
  asset management, 217
  backup, 64
  building, 58
  cloud and traditional data center
      comparison, 55–58
  cloud computing economies of scale, 53
  communications, 64
  compliance, 252–253
  computing, 52, 54
  cooling, 61
  data center operation, 50–51, 249, 251
  disaster recovery, 64, 249
  economic cost model, 253–254
  electric power, 57
  hardware, 60–63
  heating and air, 58
  help desk support, 250
  infrastructure software, 250
  in-house software, 249
  investment incentive and taxation, 58
  labor, 52, 56
  land, 58
  location, 58
  network, 248–250
  operational support, 250–251
  package software, 249, 251
  platform, 249, 251
  power distribution and cooling, 52
  private cloud versus allocation, 251–252
  recovering, 250–251
  revenue model, 143–144
  security, 65

server, 248, 250
service level, 252–253
software maintenance, 249
staff, 58
storage, 248, 250
strategic consideration and, 253
system management, 64–65
Cost of a Cloud: Research Problems in Data Center Networks, The (Greenberg, Hamilton, Maltz, and Patel)
CouchDB database, 83
CPU, 61
Craigslist, 155
CRM (customer relationship management)
  defined, 278
  PaaS, 137
  as SaaS strategy, 21
  Salesforce.com history, 128
CSA (Cloud Security Alliance), 166–167, 269
CSC (Computer Sciences Corporation), 98–99
cultural issue
  anticipating, 255–258
  executive support, 257
  getting people involved, 258
  smoothing transition to cloud model, 257–258
  training the staff, 258
customer management, 234–235
customer relationship management. *See* CRM

• *D* •

DaaS (Desktop as a Service), 213–214
dashboard, 12, 195
data analysis, 181
data and application architecture, 33
data audit, 184
data center. *See also* cloud data center; traditional data center
  benefit of, 49
  cost to operate, 50–51, 249, 251
  economic model of, 248–250
  embedded software cost, 62–63
  per-user cost example, 53
  strategy, 42–43
  where you are today assessment, 43

data cleansing, 279
data diversity, 75
data fabric, 279
data federation, 279
data management
  access control, 78
  Amazon SimpleDB database, 83
  archive, 84
  backup and recovery control, 78
  change management control, 78
  cloud database, 83
  cloud-based SQL database, 83
  co-mingling of data, 77
  compliance, 85
  continuity plan, 85
  contract, 85
  CouchDB database, 83
  data destruction control, 79
  data integrity, 85
  data ownership, 85
  data transfer across country border, 77
  data transport security, 79–80
  database as a service, 83
  encryption, 79–80
  file control, 78
  firewall, 79
  Google Bigtable database, 83
  input validation control, 78
  large-scale data processing, 81–82
  latency requirement, 76
  laws governing data, 77
  loss of data, 85
  LucidDB database, 83
  metadata, 84
  MongoDB database, 83
  output reconciliation control, 78
  privacy and compliance issue, 43, 76–80
  processing control, 78
  relational database model, 82
  risk assessment, 260
  secondary data use, 77
  security, 43, 76–80
  strategy, 43–44
  uptime, 85
  vendor, switching, 85
data profiling, 279
data quality, 279
data storage, 61

data store, 82–83
data transformation, 33, 279
data warehouse, 279
database
  incident and problem management, 239
  MySQL, 283
  Salesforce.com software
    environment, 138
database-bound application, 14
datastore, 124
de facto standard, 163
decoupling, 198
dedicated hosting, 279
dedicated server, 279
delivery model, 17–19
department meeting, 257
Desktone Web site, 214
desktop
  asset management, 216–217
  change management, 216
  client, 210–212
  governance, 216
  KPI, 215
  moving to cloud, 212–213
  security, 216
  service management, 216
  virtual, 209–212
Desktop as a Service (DaaS), 213–214
detection, 182–184
development as a service, 150
development sandbox, 129
Development Suite (LongJump company),
    132–133
development tool, 34
digital deception software, 183
directory, 279
disaster recovery
  as business process, 159
  cost, 64, 249
  data management, 79
distributed processing, 279
distributed resource scheduler
    virtualization, 201
diversity, data, 75
DMTF (Distributed Management Task
    Force), 164, 167

downtime, 242
dramatic economies of scale, 23–24
dynamic economic environment, 7
dynamic scaling
  IaaS and, 19
  ISP pattern, 109
  PaaS and, 20
dynamic virtualization, 206–207
dynamic workload, 70

• E •

early binding, 279
eBay
  as massively scaled application, 154
  as massively scaled SaaS, 23
EBS (Elastic Block Storage), 103, 111
Eclipse Foundation Web site, 269
economies of scale
  communications cost, 64
  network virtualization, 64
  predictable network traffic, 64
  SaaS, 23–24
ecosystem
  Salesforce.com, 140
  value of, 144
EC2 (Elastic Compute Cloud)
  Compute Units, 110
  customer, 112
  hourly charge, 112
  as IaaS operation, 109–112
  operating system support, 110–111
  platform and storage, 110–111
  resource allocation based on, 111
  Xen virtualization, 110
efficient server, 54
Elastic Block Storage (EBS), 103, 111
Elastic Compute Cloud. *See* EC2
elasticity
  defined, 280
  infrastructure resource, 19
  scalability and, 10
electric power cost, 57
email, 157
embedded hypervisor, 201
embedded software cost, 62–63

EMC company
  Atmos cloud storage service, 98
  private cloud offering, 97–98
encapsulation, 198
encryption
  basic description of, 80
  performance penalty, 184
  public key, 80
  symmetric key, 80
end user, 9
end-of-month workload, 112
end-of-year workload, 112
end-to-end service, 225
enhanced Telecom Operations Map
    (eTOM), 280
Enterprise Edition (Force.com), 130,
    225–226
ERP (enterprise resource planning),
    147, 280
error. *See* support desk
ESB (Enterprise Service Bus), 224–226, 280
eSCM (eSourcing Capability Model), 280
Etelos company, 21
ETL (Extract-Transform-Load) tool, 280
eTOM (enhanced Telecom Operations
    Map), 280
Eucalyptus Systems company
  as IaaS company, 115–116
  private cloud offering, 103
evaluation
  of cloud service provider, 31
  software, 246
  strategy, 41
  technology, 73
executive support, 257
expenditure
  capital expenditure reduction, 15
  expense structure assessment, 44
Extensible Markup Language (XML),
    70, 289
Extensible Stylesheet Language
    Transformation (XSLT), 289
Extract-Transform-Load (ETL) tool, 280

• *F* •

Facebook
  as massively scaled application, 155
  as massively scaled SaaS, 23
fault tolerance, 280
Federated Applications service, 130–131
federated identity management, 180
federation, 92, 280
fee. *See also* cost
  Force.com, 130
  Google App Engine, 124–125
  Microsoft Azure, 126
file control, data management, 79
file system virtualization, 201
fine grain multi-tenancy, 22
firewall, 79–80
Flexiscale company, 114
Flickr company, 155
Force.com
  AppExchange marketplace, 129
  database as a service, 129
  Enterprise Edition, 130
  fee, 130
  Free Edition, 130
  logic as a service, 129
  metadata architecture, 128
  multi-tenancy architecture, 127
  as PaaS example, 21, 127–130
  service delivery infrastructure, 129
  Unlimited Edition, 130
  user interface, 129
forensics program, 182–184
form, virtualization, 198–199
free cloud service, 11
Free Edition (Force.com), 130
functional testing, 149

• *G* •

GFS (Google File System), 123
GNU (GPL General Public License), 280
GoDaddy Web site, 109

GoGrid company, 114
Google
  Bigtable database, 83
  MapReduce software framework, 82
  as massively scaled application, 155
  Web site, 13
Google App Engine
  fee, 125
  infrastructure service, 123
  load balancing, 123
  as massively scaled SaaS, 23
  as PaaS example, 21, 123–125
  persistent storage, 123
  programming interface, 124
  scalable serving infrastructure, 124
  scheduled task, 124
  sorting and transaction, 123
  Web site, 123
Google File System (GFS), 123
governance
  basic description of, 187–189
  concerns, 190
  desktop management, 216
  do's and don'ts, 272
  governance body establishment, 194
  KPI, 189
  making it work, 194–195
  risk level assessment, 190–194
  as a service, 151
  service catalog, 195
  strategy, 44–45
governance issue
  company strategy challenge, 29
  coping with, 28–29
  IaaS approach, 28
  IT strategy challenge, 29
  PaaS approach, 28
  SaaS approach, 28
GPL (GNU General Public License), 280
granularity, 280
Greenberg, Albert (*The Cost of a Cloud:
  Research Problems in Data Center
  Networks*), 52
grid computing, 54, 281
Gridlayer company, 114

• *H* •

Halper, Fern (*Service Oriented Architecture
  For Dummies*), 32
Hamilton, James (*The Cost of a Cloud:
  Research Problems in Data Center
  Networks*), 52
hardware
  cost, 60–61
  software dependencies, 38
  virtualization, 198
hardware provisioning, 205–206, 218
heating and air cost, 58
help desk support cost, 250
Hewlett-Packard (HP) company, 96–97
HIPPA (Health Insurance Portability and
  Accountability Act), 77, 281
HIPS (host-based intrusion protection
  system), 182
honeynet, 183
honeypot, 183
hosted hypervisor, 201
HTML (Hypertext Markup Language), 281
HTTP (Hypertext Transfer Protocol), 281
human resource system, 181
Hurwitz & Associates Web site, 4, 267
Hurwitz, Judith (*Service Oriented
  Architecture For Dummies*), 32
hybrid cloud, 8, 91
hybrid environment, 236
hypervisor
  defined, 110
  embedded, 201
  hosted, 201
  native, 201
  security issue, 206
  in virtualization, 199, 201

• *I* •

IaaS (Infrastructure as a Service)
  AppLogic 3Tera company, 115
  defined, 18, 281
  dynamic scaling, 19
  embedded software cost, 62

EC2 (Elastic Compute Cloud), 109–112
Eucalyptus company, 115–116
Flexiscale company, 114
GoGrid company, 114
governance challenge, 28
Gridlayer company, 114
ISP and, 107–109
Joyent Accelerator company, 114
MediaTemplate company, 114
most high-profile operation, 19
potential cloud gain, 117
Rackspace company, 113
research-intensive companies as
    fit for, 20
SOA, 229
trusted cloud, 116–117
IBM company
    Cloudburst appliance, 96
    consumption model, 95
    private cloud offering, 95–96
    Smart Analytics System, 96
identity management
    aspects of, 180–181
    authentication aspect, 180
    benefits of, 179–180
    comprehensive security importance, 34
    corralling the data aspect, 180
    data analysis aspect, 181
    defined, 281
    federated, 180
    integration aspect, 180
    provisioning aspect, 180–181
    security administration aspect, 181
    single sign-on aspect, 181
incident, 235
incident management, 239
independent software vendor (ISV), 130
inefficient server, 54
information integration, 281
information risk, 192
Information Systems Audit and Control
    Association (ISACA), 166
Information Technology Infrastructure
    Library (ITIL), 236, 282
infrastructure, 281

Infrastructure as a Service. *See* IaaS
infrastructure service, 281
infrastructure software cost, 250
in-house software cost, 249
inMotion Hosting Web site, 109
input validation, data management, 79
instant server, 113
integrated lifecycle platform, 121
integration
    identity management, 180
    Salesforce.com software
        environment, 138
    standard, 165
integration as service, 129
integration testing, 149
integrity, data, 85
intellectual property (IP), 97
interface
    delivery model, 18
    workload, 69
International Organization for
    Standardization (ISO), 163, 282
Internet, 281
Internet connectivity, 117
Internet Movie Database, 155
Internet Protocol (IP), 282
Internet service provider (ISP)
    IaaS and, 107–109
    open-source software, 63
interoperability
    best practice, 164
    defined, 281
    risk, 192
Intuit company
    data integration, 131
    Federated Applications service, 130–131
    login integration, 131
    navigation-based integration, 131
    as PaaS company, 130–132
    packaged software market, 147
    Partner Platform, 131–132
    QuickBase infrastructure, 131
    user management and permissions
        integration, 131
IP (intellectual property), 97

IP (Internet Protocol), 282
ISACA (Information Systems Audit and Control Association), 166
ISO (International Organization for Standardization), 163, 282
isolation, 198
ISP (Internet service provider)
  IaaS and, 107–109
  open-source software, 63
ISV (independent software vendor), 130
IT cost management, 30
IT environment, 37
IT governance. *See* governance
IT security, 35
IT service provider
  cloud service provider comparison, 12–14
  problems, addressing, 13–14
  roles of, 12
ITIL (Information Technology Infrastructure Library), 236, 282

• J •

Java runtime, 124
JCA (J2EE Connector Architecture), 282

• K •

Kaufman, Marcia (*Service Oriented Architecture For Dummies*), 32
knowledge management, 239
KPI (key performance indicator), 189

• L •

labor cost, 52, 56
LAMP open-source program, 282
land cost, 58
late binding, 282
latency requirement, 76
legacy application, 282
leveraging the cloud, 262–263
license management
  asset management, 73, 217
  virtualization, 203
lifecycle management, 20

LinkedIn company, 155
Linux operating system, 111, 282
Linux Web hosting, 282
Live Services, Microsoft, 126, 148
load balancing, 123
location cost, 58
log-file monitor, 182–183
logic as service, 129, 138
LongJump company
  Development Suite, 132–133
  fee, 133
  as PaaS company, 132–133
loosely coupled service, 37, 222–223, 282
LotusLive company, 148
low-hanging fruit, 261
LucidDB database, 83

• M •

Maltz, David A. (*The Cost of a Cloud: Research Problems in Data Center Networks*), 52
malware, 283
managed hosting, 283
Management and Administration, 24–25
management as a service, 150
manager, service, 224
MapReduce software framework, 82
market-managed service, 97
markup language, 283
mashup, 120, 160, 283
massively scaled application
  basic description of, 153
  company listing, 154–155
  economic, 247
  Web-based business service, 156
massively scaled SaaS, 23
master-slave, 283
MDA (Model Driven Architecture), 169
MediaTemplate company, 114
memo, 257
memory
  cloud versus traditional data center, 61
  virtualization, 198
message-oriented middleware (MOM), 283
metadata, 84, 128, 138, 283
metering of service, 11

Microsoft
  Azure platform, 125–126
  Live Services, 126, 148
  .NET Services, 126
  SQL Services, 126
  Windows Server 2003 operating
    system, 111
mirrored system, 203
mission critical, 283
Model Driven Architecture (MDA), 169
modity server, 113
molecular modeling program, 157
MOM (message-oriented middleware), 283
MongoDB database, 83
monitoring
  application, 217
  business process, 29
  as a service, 150
multi-tenancy
  defined, 9, 283
  fine grain, 22
  Force.com company, 127
  PaaS, 120
  SaaS, 138
  simple, 22
MySQL database, 283

• **N** •

NAS (network access storage), 204
National Institute of Standards and
    Technology (NIST), 121, 167–168, 268
native hypervisor, 201
navigation-based integration, 131
.NET Services, Microsoft, 126
Netsuite company, 147
network
  cost, 248–250
  incident and problem management, 239
  scan, 240
  virtualization, 198
network access storage (NAS), 204
network intrusion-detection system
    (NIDS), 183

network management
  cloud versus traditional data center, 61
  service management, 37
  virtualization, 203
network monitoring, 206
network traffic, 64, 108
NIDS (network intrusion-detection
    system), 183
Nikitin, Alex (*Storage Area Networks For
    Dummies*), 204
NIPS (network-based intrusion protection
    system), 182
NIST (National Institute of Standards and
    Technology), 121, 167–168, 268

• **O** •

OASIS (Organization for the Advancement
    of Structured Information Standards)
    Web site, 269
OCC (Open Cloud Consortium), 168
OCCI (Open Cloud Computing
    Interface), 168
OGF (Open Grid Forum), 168
OMG (Object Management Group), 169
on-demand provisioning, 11
open cloud, 165
Open Cloud Manifesto document, 165, 270
Open Platform as a Service, 21
Open Virtual Format (OVF), 164, 167
open-source software, 63
operating expense, 30
operating system, 198
operating-system streaming, 211
operational support cost, 250–251
optimization, 88
organization
  about this book, 2–3
  how cloud services impact, 27
  readiness assessment, 45
  strategy, deciding on, 28
Organization for the Advancement of
    Structured Information Standards
    (OASIS) Web site, 269

output control, data management, 79
OVF (Open Virtual format), 164, 167

• P •

PaaS (Platform as a Service)
  advantage, 20
  anchored lifecycle platform, 122
  basic description of, 119
  composite application, 120
  defined, 284
  disadvantage, 20–21
  dynamic scaling, 20
  embedded software cost, 62
  enabled technology as platform, 122
  example of, 21
  Force.com platform, 127–130
  Google App Engine, 123–125
  governance challenge, 28
  integrated lifecycle platform, 121
  integration service, 127
  Internet leverage, 120
  Intuit platform, 130–132
  large customer database
    characteristic, 127
  lifecycle management, 20
  LongJump company, 132–133
  mashup, 120
  Microsoft Azure company, 125–126
  multi-tenancy architecture, 120
  NIST, 121
  Open Platform as a Service, 21
  portal, 120, 135
  programming language, 127
  service interface, 120
  service management, 134
  SOA, 229
  social network, 135
  solution stack, 20
package software cost, 249, 251
packaged software as a service, 146–147
partitioning, 198
partner, 8
Partner Platform (Intuit company), 131–132
patch and update management,
    37, 151, 218

Patel, Parveen (*The Cost of a Cloud:
    Research Problems in Data Center
    Networks*), 52
payment technology, 159
PayPal, 154
peak loading, 246
peer to peer (P2P), 284
performance management
  bandwidth, 36
  connection point, 36
  resource management, 35–36
  risk management, 193
  software service, 35–36
performance monitoring and
    measurement, 12, 30
performance risk, 192
performance testing, 149
perimeter security, 177, 207
Perl programming language, 284
perpetual license, 142
physical environment, 37
pilot project, 273
platform
  anchored lifecycle, 121
  cost, 249, 251
  enabling technology as, 121
  integrated lifecycle, 121
  software dependencies, 38
Platform as a Service. *See* PaaS
Platform Computing, Inc., 101–102
Podcast, 257
Poelker, Christopher (*Storage
    Area Networks For Dummies*,
    2nd Edition), 204
policy, 69
portability, 164
portal, 120, 284
POS (point-of sale), 82
power distribution and cooling cost, 52
privacy, data management, 43, 76–80
private cloud
  basic description of, 8
  business need, 90–91
  capital expenditure, 92–93
  cost, 251–252
  defined, 88–89, 284

optimization, 88
public cloud versus, 87–89
services-led technology vendor, 93–94
systems integrator vendor, 94
technology enabling vendor, 94
vendor private cloud offering, 93–94
virtual, 91
well-managed environment, 88
workload support, 89
problem resolution, 237, 239
process risk, 258
processing control, data management, 79
productivity, 179
programming in the large, 284
protocol, 285
provisioning
defined, 285
hardware, 205–206, 218
identity management, 180–181
resource management, 36
software, 204–205
P2P (peer to peer), 284
public cloud
about this book, 1
basic description of, 8
business need, 90
private cloud versus, 87–89
public key encryption, 80
Python runtime, 124

• Q •

Qrimp company, 21
Quad Core Xeon server, 112
QuickBase infrastructure, 131

• R •

Rackspace company
as IaaS company, 113
private cloud offering, 102
radio frequency identification (RFID), 285
reactive, 271
real time, 285
real-time event processing, 285

register
asset, 216
software, 217
registry, 224, 226–227, 285
reliability, 259
remote management, 217
remote procedure call (RPC), 285
rent infrastructure, 108–109
repository, 224, 227, 285
Representational State Transfer
(REST), 164
requirements testing, 149
research, as business process, 159
resource management
development tool, 34
IT security, 35
performance management, 35–36
provisioning, 36
service management, 37
response time, 242, 285
REST API, 132
REST (Representational State
Transfer), 164
RFID (radio frequency identification), 285
RightNow company, 147
risk
audit, 192
availability, 192, 259
billing, 192
compliance, 192
contract, 192
data management, 260
governance strategy, 190–194
information, 192
interoperability, 192
measurement method, 193–194
people, 258
performance, 192
process, 258
risk list, 192
security, 175–176, 192
technology, 258
top company concerns, 259–260
vendor, 260
road map development, 45–46
root cause analysis, 37, 218

RPC (remote procedure call), 285
Ruby on Rails programming language, 285
Runbook automation, 73

• S •

SaaS Showplace Web site, 268
SaaS (Software as a Service)
 advantage, 21
 APS and, 21
 collaboration as a service, 146, 148–149
 continuity planning service, 151
 CRM strategy, 21, 137
 defined, 21, 285
 dramatic economies of scale, 23–24
 embedded software cost, 63
 enabling and management tool, 149–151
 fine grain multi-tenancy mode, 22
 governance challenge, 28
 history of, 139
 massively scaled, 23
 multi-tenancy architecture, 138
 packaged software as a service, 146–147
 patch management service, 151
 Salesforce.com, 21, 138–140
 simple multi-tenancy mode, 22
 SOA, 229–230
 third-party solution, 40
 VPN, 23
Salesforce.com
 automation application, 22
 built-in billing service, 141
 ecosystem, 140
 generalized application, 140
 modular and service oriented
  application, 141
 SaaS and, 21, 138–140
 software environment component, 138
SAML framework, 285
SAN (storage area network), 116, 204
Sarbanes-Oxley (SOX), 151, 286
Savvis, Inc., 99
scalability
 defined, 286
 elasticity and, 10
 ensuring performance level, 241

scalable serving infrastructure, 124
scan network, 240
scripting language, 286
SDK (Software Development Kit), 124
SDS (SQL Database), 83
Search Engine Optimization For Dummies,
 159
Secure Sockets Layer (SSL), 287
secure Web hosting, 286
security
 access control, 34, 219
 activity log, 183
 administration, 181
 authentication, 34
 authorization, 34
 automated, 219
 breach, 177–178
 Cloud Security Alliance Web site, 76
 common security question, 174–175
 comprehensive infrastructure
  importance, 34
 consultant, 185
 cost, 65
 customer leap of faith to trust, 12
 data audit, 184
 data management, 43, 76–80
 desktop management, 216
 detection, 182–184
 do's and don'ts, 273
 encryption, 79–80, 184
 firewall, 79–80
 forensics program, 182–184
 HIPS, 182
 identity management, 34, 179–181
 importance of, 174–175
 incident and problem management, 239
 integration, 165
 log-file monitor, 182–183
 need for well-defined process, 11
 network monitoring, 206
 NIPS, 182
 perimeter, 177, 207
 resource management, 35
 risk, 175–176, 192
 scan network, 240
 as a service, 150–151
 strategy, 185

system monitor, 182–183
threat management, 219
TLS, 288
top company concerns, 259
virtualization, 206–207
self-service provisioning, 10–11
semantic, 286
server array, 286
server blade, 212
server cost, 248, 250
server farm, 286
service. *See also* cloud service
  business process as, 28, 155
  collaboration as a, 146, 148–149
  compliance and governance as a, 151
  defined, 286
  development as a, 129, 150
  end-to-end, 225
  integration as, 129
  logic as, 129
  loosely coupled, 37
  monitoring and management as a, 150
  packaged software as, 146–147
  security as a, 150–151
  testing as a, 149–150
  user interface as, 129
service broker, 224
service catalog, 195, 227–228, 286
service delivery infrastructure, 129
service desk, 37, 286
service level, 19, 203
service level agreement. *See* SLA
service level cost, 252–253
service management
  asset management, 37
  basic description of, 14
  capacity planning, 37
  comprehensive approach to, 11
  configuration management, 37
  dashboard for, 12
  defined, 287
  desktop management, 216
  dos and don'ts, 273
  IT environment, 37
  network management, 37
  overall system performance, 12

PaaS, 134
patch and update management, 37
performance monitoring and
    measurement, 12
physical environment, 37
resource management, 37
root cause analysis, 37
service desk, 37
virtual environment, 37
workload management, 37
service manager, 224
Service Oriented Architecture For Dummies
    (Hurwitz, Bloor, Kaufman, and
    Halper), 32
service restoration, 238
service-level maintenance, 217
service-oriented architecture. *See* SOA
services-led technology vendor
  EMC company, 98–99
  HP (Hewlett-Packard), 95–96
  IBM company, 95–96
  list of, 93–94
servlet, 287
session-based computing, 211
silo, 207, 287
silver bullet, 287
Simple Mail Transfer Protocol (SMTP), 287
simple multi-tenancy, 22
Simple Object Access Protocol (SOAP), 164
Simple Query Service (SQS), 122
Simple Storage Service (S3), 103, 111, 287
SimpleDB database (Amazon), 83
single sign-on, 181
site. *See* Web site
Six Sigma, 287
Skype
  as massively scaled application, 154
  as massively scaled SaaS, 23
SLA (service level agreement)
  balancing risk and practical model, 72
  defined, 286
  importance of, 31
  negotiation, 241
  response time, 242
  tracking, 241–242
SMTP (Simple Mail Transfer Protocol), 287

SNIA (Storage Networking Industry Association), 169
SOA (service-oriented architecture)
  basic description of, 14, 32, 221
  benefits of, 230
  black-box component architecture, 222
  combining cloud and, 222
  component, 224
  consistency of, 33
  defined, 287
  ESB, 224–226
  IaaS, 229
  loosely coupled component, 222–223
  modular approach to, 32
  PaaS, 229
  registry, 224, 226–227
  repository, 224, 227
  SaaS, 229–230
  service broker, 224
  service catalog, 227–228
  service manager, 224
SOAP (Simple Object Access Protocol), 164
SOAP Web service, 129
social network
  defining the cloud, 9
  PaaS, 135
  smoothing the transition, 257
software
  cost, 249
  embedded software cost, 62–63
  evaluation, 246
  open-source, 63
  virtualization, 199, 205
Software as a Service. *See* SaaS
software dependencies
  basic description of, 37
  hardware perspective, 38
  platform perspective, 38
  software perspective, 38
Software Development Kit (SDK), 124
software register, 217
software service, 35–36
solution stack, 20
SOX (Sarbanes-Oxley), 151, 286
spoofing, 183
SQL Database (SDS), 83
SQL Services, Microsoft, 126

SQL (Structured Query Language), 287
SQS (Simple Query Service), 122
SSL (Secure Sockets Layer), 287
staff cost, 58
standard. *See also* best practice
  CCIF, 169–170
  as core set of common practice, 162–163
  CSA (Cloud Security Alliance), 166–167
  de facto, 163
  defined, 287
  DMTF, 167
  example, 164
  integration, 165
  interoperability, 164
  ISO, 163
  NIST, 167–168
  OCC, 168
  OGF, 168
  OMG, 169
  portability, 164
  security, 165
  SNIA, 169
  vertical industry group, 170
standardized API, 33
static virtualization, 206–207
S3 (Simple Storage Service), 103, 111, 287
storage
  cost, 248, 250
  virtualization, 198
storage area network (SAN), 116, 204
Storage Area Networks For Dummies, 2nd Edition (Poelker and Nikitin), 204
Storage Networking Industry Association (SNIA), 169
strategy
  company approach to, 40
  comprehensive, 28
  data center environment assessment, 42–43
  data management, 43–44
  data supporting, 43–44
  deciding on a, 28
  evaluation, 41
  expense structure assessment, 44
  key areas of planning, 39
  new application, 40
  organizational readiness assessment, 45

risk assessment, 45
road map development, 45–46
rules and governance check, 44–45
SaaS, 137
security, 185
three-data-center, 64
where you are today assessment, 42–44
streaming, 211
stress testing, 149
Structured Query Language (SQL), 287
subroutine, 287
success target, 260–262
SugarCRM company, 147
Sun Microsystem OpenSolaris operating
system, 111
Sun Microsystem Solaris Express
Community Edition operating
system, 111
supply-chain system, 181
support, 32
support desk
change management, 239
communication via multiple channel
support, 238–239
incident management, 239
knowledge management, 239
problem resolution, 237, 239
service desk goal, 237–238
service restoration, 238
system support, 238
varying levels, 238
symmetric key encryption, 80
symmetric multiprocessing
virtualization, 201
system integrator vendor
Accenture company, 99
basic description of, 94
CSC (Computer Sciences Corporation),
98–99
Savvis, Inc., 99
Unisys company, 98
system management, 64–65
system monitor, 182–183
system support, 238
system testing, 246

• T •

tag, XML, 70
Taleo company, 147
TB (terabyte), 111
TCAO (Total Cost of Application
Ownership), 250
TCO (total cost of ownership), 209
TCP/IP (Transmission Control Protocol/
Internet Protocol), 288
technical interface
API and data transformation, 33
data and application architecture, 33
SAO, 32
security infrastructure, 34
technology
about this book, 1–3
cloud and traditional data center cost
comparison, 56
enabling as platform, 122
evaluation, 73
risk, 258
technology enabling vendor
basic description of, 94
CA company, 100–101
Eucalyptus company, 103
Platform Computing, Inc., 101–102
Rackspace company, 102
3Tera company, 102–103
VMware company, 100
TechTarget Web site, 268–269
Telemanagement Forum (TM Forum), 170
terabyte (TB), 111
termination, contract, 85
testing
cloud management, 241
compatibility, 149
functional, 149
integration, 149
performance, 149
requirements, 149
as a service, 149–150
stress, 149
system, 246
unit, 149
workload, 73–74

thin client, 210, 288
threat. *See* security
three-data–center strategy, 64
throughput, 288
TLS (Transport Layer Security), 288
TM Forum (Telemanagement Forum), 170
Total Cost of Application Ownership (TCAO), 250
total cost of ownership (TCO), 209
TQM (Total Quality Management), 288
traditional data center
  backup, 62
  cloud data center cost comparison, 55–58
  cost to operate, 50–51
  hardware cost, 60–61
training material, 162, 258
transaction, 288
Transmission Control Protocol/Internet Protocol (TCP/IP), 288
Transport Layer Security (TLS), 288
trusted cloud, 116–117
Twitter, 155

• U •

UDDI (Universal Description, Discovery, and Integration), 288
UML (Unified Modeling Language), 169
unified communication, 148
unified threat management, 183
UnifiedPOS, 170
Unisys company, 98
unit testing, 149
Universal Description, Discovery, and Integration (UDDI), 288
Unlimited Edition (Force.com), 130
user interface as service, 129, 138
user productivity, 179
utility computing, 28

• V •

VDI (virtual desktop infrastructure), 211
vendor
  as player in cloud computing world, 8
  risk, 260

services-led technology, 93–94
switching, 85
systems integrator, 94
technology enabling, 94
Web site, 270
vertical industry group, 170
Virtual Bridges Web site, 214
virtual desktop, 209–212
virtual desktop infrastructure (VDI), 211
virtual environment, 37
virtual LAN (VLAN), 114
virtual machine, 54
virtual memory, 198–199
virtual private cloud, 91
virtual private network (VPN)
  data security, 79
  hybrid cloud, 91
  SaaS, 23
virtual private server (VPS), 288
virtual server, 109
virtualization
  abstraction layer, 203–204
  application, 198
  basic description of, 13–14, 197
  capacity planning, 203
  client, 210–212
  defined, 288
  distributed resource scheduler, 201
  economies of scale, 64
  encapsulation characteristic, 198
  file system, 201
  form, 198–199
  foundational issue, 202–203
  hardware abstraction, 201
  hardware provisioning, 205–206
  high-availability support, 201
  history of, 200
  hypervisor in, 199, 201
  isolation characteristic, 198
  license management, 203
  migration, 204
  network management, 203
  partitioning characteristic, 198
  provisioning software, 204–205
  as requirement for data center management, 208
  security issue, 206–207

service level, 203
software, 199, 205
static versus dynamic, 206–207
symmetric multiprocessing, 201
virtual infrastructure client console, 201
workload administration, 203
VLAN (virtual LAN), 114
VMware company
  cloud operating system, 100
  defined, 288
  private cloud offering, 100
VoIP (Voice over IP), 154
VPN (virtual private network)
  data security, 79
  hybrid cloud, 91
  SaaS, 23
VPS (virtual private server), 288

• *W* •

Web service, 288
Web Service Policy Framework
    (WS-Policy), 289
Web Services Choreography Interface
    (WSCI), 289
Web Services Definition Language
    (WSDL), 289
Web Services for Remote Portlets
    (WSRP), 289
Web site
  Amazon, 13
  Canonical, 214
  CloudCamp, 268
  Deskton, 214
  Eclipse Foundation, 269
  GoDaddy, 109
  Google, 13
  Google App Engine, 123
  Hurwitz & Associates, 4, 267
  inMotion Hosting, 109
  OASIS, 269
  SaaS Showplace, 268
  TechTarget, 268–269
  vendor, 270
  Virtual Bridges, 214

Web-based administration console, 124
Web-based business process, 159
Web-based business service, 156
white-listing software, 183
Wikipedia company, 155
WordPress company, 155
workflow, 289
workload
  abstraction, 68
  ad-hoc, 112
  asset management, 73
  combined, 70
  configuration management software, 74
  container, 71
  dynamic, 70
  end-of-month, 112
  end-of-year, 112
  executed at any time, 69
  interface, 69
  real-time, 69
  risk and practical models, balancing,
    71–72
  rule or policy, 69
  as self-contained entity, 69
  testing in real world, 73–74
  types, 69
  as well-planned service, 68–69
  XML-based interface, 70–71
workload management
  business planning, 67–68
  history of, 68
  service management, 37
World Wide Web Consortium (W3C), 288
WSCI (Web Services Choreography
    Interface), 289
WSDL (Web Services Definition
    Language), 289
WS-Policy (Web Service Policy
    Framework), 289
WSRP (Web Services for Remote
    Portlets), 289
W3C (World Wide Web Consortium), 288

• X •

Xen virtualization (3C2), 110
XML (Extensible Markup Language),
    70, 289
XML Schema, 289
XSD (XML schema definition), 289
XSLT (Extensible Stylesheet Language
    Transformation), 289

• Y •

Yahoo!, 155
Yahoo Mail, 23
YouTube, 155

• Z •

Zoho company, 148

siness/Accounting
ookkeeping
ookkeeping For Dummies
-0-7645-9848-7

ay Business
-in-One For Dummies,
 Edition
-0-470-38536-4

 Interviews
 Dummies,
 Edition
-0-470-17748-8

sumes For Dummies,
 Edition
-0-470-08037-5

ck Investing
 Dummies,
 Edition
-0-470-40114-9

ccessful Time
nagement
 Dummies
-0-470-29034-7

mputer Hardware
ckBerry For Dummies,
 Edition
-0-470-45762-7

mputers For Seniors
r Dummies
-0-470-24055-7

one For Dummies,
d Edition
-0-470-42342-4

Laptops For Dummies,
3rd Edition
978-0-470-27759-1

Macs For Dummies,
10th Edition
978-0-470-27817-8

Cooking & Entertaining
Cooking Basics
For Dummies,
3rd Edition
978-0-7645-7206-7

Wine For Dummies,
4th Edition
978-0-470-04579-4

Diet & Nutrition
Dieting For Dummies,
2nd Edition
978-0-7645-4149-0

Nutrition For Dummies,
4th Edition
978-0-471-79868-2

Weight Training
For Dummies,
3rd Edition
978-0-471-76845-6

Digital Photography
Digital Photography
For Dummies,
6th Edition
978-0-470-25074-7

Photoshop Elements 7
For Dummies
978-0-470-39700-8

Gardening
Gardening Basics
For Dummies
978-0-470-03749-2

Organic Gardening
For Dummies,
2nd Edition
978-0-470-43067-5

Green/Sustainable
Green Building
& Remodeling
For Dummies
978-0-470-17559-0

Green Cleaning
For Dummies
978-0-470-39106-8

Green IT For Dummies
978-0-470-38688-0

Health
Diabetes For Dummies,
3rd Edition
978-0-470-27086-8

Food Allergies
For Dummies
978-0-470-09584-3

Living Gluten-Free
For Dummies
978-0-471-77383-2

Hobbies/General
Chess For Dummies,
2nd Edition
978-0-7645-8404-6

Drawing For Dummies
978-0-7645-5476-6

Knitting For Dummies,
2nd Edition
978-0-470-28747-7

Organizing For Dummies
978-0-7645-5300-4

SuDoku For Dummies
978-0-470-01892-7

Home Improvement
Energy Efficient Homes
For Dummies
978-0-470-37602-7

Home Theater
For Dummies,
3rd Edition
978-0-470-41189-6

Living the Country Lifestyle
All-in-One For Dummies
978-0-470-43061-3

Solar Power Your Home
For Dummies
978-0-470-17569-9

ailable wherever books are sold. For more information or to order direct: U.S. customers visit www.dummies.com or call 1-877-762-2974.
K. customers visit www.wileyeurope.com or call (0) 1243 843291. Canadian customers visit www.wiley.ca or call 1-800-567-4797.

Internet
Blogging For Dummies,
2nd Edition
978-0-470-23017-6

eBay For Dummies,
6th Edition
978-0-470-49741-8

Facebook For Dummies
978-0-470-26273-3

Google Blogger
For Dummies
978-0-470-40742-4

Web Marketing
For Dummies,
2nd Edition
978-0-470-37181-7

WordPress For Dummies,
2nd Edition
978-0-470-40296-2

Language & Foreign Language
French For Dummies
978-0-7645-5193-2

Italian Phrases
For Dummies
978-0-7645-7203-6

Spanish For Dummies
978-0-7645-5194-9

Spanish For Dummies,
Audio Set
978-0-470-09585-0

Macintosh
Mac OS X Snow Leopard
For Dummies
978-0-470-43543-4

Math & Science
Algebra I For Dummies
978-0-7645-5325-7

Biology For Dummies
978-0-7645-5326-4

Calculus For Dummies
978-0-7645-2498-1

Chemistry For Dummies
978-0-7645-5430-8

Microsoft Office
Excel 2007 For Dummies
978-0-470-03737-9

Office 2007 All-in-One
Desk Reference
For Dummies
978-0-471-78279-7

Music
Guitar For Dummies,
2nd Edition
978-0-7645-9904-0

iPod & iTunes
For Dummies,
6th Edition
978-0-470-39062-7

Piano Exercises
For Dummies
978-0-470-38765-8

Parenting & Education
Parenting For Dummies,
2nd Edition
978-0-7645-5418-6

Type 1 Diabetes
For Dummies
978-0-470-17811-9

Pets
Cats For Dummies,
2nd Edition
978-0-7645-5275-5

Dog Training For Dummies,
2nd Edition
978-0-7645-8418-3

Puppies For Dummies,
2nd Edition
978-0-470-03717-1

Religion & Inspiration
The Bible For Dummies
978-0-7645-5296-0

Catholicism For Dummies
978-0-7645-5391-2

Women in the Bible
For Dummies
978-0-7645-8475-6

Self-Help & Relationship
Anger Management
For Dummies
978-0-470-03715-7

Overcoming Anxiety
For Dummies
978-0-7645-5447-6

Sports
Baseball For Dummies,
3rd Edition
978-0-7645-7537-2

Basketball For Dummies,
2nd Edition
978-0-7645-5248-9

Golf For Dummies,
3rd Edition
978-0-471-76871-5

Web Development
Web Design All-in-One
For Dummies
978-0-470-41796-6

Windows Vista
Windows Vista
For Dummies
978-0-471-75421-3

Available wherever books are sold. For more information or to order direct: U.S. customers visit www.dummies.com or call 1-877-762-297
U.K. customers visit www.wileyeurope.com or call (0) 1243 843291. Canadian customers visit www.wiley.ca or call 1-800-567-4797.

DUMMIES.COM®

ow-to?
ow Easy.

Go to www.Dummies.com

From hooking up a modem to cooking up a casserole, knitting a scarf to navigating an iPod, you can trust Dummies.com to show you how to get things done the easy way.

Visit us at Dummies.com

Dummies products make life easier!

DVDs • Music • Games •
DIY • Consumer Electronics •
Software • Crafts • Hobbies •
Cookware • and more!

For more information, go to
Dummies.com® and search
the store by category.

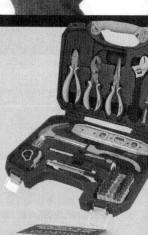

FOR
DUMMIES
Making everything easier!™

Get More and Do More at Dummies.com®

Start with **FREE** Cheat Sheets

Cheat Sheets include
- Checklists
- Charts
- Common Instructions
- And Other Good Stuff!

To access the Cheat Sheet created specifically for this book, go to
www.dummies.com/cheatsheet/cloudcomputing

t Smart at Dummies.com

mies.com makes your life easier with 1,000s
nswers on everything from removing wallpaper
sing the latest version of Windows.

ck out our
- Videos
- Illustrated Articles
- Step-by-Step Instructions

each month you can win valuable prizes by entering
Dummies.com sweepstakes. *

t a weekly dose of Dummies? Sign up for Newsletters on
- Digital Photography
- Microsoft Windows & Office
- Personal Finance & Investing
- Health & Wellness
- Computing, iPods & Cell Phones
- eBay
- Internet
- Food, Home & Garden

nd out "HOW" at Dummies.com

pstakes not currently available in all countries; visit Dummies.com for official rules.

CPSIA information can be obtained at www.ICGtesting.com
Printed in the USA
LVOW03s1926070214

372824LV00014B/790/P